Leading with Love

CW00538855

'Just wow! If you are curious about yourself, leadership, and love then Vic will take you on a reflective ride through her and (more importantly) your life. With loads of stories to help you think, links to threads you might want to explore and practical nudges, I now have a book covered in ink and a mind that has been lit up. Enjoy!'

Russell Earnshaw
Rugby Player and Coach, The Magic Academy

'Vic is a well-respected and successful Headteacher, with a proven professional track record. She supports numerous leaders in a range of spheres of influence and is widely recognised as a leadership and life coach and source of support to all. Dr Vic's TEDx talk has been viewed thousands of times and has provided inspiration to countless people as it resonates on many levels. She is also up to date with current research and is a skilled academic, but this book makes tangible what all leaders face in the ever-changing world we live in. SHE IS AMAZING!'

Sarah Watkins
Reception Teacher and Forest School Leader

'What an emotional rollercoaster – I've gone from tears to smiles and back again reading this book. It's lovely and hopeful and positive in spite of all the pain in it. But then that's what it's about isn't it – transcending all that and finding beauty and love among it all.'

Debra Kidd
Educator

'Gold dust to any teacher or aspiring teacher, very personal and obviously from the heart. I genuinely enjoyed it. I know it will resonate most strongly with those who are, or aspire to be, school leaders. You offer a heart-felt insight into leading in education, offering many practical tips that many will find useful as a guide and hand rail. I see the book as more of a reference book that education professionals will use often – not just read once. But, the book will be of interest to a far wider audience. It offers us all a different perspective on leadership, based on an intensely personal journey. You deal not only with the professional world, but relate leadership to normal life – and I might add you are not afraid to cover some extremely sensitive ground such as illness and therapy. There are some practical leadership tips for us all – life skills – such as your Top 10 list. It also offers some excellent insights on leading our kids; it certainly made me think.'

Paul Anthony Edward Nanson
CB, CBE, Major General (retd.)

'For those like Victoria and I, both who have survived adverse experiences, at work and in our personal lives, it is crucial that when we reach a point of confidence, we share our stories to benefit humanity.

This is a book for people who like to wear their "heart on their sleeve". An encapsulating account of life for people who want to learn how others overcome anxiety and a lack of confidence; something we all experience in life and at work.

In all sorts of scenarios, particularly in leadership, Dr Victoria Carr models how she is not only an inspirational woman, she is a mother, an author, an academic and an energetic school leader! She is a teacher full of integrity and resilience. This book has it *all*, from abuse to divorce, from growing up in Liverpool and Kenya to surviving the British Reserves application process – with flying colours – and Ofsted inspections.

Get this book! Have a box of tissues or chocolates to hand, because it's a gripping read, and when you come up for air, you'll be in awe of the human potential in all of us and how resilient we truly can be. It has taken me almost 30 years working in education, to truly understand that what our young people need more than anything else, is love and *then* an education. Learning to lead with love rather than just with your head requires phronesis, and this book has boundless lessons for us all. It's an epic book!'

Ross Morrison McGill
Author of '100 Ideas – Outstanding Lessons',
'Teacher Toolkit' and 'Just Great Teaching'

'Authentic, gritty and powerful. This deeply personal story shows how closely "life leadership" and "school leadership" are aligned. Despite tragedy and hardship this is a motivational and optimistic read. Packed with examples of integrity, self-knowledge and resilience, this book clearly illustrates how our best school leaders work as a protective force for others.'

Professor Dame Alison Peacock
DBE, DL, DLitt, Chief Executive, Chartered College of Teaching

'It is very moving and full of insights into how to turn painful to positive. What a difference belief in someone can make, for all of us.'

Mary Myatt
Education Writer and Speaker

'Vic traces her professional journey from a difficult childhood to school leadership, university lecturer and, ultimately, a reservist in the British Army as well. This book takes the mantra "You can't do that!" and turns it on its head.

It is self-affirming, reaffirming and full of reflection on a life full of challenge, demanding and even chaotic at times.

The recurrent message threaded throughout this vivid portrait of a life packed full of change and challenge is the need to give people the time they need to talk, to share problems and to have someone who listens to you with empathy and wisdom. Vic is that person. Her patience and positivity are exuded throughout this publication and are a message and a model for all of us.

When Vic says: "I will never know the influence I have had, if any, I know that people tell me publicly and through direct messages, emails and gifts that they are thankful, but we never know the impact of supporting someone to achieve. My take on this is I don't need to know, what I do know is that everyone I help out is more likely to then help others, and who would not like the idea of that?" she speaks from the heart with caring and wisdom. The miracle is that her generosity of spirit and compassion have grown out of a childhood of crisis and abuse.

The wisdom is repeated in Chapter 9: "People may forget what you said, but never how you made them feel." Here Vic reflects that ". . . you will see how difficult it is to extract your human self from the leadership persona you have, and in fact it is perhaps much more healthy to align the two, integrating the lessons learned in both to gain deeper understanding of yourself and how you can improve." Wise words indeed.

We are reassured that exceptional leaders are kind and generous with their time, but move on if they are not valued – accepting that some things are time limited. Making yourself "redundant" is part of succession planning and is healthy.

This book leaves you wondering . . .

Where next for me? Where next for you? Where next for a school?

There is always a new page, a new ending and a new beginning with caring and with love.'

Ros Wilson
Cert.Ed; Dip.Ed; M.Ed.; Education Consultant

'Leading with love . . . A very open, honest and personal journey from a Headteacher that passionately wants to make a difference. There are some little gems of advice for any educator and a clear message throughout that you don't need to be a perfect leader but if you lead with positive intent and love then you can make a real difference.'

Mike Hamilton
Founder of Commando Joes

'Deeply moving, incredibly honest and totally inspiring – a must read for anyone interested in understanding where humanity in their leadership comes from, with simple, yet practical, signposting at the end of each chapter.

What a fantastic read! Some great insights into leading with love, anchored in a rich seam of experience and grounded in authenticity. It takes real courage and a leap of faith to do something like this. Just brilliant.'

Colonel Lucy Giles
Deputy Director, Army HQ

Leading with Love

Leading with Love reveals how focusing on relationships, wellbeing and core moral and ethical values can transform the motivation and engagement of teachers, parents and pupils, increasing their overall happiness as well as academic standards.

In each chapter Victoria Carr presents accessible and relatable personal life lessons, leadership observations and anecdotes, drawing on her leadership experiences in a wide range of schools to show how leading with integrity is possible for all. Her methods are simple and authentic and have transformed failing schools into thriving ones, improving whole-school systems, the culture of staff and pupil wellbeing and mental health, and standards.

Full of practical tips and end of chapter summaries with further suggested reading, *Leading with Love* will appeal to anyone who has suffered from imposter syndrome, who thinks they are not good enough to succeed, who thinks they are too old or don't have the right background.

With a Foreword from Paul Garvey, this is essential reading for all school leaders and aspiring school leaders.

Victoria Carr is Headteacher at Woodlands Primary School, UK. She has been a leader in several contexts in her life, from parenthood to headship, lecturing to headteacher, research to relationships. Dr Vic always leads with love and this book exemplifies how and why!

Leading with Love

How Compassionate Leadership Enables Schools to Thrive

Victoria Carr

Routledge
Taylor & Francis Group

LONDON AND NEW YORK

Cover image: © Getty Images

First published 2023
by Routledge
4 Park Square, Milton Park, Abingdon, Oxon OX14 4RN

and by Routledge
605 Third Avenue, New York, NY 10158

Routledge is an imprint of the Taylor & Francis Group, an informa business

British Library Cataloguing-in-Publication Data
A catalogue record for this book is available from the British Library

Library of Congress Cataloging-in-Publication Data
Names: Carr, Victoria, author.
Title: Leading with love : how compassionate leadership enables schools to
    thrive / Victoria Carr.
Description: First Edition. | New York : Routledge, 2023. | Includes
    bibliographical references and index.
Identifiers: LCCN 2022023248 | Subjects: LCSH: Educational leadership—
    Moral and ethical aspects—Great Britain. | Moral education—Great
    Britain. | School management and organization—Great Britain.
Classification: LCC LB2806 .C297 2023 | DDC 371.2/0110941—dc23/
    eng/20220727
LC record available at https://lccn.loc.gov/2022023248

ISBN: 978-1-032-25049-6 (hbk)
ISBN: 978-1-032-25051-9 (pbk)
ISBN: 978-1-003-28131-3 (ebk)

DOI: 10.4324/9781003281313

Typeset in Melior
by Apex CoVantage, LLC

To all whom I have loved, to all who have loved me, but especially for the loves of my life, Tom and Iz, after all, 'What's it all about?'

Contents

Foreword

Paul Garvey

Teaching is a tough profession, but leading teachers and the rest of the amazing professionals in a school is a mind-bogglingly difficult one much of the time. It can be damaging, if you are not on top of your game, but upon what do you draw when things get really tough and you feel your professional life crumbling?

I've worked with hundreds of Headteachers, some of whom, unfortunately, have packed in leading their schools because the pressures; from the DfE, from Ofsted, from parents, or the day-to-day myriad tasks which can become too great. They found that even their vast well of resilience was tested beyond breaking point. I wish they'd had Vic's book to read before they'd made the decision.

This life-affirming book is about incy-wincy spider, or Bruce's spider, climbing back up following setback after setback and in Barton's words:

> *'One effort more, his seventh and last!–*
> *The hero hailed the sign!–*
> *And on the wished-for beam hung fast*
> *That slender silken line!'*

This is a book that shouts 'YOU CAN DO IT' from every chapter and as Vic says – 'If I can do it, you can do it. This is a tale of 'Legs' from Liverpool. A girl who didn't fit in. A girl who used the difficulties and setbacks in a difficult childhood to overcome obstacles and learn, hand over fist, what is needed to succeed – eventually in the most difficult, but most rewarding of professions. A girl whose experiences taught her that listening to others, forming relationships with everyone in her school and taking all the opportunities that came her way, hard as they may have been, led her to lead with love'.

I've called the book you are about to read 'life-affirming', and I believe it is. It's leadership-affirming too. It's about much more than a Headteacher's journey. This is about resilience and its place in our human make-up. It will help you, as a leader, or a future leader, to gather your past experiences and use them to create a moral base of steel on which to ground your decisions in difficult times.

Leadership is a unique practice to each of us who are in a leadership role. Vic tells us that we need humanity and emotional intelligence. We need to learn from our mistakes. We need to weave our life's path to become a patchwork leader! Each chapter is a patch in a leadership quilt. Overall, to lead well and with love, we need integrity. Basically, we need to be a good human being and model that for others in our daily actions.

There are difficult moments in this read; Vic's was not an easy path to leadership, or to being the woman she is today, but there are many moments that you'll empathise with and smile about. You'll learn a great deal about how, as a leader, or a future leader (and we all are, or will be in one form, or another), your journey will be shaped by your past, but not dictated by it.

Damage begets damage – Maybe the greatest task of humanity is to break that cycle. There is catharsis in this book, but there is also huge hope. The steps people have to take to gain the skills and resilience to run a school are not easy.

I was one of the early recipients of #AVicCarrCalls – a phone call out of a clear blue sky one day that took me so much by surprise, I didn't know what to make of it at first. It was Vic simply asking me if I was doing OK. I was gobsmacked that someone would do this for me. The experience has prompted me to do exactly that for others, and I know others too have done exactly the same. It was also why I jumped at the chance to write this foreword. Do unto others how you would like others to do for you. Karma, in my view. You get back far more than you give, and I talked about exactly this in 'Talk for Teaching'. Victoria Carr's influence is extending a long way. As Vic says; 'All it costs is time!' This book is imbued with how to lead well and Vic askes the question 'Who are you actually making decisions for?' Something we should all consider.

Vic talks about her 'Go to' strategy of 'Do all things with love'. In many ways you'll read a book that is not about leadership, but about growing to be the person that you are, which, of course, is really everything about leadership! About compassionate leadership. Leadership which is forged in the furnace of resilience and the product is a deep empathy with what others are facing – a love for the other people in our organisation. There are so many of us who come into teaching – and into leadership – determined not to repeat the mistakes of those who taught and led us. In reading 'Leading with Love' you'll recognise – or perhaps you already know – that you yourself may have been driven by this.

Could you be the person who makes the sliding doors connect to a child that opens up a world of future possibilities for them, simply by your spoken support, or will you be someone who likes to close doors to others? 'Pivotal moments', as Vic explains, saying that words count and she's right. You'll learn how Kenya on a carton of milk sowed a seed for a life path. You'll see just how much teachers can influence young lives. I wrote on Twitter, recently: 'Don't close doors. Instead, show them doors that they didn't know existed!' I wrote it while reading and absorbing Vic's messages, and it's really what Vic tells us to do all through this book.

Build relationships, Vic tells us. Take the time do so, as they are crucial. Make people feel they are invaluable members of the team. It's people that cause change, not systems, and Vic's quote from Barack Obama, amongst many aptly chosen quotes, stands out: 'You are the change you seek'. And look after yourself – there's only one you – even though you may not quite be the woman who wrote this book! I promise you this is a read you will enjoy and from which you will learn so much.

Lead from the heart and lead with love!

Go well, Paul

Paul Garvey was a teacher for 22 years and is a former lead inspector for Ofsted. He has also supported many schools in preparing for inspection. He uses his experience as a teacher, inspector and a National Strategies consultant to advise educators and schools on how to take control of professional development.

Introduction

Who am I?

I was going to start this book a little tongue in cheek, but several 'draft readers' told me I should introduce myself before I start the self-ridicule! I am Dr Victoria Carr. I describe myself firstly as a mum, which I am, to two wonderful teenagers, Thomas and Elizabeth – in actual fact I am a single mum and have been for a lot of the time I was up to the shenanigans I will share with you in this book. Secondly, I describe myself as a good human being. Truth be known, this is easier than it looks, despite us all witnessing the opposite from people in our slightly broken world on a daily basis. Being a good person for me is inextricable from being a good leader, which means many of the life lessons I learn inform my leadership and vice versa.

I am currently a Headteacher of a fabulous school full of shamelessly amazing staff and children (naturally), but I haven't always been (some decades ago I too was a student, NQT, Head of Key Stage, supply teacher etc.). I have lectured at master's degree level, in leadership; I have done two MAs myself, and a doctorate, and I am also currently doing a third MA in Military History. I am a TEDx speaker. Although I was asked a couple of times, it took me years to build the courage to do that, and if you watch it, you will see my nerves are evident.

Latterly I also count myself as a British Army Reservist and have not long finished the commissioning process to become an officer (and yes, I am pretty old to have done so, and clearly female, but I don't let things like age and gender get in the way – nor should anyone!). I count amongst my 'talents' the fact I am a consummate mistake maker, always 'lead with my chin', learn all my lessons the hard way, wear my heart on my sleeve and am probably the luckiest person I have ever met . . . still interested in what might be in the book? Then read on!

What am I writing about?

We all have something to say and share, if we are brave enough. I think it fair to say that I have found my voice, and the courage to use it, in the last couple of years. If

DOI: 10.4324/9781003281313-1

you have reached this point then something about the book cover, my career journey, or my social media presence has caught your eye, piqued your interest or resonated with you. Maybe you have heard one of my podcasts or read a blog I have written; maybe you have watched the TEDx talk or maybe it was the title, and you wondered about the juxtaposition of the words 'leadership' and 'love'? Hopefully it is *not* because you are searching for 'The Holy Grail' of leadership and want a simple recipe, a 'paint-by-numbers' for rapidly 'turning around' the fortunes of a school that you are currently working in or the definitive answer to leadership in our capitalist, market-driven world because I hate to disappoint people, and I am afraid that this would be the outcome if you wanted from this book the ubiquitous 'quick fix'!

It is not academically rigorous; it is not designed to be. You can read it cover to cover, folding pages as you go, covering it in coffee rings or red wine stains. If you are like me then this is the only way to read a book; others would disagree and may choose to dip in and out, and either way is fine. There is absolutely no way, for example, that my lovely 'Yozzini' could or would ever read a book from front to back – not even one written by me – so I have written each chapter as a stand-alone, a patch in a leadership quilt. The golden thread that binds the patches together is the recurring theme of love in leadership – its inception and its lived reality.

So, having told you what the book isn't, if you are still with me and haven't chucked it to one side in the downstairs loo, let me now explain what it is. The book will offer you some insights, observations and honest reflections on leadership as I have experienced it and grown into it, and for many of you this will be affirming. I will talk to you about mistakes I have made and lessons I have learned from those mistakes that have helped me become the leader I am. I may offer suggestions of practical things you can adopt, adapt or cogitate over, perhaps some of which you may already have in place. I may make recommendations, state the obvious, provoke debate and discussion, but I won't tell you how you need to lead. All of our schools, or workplaces, are different and you can easily contextualise some of what I say to find the relevance for you (or simply ignore it!).

It has been said that while leaders are concerned with '*doing the right thing*', managers are concerned with '*doing things right*'. I think there is a case to be argued that modern leadership, in particular for the purposes of this book, can be a hybrid of both. The problem with trying to distil leadership into digestible chunks is that it is a unique practice to each of us who are in a leadership role – whether we are considered good or bad at it – and is enacted as such. This book is my unique take on it and as such there may be things I say that you disagree with.

As a leader, I have found that what endures, what is central to the efficacy and successes of any leadership role I have had even in my earlier years, particularly in the schools that I have led, are the relationships that I have forged – as they are the vehicle by which my team have collectively achieved our outcomes. It is a truism that as a leader, my ability to communicate and share my vision, to instil my values and to demonstrate emotional literacy have been crucial to successful attempts to transform schools in which I have worked, and none more so than my current school, in which I can exemplify the message of leading with love in so many ways. The anecdotes and stories are not prescriptive or formulaic, but if what I do resonates, then you can adapt it to your own context.

Why am I writing about this?

It is my belief that your social, cultural and educational background matters a lot less to your potential success in life, or as a leader, than your self-awareness and determination to make a difference does. If you remain focused on your legacy, remain driven by values such as excellence in yourself and others, integrity and honesty, if you retain a sense of curiosity, and you remain eager to learn, then you can create magic in your workplace (whatever that may be) that has long-reaching impact.

But you will likely not be able to do this alone; you therefore must learn to trust and empower others. You must be prepared to embrace your fears and take calculated risks; you must be prepared to do better when you know better. You must be self-reliant yet prepared to embrace the advice of a critical friend. Above all is the ability to be able to manage physical and mental health and 'switch off' to prevent becoming overwhelmed.

Of course, these statements could be obvious, but what may not be obvious, if you have not been led in this way and not had a good leadership role model, is how you may develop these attributes, how this may actually look and how you can emulate these things in your life and thus leadership. This book is my attempt to make accessible some of those conceptual ideas and give concrete examples of how you can implement them in your own leadership journey, no matter your context, age or stage – whether you are at the start and about to commence a Post Graduate Certificate in Education (PGCE), well into a Headship or Principle role, or even if you are a leader outside the vast world of education.

There are few inevitable certainties in life: one is death and one is change. Nothing remains static and that includes each of us, and preparing for change, in relation to expectation and behaviour management, is key to thriving within it.

On the way through your leadership career, I would recommend that you hang on for dear life to a few leadership traits that are not confined to the Western world: key amongst which is your humanity. We all have the same hopes, fears and concerns as everyone else – even those tricky parents/clients or pesky inspectors/assessors. Remember, as leaders we are not the hero of the hour; our job is to create an internal climate in our setting where sustainable change is nurtured, and this will involve us being empathetic and able to model how we expect others to behave. If we are able to embrace emotional intelligence (vital because our leadership will be tested when we need to manage emotions within a group, providing direction in times of high anxiety and stress), then we are assured of cohesion, collaboration and support through any change process, in any professional arena.

Wanting to achieve the best outcomes, knowing yourself, being able to laugh and also to self-regulate, being able to keep things in perspective and being resilient in the face of adversity are all transferable skills for leaders across the globe, in all sectors, at all phases of their careers. The same could be said for dealing effectively with conflict, making difficult decisions and having the ensuing conversations in a sensitive way, learning from our mistakes and making effective contributions to team projects, all of which are essential in leadership and which I will touch on anecdotally in the book.

What could you gain from reading it?

What better time to write about leading with love than during the 'hangover' following the world being tipped on its axis, a period in history that will be analysed and written about for hundreds of years to come, and may perhaps be remembered for only a few things: the 'Brexit shambles' and imminent recession, the estimated world Covid-19 death toll passing the 6 million mark, and the humanitarian crises of Russia invading the Ukraine as 'The West' exited Afghanistan?

What better time to reflect on which experiences have brought me to this point in time, in the roles I currently occupy in the little town where I live in the North West of England, and to try to share some of those experiences in a way that demonstrates how we are all capable of growth, all capable of becoming the poppy that grew through the cracks in the pavement? Each of us must build on the foundations of our own childhoods, and if we recognise this and are lucky enough to work with children, or have children of our own, then we can actively give them some of the necessary experiences in their learning to provide them with skills for life we may not have had access to.

What I will remember about this period, set against the grim backdrop of 2020–2022, is that when the protracted measures to address a pandemic meant we were all isolated, and physical connection with others was no longer permitted, when normality ceased, and when people began to dissemble, I was asked repeatedly to reflect on my views of leadership in one podcast after the next, through one blog after another, and something in me grew. Simultaneously, I realised that several people considered me 'inspirational' and that made me feel extremely uncomfortable – mainly because I really am quite ordinary, but also because something about that concept made me seem special, and as if my accomplishments were beyond reach of other people, unattainable, and that is simply not the case.

Our experiences, and how we absorb and then manifest them, can define us, and the perspective we gain from our lives can be moulded into powerful narratives that can enable us to authentically situate our leadership, in turn perhaps inspiring and motivating others. Now, let's be clear, this isn't a navel gazing exercise and not at all self-aggrandising, rather a consideration about how and why we might inspire others – what it is about who we are and what we model that others connect with on a profound level.

This book will hopefully take you with me as I reflect on 25 years as an educator, of one sort or another, and 47 years on the planet, trying to navigate the curve balls that life tends to throw at us all, whilst discovering (and latterly maintaining) a sense of gratitude and an awareness of the everyday joys that can be found, despite the difficulties. I will touch on leadership theory a little, but mainly the lived experience of it, which may involve one or two of you starring in the narrative, and hopefully all of you engaging with it at one level or another. It aims to bring to life the realities of school leadership and how I successfully enact it, by reflecting on and drawing together experiences from both life and the joys and trials of leading.

I may have a doctorate, but you will see there are less 'big' words, rather more 'real' ones, and a lot of naked truth. It does not claim that experience has made me an expert; I have no awards for 'Services to Education', and I am, by and large, quite a simple soul, lacking the kind of charisma that sees others in our field carrying many tens of thousands of followers on multiple social media platforms, and (until now) I am unpublished. You may discover some pearls of wisdom, quite by accident probably (as I am not sure wisdom is something I am known for!). If you do find any, then all I ask is that you share them far and wide and in doing so pay forward what I have learned in the hopes that others will gain from the cornucopia of mistakes I have made in this mortal endeavour we call 'living', and try to emulate, as I do, those who have carried me, or reached out, when I have needed it.

The pathway to what I consider my 'successful life', including my successful professional life (more about this as you hopefully read on), has not been linear, easy or straightforward and has withstood significant heartache. Equally, it has been so rich and wonderfully diverse.

If you have ever felt that you are 'not enough', if you have ever been told that 'you will never', or ever felt like you will always be standing on the outside looking in, then perhaps this book can outline to you that if I can do it, then anyone can, you included. I should say that at times the content of this book may trigger you; it may remind you of painful things you would rather forget because, let's be honest, life *is* tricky, and our best lessons are not necessarily learned in the classroom or lecture theatre but in the melting pot of life. A word of caution: if you are upset by anything in this book, reach out to someone, don't suffer alone.

What I know to date, from a life well lived, and several leadership roles, is perhaps distilled into this book; many of you who know me will find yourselves, or how I am in our relationship, within its pages; essentially though there are many aspects of leadership that are generic, thus, the same challenges present themselves no matter the school, country or phase, even the organisation.

As I have already said, in addition to my day job, I am also a mum of two teenagers, aunt to nine living nieces and nephews, and I have supported them throughout each of their developmental and transition phases from birth to adulthood and into the workforce, through friendships, romance and bereavement, in one way or another – by and large, parenting presents people with relatable complications to leadership. I am a Reservist in the British Army, and anyone who has completed any training with the Army may well echo my shared sentiments. I have been a lecturer in leadership at MA level in three universities, with the joys that working with likeminded professionals has brought me, and finally, I am considered an 'academic' (in the same way that having run two marathons, I can be considered a marathon runner!). Despite my best efforts, I cannot give this up – if you have done any kind of study on top of work, and/or parenting, then you will definitely understand some of the angst I will talk about. I have given parts of my heart, my soul and even my actual body to many deserving, and some not so deserving (yet nevertheless needy), people across the decades of my life, and others have given pieces of themselves to me so I could conduct 'essential repairs'. I am literally like a well-loved, patched up, children's bear. A 'Patchwork Leader', and it is all of those glorious patches that lend the meat to the bones of the leadership narrative contained within this book.

The beginning . . .

After many years of being told that I should write a book, and telling myself that I would have nothing to offer, that nobody would want to read what I had to say, and letting *imposter syndrome* win, I decided to take the fight to the enemy that is self-doubt, and this book is the result of me maybe winning this battle, if not the war, against it.

There is, of course, intellectually robust research evidence for the educational efficacy of leaders constructing caring communities that does lend credibility and validity to me exploring what this means for me in practice. It is also echoed in the processes by which creating a loving or 'caring community' may be authentically achieved, or how I have attempted to achieve it – and that pretty much sums up the book!

The first barrier to overcome was 'where to start?' and naturally, having spent some time obsessing over this (about 10 years), the most profound thought occurred to me following a recent podcast I did.

The beginning, Vic. Begin at the beginning!

Taking the hand of my inner child

The beginning of my leadership journey

Life can only be understood backwards, but it must be lived forwards.

Soren Kierkegaard

I was asked to do a talk for MA students at Liverpool Hope University recently, with a focus on my leadership journey. I thought that this would be a bit boring, hearing a potted history of my career over Zoom, so instead I gave them a kind of list of 'takeaways' from my career, in non-chronological order (sorry for all of the history buffs reading this) that underpin my leadership and that each person could discuss, reject, adapt or adopt. I have elaborated on the points I made, off the cuff that night, in the following chapters, and I hope that somewhere in them you can see that we don't tend to grow *before* we are immersed in something, but *after* we emerge from it, always on reflection, and always acknowledging the default settings we have. Leadership I think starts internally, with self.

In order to try to give some structure to this book, I have made it thematic, attempting to show growth over time in each theme, with early chapters focusing internally and working outwards, from self to community to society.

I know that my inner child tells me I am not good enough. It tells me that if I had been attractive enough I would . . . , if I had been clever enough I would . . . , if I was strong enough then . . . , but this voice can be taken to task, and is regularly. When I am telling myself I am not brave enough to . . . I list in my mind all of the times that I *have* been brave and remind myself how I felt before, during and after. In doing so, I familiarise myself with the discomfort of my feelings, label and compartmentalise them so that when they next arrive, I can greet them head on rather than be afraid and run from them.

Who is my inner child?

'Jump and I will catch you,' said my dad, smiling beatifically. So I did. I jumped into his open arms from the third or fourth step, and he caught me, laughing, and

DOI: 10.4324/9781003281313-2

the pure joy that I felt, usually so absent in our existence then, was priceless, and addictive.

'Again!' he said, 'this time, go up a step!' I did. He caught me. In the unusual elation that I found myself immersed in, it never occurred to me that this heightened sense of happiness was a warning, that before all great catastrophe would come great delight, and yet . . . 'Again!' he said, 'this time, another step up!'

Only this time there were no open arms to catch me, there was the hard, and particularly unforgiving, thinly carpeted floor of the hallway in our terraced house, in the heart of Liverpool 8. I landed awkwardly and was winded, the atmosphere changing in an instant and a sense of foreboding arriving in the pit of my stomach. Apologising profusely, and picking me up, he implored me to do it again, promising this time that he would definitely catch me and reassuring me that he hadn't meant to let me fall and hurt myself. Fighting the tears that threatened to spill from my watering eyes, I did as I was told – you always did as you were told in our house, for fear of the repercussions not just to you, but to our mum, who would definitely pay the 'blood price' of any real or perceived disobedience or deviation from the expected.

'Ok, this time!' he said, 'Another step up, the big one!' My knees were shaking, and I was afraid. It seemed a very long way to jump, especially when I was not absolutely sure that I would be caught, but I had no choice. 'I will catch you,' he cajoled, a strange and bright look in his eyes.

I jumped. Although the sixth sense that I had developed over my limited years had already told me that something was amiss, I wasn't prepared for the bone-breaking landing and the white-hot pain that greeted me as my dad stepped out of the way a second time. The first experience in leadership that I had was there on the hallway floor, at age five, screaming in agony, as my dad said, looming over me before walking away, 'That's the best lesson in trust that I will ever teach you'.

Why she needs love first . . .

As a human being, I have had to learn not to despise the weakness in that broken child, not to be ashamed of her impotence when someone bigger and more powerful hurt her, and not to let her raise her head when, 40 years later, she is faced with other 'bullies', for want of a better expression (but in keeping with the immaturity of that inner child), now that she has 'found herself' and is also big and strong.

That in itself is the most profound lesson in love and benevolence anyone can learn, the wisdom to treat yourself with considered compassion, something that I will discuss later. What I learned very quickly however is that, both metaphorically and literally, there is nobody there to catch any of us, personally or professionally. There will be adults and colleagues who we love and care for who tell us they will not hurt us or let us down and yet see us crash to the ground repeatedly if we allow it. Therefore, we must prepare to take each jump in life ready to land on our own feet, and never expect to be caught. Sometimes the landing will be painful, and I have learned as much from those painful occasions as I have from the ones where I have been fortunate enough to have found the loving arms there to swing me upwards.

Superficially, as a teacher, it taught me to always look out for the quiet and supremely well-behaved child in the class, who is tightly wound and keen to do everything right, who appears to not understand or know how to have fun and be carefree, the one who is aware and vigilant, who jumps at the slightest noise, always sits with her back to the wall and her eye on the door and who is essentially a swan in the making. I was, and am to a degree still, both heart warmed and slightly envious of those who have a catalogue of fun stories from their early lives and the inner contentment, the healthy attachments that it takes to enjoy things in adult life with complete abandon. It isn't my story, but it is something I am continually working on to this day, something that we can all take cognisance of when working with others, particularly children or the vulnerable, but as leaders in schools, then we must also be aware of it when working with staff and parents.

How to relate self to leader

What has inner child theory got to do with leadership, though? For me, fundamentally, being a good human being is central to being a good leader and begins *internally* as you navigate the expressions of your inner child. Knowing this taught me on reflection (where much of leadership learning lies, actually) that *each of us has an 'inner child', and we are not responsible for the creation of it, just its management.* I now look for that inner child in myself when faced with a dilemma in any of my roles, and I also look for it in the staff that I support, the children with whom I work and the parents that co-create the educational reality for our children. I own my inner child, and I articulate how it makes me feel to my senior leadership team so that they can act as a 'check and balance' for my responses, as I do for them when their inner child reacts and attempts to hijack their amygdala (the technical expression for 'make them freak out'). There is a close relationship, I think, between the 'chimp brain' and the inner child; both are capable of hijacking our reactions to things and both are not in the realm of the conscious decision-making mind, but both can be trained to not derail us completely.

I am not a psychologist, and there are many books out there on trauma, attachment and the importance of cognitive development between birth and five, so I won't try to summarise them here. What I will say is, undoubtedly, each of us is the product of the lottery that is our parenting, combined with our social strata and circle, and our physical attributes. Social capital is as real as emotional capital. None of us gets to choose the factors that shape us in our early years, any more than we get to choose if we are born with one leg or two, Welsh or Scottish, yet we can choose the way we embody those unique elements and allow them to affect our future as we grow – provided we both learn the language of feelings and also have something other than what we have always known and experienced to aspire to that broadens our thinking.

Growth and why it is key to developing emotional literacy

Elizabeth Marvel said, 'If you can see it, you can be it'. This is where true leadership lies, creating the space for people to learn about themselves and others, think about who they want to become and then have the courage to build steps towards that goal so that each can know better, in order to be better. In short: growth. Understanding relational exchanges and having a working knowledge of emotional literacy and intelligence are key in being able to create cultures where individuals can become an improved version of themselves, and that begins close to home.

If you are lucky, then you will have avoided working for a chaotic leader who cannot 'self regulate'; if not, then you will have been subject to the impact of it on staff. Let's be honest, if we all enacted our inner child in the workplace each day, unrestricted, if we interacted with everyone based on our inner child, then the world would be a very chaotic place for everyone. Sentient adults know this, but it shouldn't be a 'given' that everyone knows it, or that everyone is able to contain themselves and their behaviour even if they are aware of it. The nuanced part of leadership that I have come to realise makes such a difference in any organisation, particularly an educational one, where emotive and emotional transactions are central to daily life, is giving everyone agency to both be the individual they are, with all of their perfections and also all of their failings, yet facilitate their personal growth so that neither adversely affect either the individual or the organisational integrity.

This is 'big' stuff for leaders in a marketplace because there are many other unrelenting issues that a leader may feel take precedence over 'knowing self', but for me, placing self-awareness and emotional intelligence at the heart of how I lead has enabled me to build brilliantly effective and efficient teams in different settings. Therefore, I am sticking with my tried and tested method!

How is this possible in a school? Model it!

I will say to my senior leadership team, in the 'green zone' of all round safety that is my office when the door is closed, that my initial reaction at times is hurt or distress about an issue; or I am unable to understand the motivations of a particular individual and feel frustration or disbelief and need to talk my feelings through. I will articulate the topic with as much information as I have, ask them openly to challenge my thinking and feelings with their understanding, acknowledging that I am struggling to consider the situation impartially, and offer coherent reasons why. It is this routine occurrence that sets the tone for them as developing leaders to be able to do the same. In modelling to the team how cognitive dissonance manifests, and being authentic, it permits each of them to replicate this. We always (using all of our combined strengths) respond professionally, fairly and appropriately as a team. Following each action taken by me as the final decision maker, my 'After Action Review' (written, verbal or internal; an expression brazenly nicked from the military and firmly embedded now as our reflective practice has matured) elucidates some learning that has taken place for me on a personal and professional level, again to model the process full circle to the team.

As a leader, then, your first responsibility, *is* perhaps to yourself. Not just for literal 'self-care', eating well, drinking water, sleeping, which are obviously vital for maintaining physical and mental wellbeing; but to *knowing* yourself and reflecting on who you really are and what motivates, triggers and satisfies you. It is as important to know what makes you happy as it is to know what makes you angry. If you have a menu of happiness-inducing activity to choose from, then when the going gets tough you can pull that out and select appropriate countermeasures to the stresses of leadership or life. Hero leadership is something of the past. As a leader I know I am not the most important, but my decisions, language and behaviour *are* the most important influence on the culture of my school, and my inner child, and the way I handle her impact on me, is what influences my decisions, language and behaviour. It is impossible to extract ourselves from our leadership.

Where can I start to learn about myself?

These kinds of things are love/hate usually, but one of the tools that I do every few years or so is the 'Myers Briggs' personality assessment – mainly because I wonder if I change or have changed over time. I do this out of curiosity, but I have to admit, something about the random questions (which clearly are not random at all!) is so intriguing. I am, without fail, always surprised at the accuracy of the outcome, and indeed, the fact that it remains the same despite any changes in life, job, or the world. Another self-awareness tool that I have used and found quite thought provoking is the Johari Window (and its opposite, the Nohari Window). This is a technique designed to help people better understand themselves and their interactions with others. Created by psychologists Joseph Luft and Harrington Ingham in 1955, it is still used as a heuristic exercise for people to begin to explore the impact of their personality on other people.

I am aware that I am an 'INFJ-A', one of the 16 personality types created by Katharine Briggs and Isabel Myers, creators of the Myers-Briggs Type Indicator (MBTI). I have a framework through this for examining to what degree I exemplify the traits and therefore the aspects of myself I need to be acutely aware of in my work environment. Incidentally, INFJ stands for introversion, intuition, feeling and judging – if you know me in real life, and you have googled the INFJ-A description, you will be hitting your forehead in agreement right about now. I challenge you, however, to go and do the test and look at your own without cringing!

By definition, INFJs are re-energised by time alone (which can be a huge irritant for many people who want to be around me). We focus on ideas and concepts rather than facts and details (and this means I need at least one 'detail expert' in my team because I know I am not blessed in this area). I make decisions based on feelings and values (sometimes to my detriment, but never compromising my own integrity), and yep, I am not controlling, I just prefer to be planned and organised rather than spontaneous and flexible, like the rest of my INFJ brethren.

An INFJ personality type can also be referred to as the 'Counsellor' because of our tendencies to be idealistic, compassionate and sensitive, and if you work with me, you will know that I spend a lot of time doing just this. Other diminutives for an INFJ include the Insightful Visionary and the Advocate.

Are there any patterns in my life and leadership responses, and how do I address them?

Whether you are a leader, university student, teaching assistant, mid-day assistant, governor, visiting lecturer, trainer or a school child, if you are human, awareness of what evokes a response in you will help you shape the kinds of situations that you put yourself in and the learning that takes place as a result. For example, it can inform you about when to place yourself out of your comfort zone and how far you are prepared to go, and it can help you both anticipate and articulate how you feel when you are in that uncomfortable place – at any age or stage in your life or career.

In my mid-forties, for example, I decided to embark on the (as it happens) lengthy process of becoming a Reserve British Army Officer. I passed the initial stages of 'soldier selection', having attended Lichfield for a three-day assessment. I am pretty fit (for my age), intelligent (albeit not really blessed with common sense) and quite 'driven', yet I felt such apprehension before attending that I nearly didn't go (I cover this phenomenon in later chapters, but for now, it was 'fear of failure').

Everyone around me told me I was going to 'smash it' (they also said I was utterly bonkers for doing it), but no amount of encouragement or positive affirmation would shift the raging doubts I had. Those of you reading who have lacked self-confidence and belief at times will be able to appreciate what I mean, and the older we get, perhaps in line with a decreasing sense of usefulness, the more these increase – or they have done for me. To the outside world I was an 'Alpha', a total success, good at everything, and therefore there was no way on Earth I could or would not pass. To me, I was venturing into the unknown, at twice the age, at least, of any other 'recruit', and this meant the very real possibility that I may fail and embarrass myself in what I assumed was a largely physical domain.

Sitting in a lecture room on arrival the first evening and looking around, my heart sank when I realised that I truly was double the age of the youngest candidate, and I was likely to really disgrace myself the next day. As you may expect, I passed the academic assessments, passed the medical, which was actually the biggest relief for reasons I won't go into here, and headed into the second evening feeling pretty okay. I then spent the entire evening coaching two young girls on their academic skills, as I could see that they lacked confidence and that in failing the academic tests themselves that day, they may fail the entire selection. For those girls, it was a social imperative to pass in order to begin to climb out of the very difficult circumstances each was in at 'home'. Thus I found my niche.

My anxieties were eased by helping others, and I was delighted when, the next day, both girls had the confidence and understanding of what they needed to do to pass the tests at re-sit. I sat with the other female candidates, about 20 of them, awaiting the two girls coming back from their assessment, and I asked myself what it was I was anxious about. I really dug around in my head, a place I very rarely like to venture, and realised that I had nothing to be worried about other than the inner child in me who feared failure, feared judgement and thought she was not good enough – it was an eye-rolling moment when it became clear that the fears were not based in reality but in a construct of my own creation. When we were all reunited, the girls were effusive in their thanks for the coaching the previous night and shared what it would mean to pass.

As the eldest there, I felt like it was time for a little motherly 'pep talk', particularly given the life stories both girls had and the fact they did not have mums. They were all speechless when I told them that unlike the powerhouse and determined version of me they were seeing, there was another version that I struggled with based on some elements of my childhood. I confessed that I was once a vulnerable 17-year-old with a back story. I told them this was their chance, that nobody was going to 'catch them' and that nevertheless, they could survive, and had survived their childhood and that it did not need to limit them. I said that 25 years from now they wanted to be looking back on defining moments like this, from the security of their own homes and with a loving family of their own around them, knowing they had seized opportunity, gone with it and that life had unfolded.

In giving this talk and sharing with them that we all have our inner voices telling us one thing, and by listening to that voice, then rationalising what it said and creating a counter argument, we could achieve goals that previously we did not think were possible, I came to realise the message myself. I talked to those young women about overcoming fear and adversity, learning to understand their inner child, being financially independent and self-sufficient and looking to the people on their left and right for support. Having gained from my own pep talk, I then to my surprise passed the physical assessment the following day, as everyone else thought I would, and was delighted, if slightly dazed, to return home and realise that I had to plan to attend basic training. I began to tell myself then that I had nothing to lose other than pride, and given that my ego was fairly small, this was something I could tolerate as I realised that I was only competing with myself.

If I thought that soldier selection was a challenge, I had another thing coming when I attended both Basic Training in Exeter and, following that, two layers of Officer Selection at Westbury. At times I was so out of my depth – for example, weapon handling tests and 'pairs fire and manoeuvre' (a way of advancing in two sets of two whilst firing your weapon and remembering all of the drills you have been taught) – that I felt physically sick.

I told myself, and the youngsters that I was training with, that everyone must fail, despite us all being pre-disposed to try not to, and that failure gave us the determination to succeed. I may have led by example, asking for help and doing extra lessons in the evening, facilitated by Staff Styler and Cpl Muchmore who happily invested their time in my learning and development, but I felt ridiculous all of the time. I was arguing in my head on a daily basis that I should know better than to undertake something like basic training at my age, and on the other hand that I was doing it and passing each day; telling myself I was too old, yet being fitter than some of those younger than me – it was four weeks of constant mental conflict (inner voice is also covered later in the book). Yet I did it, tears, sweat, oil, skinned elbows, one of the most demanding months of my life, but I did it. Not only does it take self-awareness and a bit of courage to speak up, but it takes others who are prepared to help you when you do in order to realise success, and thankfully this was the case for me – as it has ever been. I have been lucky to have come across so many people willing to give assistance. One of the key people in maintaining that equilibrium for me at Wyvern Camp was the Platoon Commander, Dan Mills, a wonderfully patient and warm man who coached me through the fear of weapons and taught me I could shoot and who has since become a very close friend!

How does self-reflection in all aspects of my life underpin my leadership?

I was reminded during that training about learning any new skill and how it is a cognitive endeavour alongside a physical one, with muscle memory playing an important role. Excellence is merely repetition and relentless attention to detail, and that can be a metaphor for any part of our lives and all interactions. I tried to find the familiar in the unfamiliar and clung onto that, despite being in what felt like a hostile and alien environment. The Army didn't make it that way, I felt it, because I only feel 'safe' in my own home – something I didn't realise until I was there. What was familiar to me was helping others, and this was what made the experience feel real, supporting young people (some of whom had never made a bed themselves!) to rapidly develop skills of self-care and also to talk through the barriers they had in their lives and help them silence their own inner child, even if only briefly.

It was rewarding, yet it was an acutely humbling experience to literally go back to the bare basics of something in a way that I hadn't done for more than 20 years. I was not learning the ropes of being a teacher, but lying on Salisbury Plain in the night beneath a 'basha', with the rain pouring on the poncho, reflecting on the day like mental journaling, and it helped me make sense of it all.

When I returned to my day job, it made me think twice about the work we do in school with student teachers, and those who are newly qualified, to induct them into what is (for us) a familiar and supportive environment simply because we know the patterns of the day, the usual layout of the school and the expectations on us. Having felt the anxiety of learning 'at pace' many new subjects, with a lot of unusual equipment, and publicly with people I did not know, not only did my empathy for student teachers grow exponentially, so did my empathy for the plight of our children who are bombarded with many new things on a daily basis, whilst simultaneously being expected to rise to those challenges without issue.

During my adult life, as I have learned the art of self-reflection and analysis, I have been able to look back on when I have felt my most vulnerable and exposed, questioning the reasons for those feelings. I've considered my motivations, triggers and joys and been satisfied with knowing them – even if I wasn't always satisfied with the behaviours I demonstrated or the outcomes. But I went through the process, nevertheless. It transpired that learning to look for and look after my inner child, challenge it with grace and compassion, and tell it what it needed to hear when it was seven, or eight, was vital to being a good person. In learning to be a good person, I suppose from acknowledging my inner self, I have become a good leader – a leader who does all things with love.

What I know about myself and my beliefs in leadership all began at the point I lay on the floor, with my dad looming above me, and that knowledge has matured ever since. Leadership is not something I always wanted to do; it has been something that I have ended up doing, and for which I now feel a moral obligation, but it was never the purpose or the end goal for me. My main focus in life has always been, and is, to do all things with love, in the sincere hope that I can leave each life I touch the better for me having been in it. I have been let down and make it a mission never to let anyone else down. If I ask myself each day, what I have done that day to contribute to the world, and I can give myself an example of something that has made a difference to one person, then I think it has been a good day. This isn't just rhetoric or hyperbole; it really is how I live my life.

Supporting others to understand how their personal journey can support professional development

What has all of this to do with leadership, leading with love or with you?

A product of the Labour 1970s, I come from humble beginnings, like most of us. I am the eldest of four children, I have two sisters and a brother and all of us carry our scars from our early years – their stories are for them to tell, but my scars have taught me so much. One thing is for sure, when I was younger, I had no aspiration to be or do anything – my mind was occupied nearly all of the time either with survival or alternatively getting lost in the worlds crafted by others in their books. What my own primary and secondary school experiences gave me was the opportunity to do both.

This means that you could be the difference. Every one of us is a leader in our own way. You don't need to have the title of leader to lead, to charge ahead with love, anyone can do that, at any age. You can be the person you needed when you were struggling, or lonely or needed advice, or be the person you were lucky enough to be influenced and supported by, for someone else.

Learn to treat yourself with kindness and compassion so that you can practice what you preach and treat others with kindness and compassion. I have found this much easier to do than *love* myself; I am still a work in progress, but that doesn't stop me continually trying. As a leader, people will always look to you for the standards you set. It is this accountability that makes the role of the formally named leader so important.

So what? Practice getting to know yourself first. I won't tell you to get a journal or to meditate (I never have time for either in their purest sense). What I will say is take yourself mentally to a place you feel comfortable and be brutally honest about what goes on in your own head, heart and soul. You really don't need to share the dark parts of your personality with anyone else, just acknowledging both the darkness and the light to yourself will be enough to help you start the process of developing self-awareness.

I found it helpful to make mental lists of the things that triggered me and found the profound reasons why. I think, having come late to it, that having a coach could be so effective for this – it feels less intrusive to me than saying you have a therapist, but both would work equally well provided you choose the right person. The main point is to allow yourself the chance to see the real motivations you have and to let the realisation sit with you whilst you try to work out what the impact of those motivations is on your decision making.

I may have meandered, it is standard for me, but the point of this chapter is:

■ Know yourself (which means that you can . . .)

■ Be kind to yourself (because . . .)

■ Leadership starts with you (because . . .)

■ Each of us can be, and usually is, a leader (also . . .)

■ If you know yourself, then you can look for complementary skill sets in others (to make the best team you can).

'The past can hurt. But the way I see it, you can either run from it or learn from it.'

Walt Disney

Further reading/listening

If you like a podcast and 'self-awareness' is something you want to know more about in terms of leadership:

1. The High Performance Podcasts: Christian Horner: How Reflection Wins Races. https://tinyurl.com/Christian-H
2. Dina Rezk Describes How She Made a Friend of Fear. https://tinyurl.com/befriend-fear
3. TED Conferences. https://tinyurl.com/Great-Lead-TED

If you like a book and want to get the best potential out of your team in a number of levels:

1. Ferry, Korn (2017). *From Soft Skills to EI.* https://tinyurl.com/EI-K-Ferry.
2. Goleman, Daniel (1996). *Emotional Intelligence: Why it Can Matter More Than IQ.* Bloomsbury. ISBN: 978-0747528302.
3. Peters, Steve (2012). *The Chimp Paradox: The Mind Management Programme to Help You Achieve Success, Confidence and Happiness.* Vermillion. ISBN: 978-0091935580.

If you fancy doing the Myers Briggs: https://tinyurl.com/16-Personality-T
If you fancy doing the Johari/Nohari Windows:
https://tinyurl.com/JohariWi
https://tinyurl.com/NohariWin

2 The courage to continue

Resilience – where might it be found?

Leaders need resilience, we are told. It is essential. Though this concept is heavily contested. Where does resilience emerge and grow, and how can it be evidenced? Is it something that only manifests in one aspect of life, or does it present opportunities for transference no matter where you gain it?

In terms of my leadership journey, it would be difficult to extricate it from my life journey, as the previous chapter has illustrated, and subsequent ones will also show. For fear of boring you all, because my life story is known now through my TEDx talk, blogs and several podcasts, I will simply say that I have been blessed in the last nine years to be a Headteacher in two wonderful schools, working alongside dedicated and committed, talented and motivated adults and really having a transformational influence on the future generation and how they think. My ability to do this, and do it well so I am told, comes from the interconnection of lived experiences *outside* of work which translate into practice in work, and strategies developed in a professional context that I take with me into my personal life.

This chapter will illustrate how, as a direct result of several personal life experiences, a couple of which I share, I was able to internally construct a resilience overlay for my core personality enabling me to do my day job as well as I have done it – through not just multiple Ofsted inspections, but a pandemic and lockdowns also.

Resilience for sustainable leadership

For me, having resilience means that as a leader I am able to stay the distance and am not thwarted by any unexpected or unplanned adverse event, I simply use learned strategies from all aspects of my life to adapt and overcome any adversity. On a day-to-day basis, it means that when I must do things that are not universally popular, or make decisions that are right but difficult for everyone to accept, it is resilience that I rely upon.

The only problem with it is this: it cannot be bought, gifted or shared.

DOI: 10.4324/9781003281313-3

We each develop it in our own way, but resilience is often developed through suffering deep pain, failure, humiliation, being unfairly treated or being hurt. As a natural resource, it can be eroded and depleted at times, for which you then need a team to help you when your reserves are low. Equally, it can be maintained and sustained through successes shared and reflected.

The best leaders will not just show resilience, but also model how it is obtained, and this involves behaving in a way that can expose the leader or make them vulnerable, but it has to be authentic. It involves coaching those around them, supporting and encouraging them as they dive into, and then recover from, their hurt, mistakes and potential humiliation, and then guiding them to make links between what they have learned and how this has helped build resilience and future efficacy.

It is also something best viewed and understood as a retrospective exercise, where it becomes easier to evaluate the events that have assisted in the expansion of resilience as an existential concept – and hopefully when everyone involved has survived to tell the tale.

Overcoming 'ACEs' and how this can build resilience in us and others

Adverse childhood experiences (ACEs) which began really as a result of the violent nature of my father, and the latent and continued impact of them, means that I've been determined all my life to be both mentally and physically strong. Not only have I worked out physically, one of the benefits being that I have a very strong body, even at my age, but also I have exercised my mind and really given thought and consideration to my contribution to the events that have shaped me and what I have gained from them in terms of personality development. This afforded me the benefit of becoming mentally resilient.

I know that I would not have been in the position that I'm in now, would not have become the human being that I am now, without that reflection upon and the resilience created by many life experiences. Understanding how my early years, and profound life events I have experienced since, have affected so many facets of my personality has been transformational. It took me years to be able to see all of those components as part of a continuum, to perceive the start of that continuum for what it was, essentially a very complicated and, in essence, blameless situation. Once we can understand the reasons for events happening as they do, we become more adept at being able to make sense of the outcomes and able to regulate our responses to those events and future ones.

As adults we try to make things simple, to create pathways and understanding in order to make difficult things more palatable and digestible, which sometimes has the converse effect. I have found this easier the older I get because I try to exemplify my lessons learned for my colleagues and my own children, and in trying to help them make sense of things, my own understanding is enhanced.

Essentially, however, in finally understanding that my father suffered 'ACEs' of his own — as a child born at the start of World War II in Jarrow, his mum poverty stricken and starving, his father away at war for what would eventually be almost six years, and then his placement into a children's home for the care his mum perceived he would receive that she felt unable to give — I made peace with him and his legacy.

Knowing what we now know, in a different century, and after lifetimes of dedicated study in a number of countries about the psychological significance of 'birth-to-five', how children form attachment and this then informs their relationships in the future, one does not need to be a psychologist to understand that my dad, on being rescued at almost six, when his father returned from Europe, may have been emotionally and cognitively damaged for life.

I knew intuitively that it was really incumbent upon my generation to change the cyclical narrative of 'damage begets damage'. I pause here whilst that statement sits in your mind. If *we* do not change toxic and harmful cycles, then who will? I think the building of resilience and the range of life experiences of my siblings, subsidised by the care of my extended family, supported us to be able to accomplish the sub-liminal aim of changing the narrative. Mixed in for me, however, there was a lot of guilt, envy of others and profound sadness. Not having a 'dad' to turn to, not having a father figure, was a massive challenge for us all, not to mention whilst simulta-neously carrying the stigma of a dad who had killed himself. My mum did subse-quently re-marry some years later, and we were all adopted by her husband, so we did have a 'step-dad', my siblings and I, but even that was fraught with complication.

There remains a lot of sadness, if I am honest, which is the silent companion of resilience and the part that is rarely acknowledged in books or discussions on the topic. I explained to my daughter on a long journey recently that a lot of people have *sad* stories; I don't know any strong people who don't have a 'sad' or at least 'complicated' story to tell, but they are not the only stories in their repertoire, and this is what gives them strength. The strength that I have is definitely something that many people have benefited from, not least me.

As leaders, how aware are we of the experiences that have created resilience in our team members?

Can we capitalise on that resilience and help individuals and the wider team to see it for the life-enhancing and resolve-strengthening experience that it was?

Me? My youngest sister was diagnosed with a very aggressive form of blood cancer when she was 19; her chances of survival were 'limited to none'. By then I was living a wonderful life in Kenya, running a prep school, my first 'toe-dip' into educational leadership, swimming a mile a day in the open air pool in the Nanyuki Sports Club underneath azure skies, and eating lunch in my garden with the back-drop of the majestic, snow-capped Mount Kenya, my dogs Turkana and Amboseli never far from my side.

I recall having a swim in the sun that day, in January 2000 and, although gliding effortlessly through the water, having an uneasy feeling in the pit of my stomach. The call from my stepfather is hazy in my memory now, as it was so shocking, but within minutes a bag was packed, and I was on the road to Nairobi, three hours away, ready to catch the night flight back. Of all the things to recall about that night, it was the look on a famous cricketer's face, one of the other random passengers flying from Jomo Kenyatta, who must have been extremely confused to see an extremely tearful young woman talking to herself the entire time, repeating mantras and promises to herself that if her sister could only live, then she would do anything. Anything.

What greeted me in Manchester Airport that bleak January was how unprepared I was for the cold weather, and also how distracted I must have been when packing to return. My uncontrollable shaking was either the freezing temperatures and my lack of long trousers, or the terror of what was coming settling like an icy blanket around my heart; I could not tell which. I stayed with my aunt and my nan and waited at my mum's for my sister to return from her boyfriend's house – the oncologist had told my mum, not my teenage sister, the nature of the diagnosis, and within two days she was in the hospital, hair cut short, ovaries removed and with a Hickman Line implanted into her chest.

But before then, she needed to be told. My mum, recovering from extensive surgery to repair damage to her jaw caused by repeated beatings from my father, could not talk. We sat in stunned silence in the living room, and my sister walked in. To this day, the look of fear and realisation on her face about the reason for my presence, when the day before I had been thousands of miles away, is unforgettable. My reassurance that I was there not because she was going to die, but because I was going to make sure she had the strength to fight, haunts me (along with another singular moment of all-encompassing heartache that has taught me more about my strength and resilience than anything and helps me endure, which I will expose later). Having difficult leadership conversations since then has been made more manageable, finding the words to deliver unpalatable messages through the gut-wrenching feeling in the depths of your stomach is something that I am able to do now, as a result.

That defining moment, at 25, solidified the knowledge that I could not crumble and that, just as I had realised as a child, there would be nobody to catch me if I were to fall. My layers of resilience were building without me even being aware of it. I needed to step up, where perhaps my stepfather could not, and my mother was too paralysed with fear to do so. I needed to lean into this. I had to find my own fear, take hold of it and master it, or I knew it would best me.

I talk later about mastering fear as a leader, but this was the time when I first had to. My brother was away with the RAF, my grandfather had been dead for six years, my nan had breast cancer, my middle sister had an 18-month-old and was heavily pregnant, and my aunt was working full time. I was strong enough to be able to challenge the doctor, who as it happens was actually a modern-day miracle worker, the outcome of which meant that 20 years later, the only person to have survived such a prognosis and as a result of the drug trial she was placed on, a medical paper subsequently written about her, and with the product of my bone marrow running through her veins, she is still with us.

I think supporting my family through that was quite an endeavour. I was with my sister 12 hours a day, Monday to Friday 9 AM – 9 PM; my mum did the night shift, and her boyfriend (now husband) did the weekends. Other family members contributed, I am convinced of it, but my memory is so narrowed at that time through the emotional duress of it all, and I was so focused, that I recall only the *routine* of what I did, and even then, the trauma has blotted out much of the detail.

Death had terrified me since my own father's death, and this fear was heavily punctuated with the sudden death of my grandad, my only male role model, the week after I left for university. He hugged me, told me he would see me in two weeks, and I never saw him again. My aunt found a letter recently that I wrote to her after I learned he was dead (before the days of mobile phones and social media). I had been in a drama lesson at Charlotte Mason College (now University of Cumbria) and was called out of the blue to speak to someone 'in the office'. Coming from an all-girls Grammar School, the very idea of this had me petrified the entire walk from the studio to the office, and when the lady within it offered me a cigarette or a whisky, I was scandalised as I wondered what kind of bohemian world I had fallen into. I silently reminded myself to ask my boyfriend at the time, Dev, who had been to the adjoining boy's Grammar School but was two years older and automatically more qualified to tell me if this was now standard practice!

Little did that kind lady know that she was about to kick off a slightly grisly story of mistaken identity when she said bluntly, through a cloud of her own cigarette smoke, that she had bad news to impart. My parents were on their way to collect me as my grandfather was dead. I naturally assumed that it was my stepdad's dad, not my precious golf-loving, gentle giant of a 'Grandi'. It was only on the arrival of my stricken mum outside the student house, in his car, that the penny dropped, and I went from pragmatic (my step-father's dad was a 'difficult' man and much older than my Grandi, and he had also been suffering ill health) to catatonic in one nanosecond.

Needless to say, I was as terrified of the concept of 'death' as much as the 'what comes after'. I had never said goodbye to my dad, or my grandad. Yet I suddenly had to confront this huge dark pit with my sister. We talked of her death, of her funeral, her wishes, her hopes. We cried. I held her in bed. We talked of marriage, of children, of careers, of ageing. We talked about our lives in a way that we never could or did beforehand and in ways that we cannot, and have not, since. I thought of the opportunities she would miss, the finite nature of life, and (although I talk of this later on) I realised that this was something I needed to learn from and I still relate to now, 20+ years later.

I had a relentless narrative in my head – I negotiated with *any* deity I could reach with my subconscious. I bathed her with 'holy water' from Lourdes, praying to a God I doubted existed; I surrounded her with crystals and implored the spirits to surround her with a protective aura; I pestered medical professionals and begged for the scientists to make magic happen; I looked at diet and food and wondered at the extent to which what we put into our bodies can nourish them to self-heal; I read books about the power of the mind over matter and created positive affirmations around her bed. The hours were unyielding. Her acute pain, her poor ravaged body, trying to keep a grip on my own emotions and mind, remain positive for her, and support my mother and other sister are times I struggle to bring to the fore now, long since buried.

I did not give up. I was tenacious and relentless and kept my mind strong at all costs – all key leadership skills that I didn't know I was forging.

I have been told many things in my life that are not congruent with what I have seen and experienced, so I am therefore a visual person, reading what I see and what I feel, rather than believing simply what I am told. I documented everything photographically. The allergy rash from platelets, the temporary blindness, the mouth ulcers that stopped her being able to talk or swallow properly. The swollen, the emaciated, the bodily fluids, the chemicals, the transparency of life and death. I documented it all. It was visceral. It was eventually used to help other teen cancer patients and remains an historical familial artefact.

What I didn't document were the inescapable feelings of rage and desperation that I managed to contain all day, with the exception of the day she was strong enough for me to be able to take her down in the lift to walk to the entrance and see the sunshine. On this occasion, a judgemental couple made some very ill-considered comments about her being a drug addict, the scourge of society, which even had she been, she would not have deserved, and as she was fighting cancer, she definitely didn't. I am afraid that my lethally cold and pointed response may have been a result of that pent up fury at the injustice of my sister being so young and so unwell, fighting literally for her life. As a leader, I try now never to judge on the superficial; that day taught me a lesson more valuable than that couple could have appreciated, despite their profound apologies and help when my sister fainted as the lift doors opened.

Those dark, relentless, wintery days on the ward, seeing people there one day and their bed empty, only death present, the next day, took its toll. I had, and have, the most incredible sense of respect and admiration for the National Health Service (NHS) staff who are able to not just survive those wards, but to do so with such never-ending compassion, kindness and love, supporting the relatives, not just the patients, so ably. They truly are super humans. On my worst days in education, I am conscious that they do not compare to days for people in jobs such as that, and having survived a pandemic, I can only imagine the tip of their daily iceberg.

What has this to do with leadership, this superficial overview of one of the darkest times in my life?

In hindsight, it was at this time that, in the crucible of life, I was unwittingly creating my largest store of resilience. Like the formation of oil, the creation of resilience takes a significant amount of time, and my sister's illness and slow road to recovery was like my own personal Mesozoic Age (spot the person who has just reviewed their geography curriculum). At the time I was getting through each day, clinging to routine like a handrail of survival. I got home from the hospital at 2130 and went immediately out for a run, pounding the streets for quite some time in the dark, of which I had (and had until my basic training for the Army) a mortal fear, to try to clear my head and exhaust my body. What I was in fact doing was teaching myself silently that I could survive anything, as long as I had a 'release valve' and the time to ensure that stress was temporarily discharged. Running has since become a mechanism for stress relief that I rely on regularly, methodical, a meeting of body movement and breathing. I had always been a swimmer for similar reasons, but mid-winter in the UK at night there were no pools, and running became the answer, finding a way to bring body and mind together in unison.

When times are challenging now, when Ofsted are due, or a particularly unfair or harsh complaint drops in the inbox, when your heart is splintered through a breakup, when you take over a very toxic school or simply have a shocker of a day, you can ask yourself, having been through something like that, 'on a scale of 1–10, where 10 is either death or hearing the words that tell you your loved one is in imminent danger of death, where does this situation fit?'

I guarantee that each person reading this, whether you are young or old, will have had their own version of a 'Mesozoic Age'. That time when 70% of their resilience was created. The most incredible thing is that with each new and more challenging thing you experience, it is movable (unlike geological eras!), but I didn't know this until something else happened 13 years later, nor did I have the language to explain it until years after that when I read *The SUMO Guy*, by Paul McGee, who is now a friend of mine and whose philosophy is closely aligned to mine.

Surviving divorce whilst simultaneously being immersed in my first (and very challenging) headship in 2014 became my upgraded, 'pimped out' Mesozoic Age. Who could have foreseen that?

The heartache of divorce, visited in the faces of my children, in their tears, their 'Recipe for Mending Broken Hearts' notes, in their desperate selves telling me they wanted to die rather than feel the hurt, was quite the 'meat grinder'. The defining moment of agony that preceded this was some weeks after the decision was made, some months after we had bared all to one another, my ex-husband and I, and the afternoon we had crafted in order to drop the carefully constructed bomb shell. In that moment I came to learn a valuable military lesson, incidentally, that 'no plan survives first contact', somewhere around the point when I mentioned to my children, who were eight and nine, that daddy and I had some important news that we needed to share, and my son jumped up, beside himself with excitement, and declared after begging for this eventuality for years, 'You are having another baby!!'

Needless to say, the confusion etched on his face when I explained the news, the way you could almost envisage his mind make the connections, was the second most singular moment of all-encompassing heartache I have experienced. If you have been through it, you will know what I am talking about without further explanation. If you have not, it won't take a huge leap to be able to picture it. If you work with or know anyone who has been through it, and let's be honest, who of us doesn't, then you will recognise some things in what I describe next.

Children can survive just about anything, as long as they have a tribe of people willing and able to support them and make a difference. That is what I know. The chances of a child thriving or not, however, are more subtle than just surviving and are usually rooted in the parents', or adults', behaviour towards the children, and/ or the way that they relate to one another, or relate experiences to children in a way that they can understand.

I have two children, and they're very different personalities. My son fell to pieces immediately. When we sat the children down – my then-husband had come back from working abroad, and they were just extremely excited for him to come home – I said that we had some news for them. I explained that Daddy and I had not been married for about two months and established that they had noticed no difference at all. I explained that everyone was friendly, and everything was fine, that there had been no difference to them, and I tried to reassure them that this is how it would be from then on because daddy and I were not going to be married anymore.

And despite all of that careful explanation and emotional intelligence, the tone of voice, the setting, the effort, the control – the children were utterly devastated. My daughter, who was a year younger, drew pictures for how hearts could be mended, and how love could be fixed, in the way that only children can. And honestly, I can only tell you that I thought that I'd never get over it. Life became a black hole, a vortex of numbness from which I doubted survival was even possible.

Yet, I did. I got over it, at the time, for my children, because what got me through it was the love that I had for them. I think again, this proves that my go-to strategy 'do all things with love' does work. Even at my most challenged, when going through divorce, I looked at my children, and I knew that I was capable of love and that love could endure because I loved them. I knew that I had loved my ex-husband with all of my heart when my children were created. I knew that I wanted my children to only ever grow up knowing that they were loved by the both of us because it was vital for their emotional wellbeing in the long term. I hadn't had a dad. I had struggled with that fact for my entire life. I'd had a stepdad obviously, but that hadn't gone quite to plan, and I hadn't had a dad as a small child, not in the way that my friends had, my friends who would say they were 'daddy's girl', or their 'daddy would do anything' for them. I didn't have that, but I wanted that for my children desperately. So actually, it all became about my children, and love, and therefore tolerable.

Having worked with children for more than 25 years, having been a child myself who had to recover from my own childhood, and having my children grow up through that divorce process I can genuinely say, it is much easier to support children to go through the process in a healthy way than it is to fix an adult who is broken because of any kind of trauma in their childhood. And I think any kind of divorce is like a bereavement because all children ever want to do is 'fix it'. They just want it to go back to 'normal', what it was like before, and it takes a long time for them to come to terms with the changes and realise that it will not return to life 'before'.

As I said, my children reacted differently. My son fell to pieces immediately. He said he wanted to kill himself. He couldn't bear it that his heart was so hurt. And that was a huge worry for me. I ensured that he had a lot of support at school. My daughter seemed unaffected at the time, however, it came out later on with her, when she was about 14 years old; my son by this point had become quite pragmatic about the whole thing, quite accepting. He was by now a young man, and he had embarked on romantic relationships himself.

My daughter had a huge and unexpected meltdown one night at her parents' evening in school, and she struggled for about two years afterwards. Children always want to know the reasons why parents split up; they struggle to make sense where often there is little to be made. Other people's parents they saw arguing all the time; we didn't argue – I'm not a person to argue at all. In my children's minds, they thought people who argued would separate and not people who didn't, who theoretically loved one another. But I just wouldn't discuss it with them. I told them that they would understand when they were older, when they were adults, because it was tricky. Life is complicated. And I didn't ever want to say anything negative about the other half of their family.

I think I just swallowed it rather than let it consume me, it was like swallowing medicine at times, but it really was for the best. It was a horrible feeling. It was a horrible taste. But it wasn't about being righteous, it wasn't about being the person who stands out as the one who's made the right decisions, or who has the upper hand, if there even is one in a divorce. It really wasn't that. It was just about this horrible situation that nobody would have wanted, that happened, and trying to work out how to make the best of it – the best of a bad job? I haven't always got it right, but where possible I've tried to.

I felt that my children needed to be protected because, at the end of the day, they hadn't asked for any of it; they were just the young people who had to try and live through it, with limited emotional resources and vocabulary to draw upon and use to explain their fears and feelings, their hurt and the sadness, and watching their parents hurt as well. All of those changes are challenging for children who like routine, who like anchors in the day.

Interestingly, I did all my crying in the shower, away from my children. I had my smile painted on for their benefit because I didn't want them to be hurt or sad, or worried about me. Actually, some point down the line, they both shouted at me, 'you're not even bothered. You didn't even cry! We're crying, you don't cry!'

And I was shocked. I confessed to them that of course I cried, I just didn't want to upset them, so I cried in the shower. And they said, 'you need to cry with us. So we can see you hurt just as much as we do'. Honestly? I was speechless. I thought that was deep psychological stuff that they were coming out with. It blew my mind a little and made me consider the notion of 'protecting' others from challenge or adversity versus sharing how we go through it and pass out the other side. It also made me consider the way I shared my concerns on a professional basis and allowed others in my job to see how I processed them effectively.

What has this to do with leadership, another superficial overview of one of the darkest times in my life?

My personal experience, and that which I absorbed from my children, informs the way I observe children in my professional context going through similar things, and how their behaviours articulate their feelings sometimes, rather than what they say. My experience enables me to be a more pragmatic and understanding, empathetic and sympathetic leader who can try to support colleagues as they traverse the challenges of divorce and separation, of bereavement or caring for sick relatives. I don't judge whether someone's dad is more important than their great uncle, any more than I judge if it is more important to allow someone to go to the funeral of their neighbour than their child – who am I to judge the value of a relationship or another human to a member of my team?

It means that, as a leader, I try where possible, as challenging as it is, to be open with parents who come to me and tell me that they are getting a divorce, to work with them to protect their children from emotional harm. It can be a challenge because lots of people want you to take their 'side', and actually I'm only on the side of the child or the children – not on the side of either parent. One thing I know for sure is that there's always a complex story behind any kind of break up, and judging is not my job.

Resilience then . . .

Now, this isn't intended to be a sad book, as you know, but it is important to illustrate that when I talk of resilience, and the anguish that I believe one must go through to find it, I really do mean that I have been taught it by living through adversity. It has then built up in layers upon the lessons learned in childhood and teenage years, things that have happened to loved ones and things that have happened to me. Learning to thrive despite the agony, to let the pain wash through and over me rather than drown me, that is when I knew I had developed it. Gibran (1923) describes it as 'life's threshing floor' in his book *The Prophet*, which is, incidentally, my manual for life. When you see it in yourself, that you have overcome pain and made it part of you, that your pain is now part of the universe, suddenly you realise that you are strong. Then there is no stopping you.

Hence, things like being mercilessly bullied for an entire year by a leader I once had, having a double mastectomy and recovering from that, loss of profound friendships, failure to get a job or promotion when applied for all pale into insignificance when compared to a handful of truly painful experiences. I am also now smart enough to know that there will be more fundamental losses in my life, and I am already consciously preparing myself for the unspeakable to happen, not just so I survive, but also so I am able to guide my children and siblings through, if we are lucky enough to remain within the natural lifecycle of human beings, and it doesn't happen to one of us first! I hope I have the resilience that will be necessary.

What has all of this to do with leading with love, with you as a leader?

Everyone you come across will have their lives outside of work, and none of us knows the inner machinations of that life. People suffer painful experiences all the time, and the larger the school, the more likelihood you will come across someone managing a challenging situation.

Modelling how one can use those painful experiences as a fuel to create resilience is a valuable skill because it is essential in being able to manage and survive in an ever-changing world. Looking back on your own experiences as a frame for how you have built resilience may show you that you have a large store that you didn't even consider, and one that can be enhanced. Sharing how you have done so may be a very powerful lens for others.

You will become accustomed to my meandering now that we are two chapters in, but the point is:

- Don't hide from painful situations, there is no point, you must embrace them (which means that you can . . .)

- Change the narrative from 'why is this happening to me?' to 'what is this teaching me?' (because . . .)

- Resilience starts inevitably with pain (because . . .)

- Each of us can be hurt and we can all hurt others; we cannot avoid hurt, only choose to learn from it (also . . .)

- If you know how it feels, you can explain to others how it made you feel and give them agency and licence to talk through their own situations and learn from them (to make the best team you can).

Further reading/listening

If you like a podcast and 'resilience' is something you want to know more about in terms of leadership:

1. The High Performance Podcast: Jo Malone: The Power of Resilience. https://tinyurl.com/Jo-Malone
2. Resilience Institute's Podcast. https://tinyurl.com/Resilience-Inst

3. Angela Lee Duckworth. Grit: The Power of Passion and Perseverance. https://tinyurl.com/Grit-and-determination

If you like a book and want to get the best potential out of your team in a number of levels:

1. Zolli, Andrew (2013). *Resilience: Why Things Bounce Back*. Business Plus. ISBN: 978-0755360369.
2. Hanson, Rick (2018). *Resilient*. Random House. ISBN: 978-0525525103.
3. Kahn, Susan (2018). *Bounce Back: How to Fail Fast and Be Resilient at Work*. Kogan Page. ISBN: 978-0749497361.
4. Winfrey, Oprah (2021). *What Happened to You?* Bluebird Main Market. ISBN: 978-1529068504.
5. McGee, Paul (2015). *S.U.M.O (Shut Up, Move On): The Straight-Talking Guide to Succeeding in Life*. Capstone. ISBN: 978-0857086228.
6. Gibran, Khalil (1923). *The Prophet*. Suzeteo Enterprises. ISBN: 978-1947844933.

3 Do what is right, not what is easy

Integrity – why?

I think leadership begins and ends with integrity. I think good leaders live their values and don't deviate. For me, this means I can sleep at night with a clear conscience and sense of contentment, even when I feel sad or melancholy. Not that I have always been this way; as I said, I learn my mistakes the hard way (which is from ignorance, not following my intuition or from trusting people who had yet to prove their trustworthiness).

When we are young, we often react to and treat others in the way that we have been treated. The adults who care for us in those formative years guide our choices, but not everyone receives the same kind of guidance, and sometimes the messages from home and the other environments we find ourselves in are not congruent.

My motto now is always do as you would always do, based on your core value systems. If you do this then your colleagues, friends and family become accustomed to you and your reactions, and this gives them, in turn, a social road map into predicting your responses and behaviours, and it makes your interactions far less stressful. This also contributes to the culture of your school or work environment and means that if you are not there, your colleagues are empowered and best placed to be able to make decisions based on the organisational values as inspired, led and enacted by you, in your absence.

I lied quite seriously as a child – to protect myself and my siblings and also to create an alternate narrative to explain our situation once we had moved to the Wirral. I am ashamed of this, but I have long since forgiven the child who was lost and afraid, and the lies she told caused no harm – except to her own peace of mind!

We were from deepest darkest Liverpool, although my nan had her own hairdressing shop on Mill Street in 'The Holy Land' area of Toxteth, my aunty worked in Walton Hospital, my granddad worked in finance and my uncle had his own car garage. None of this mattered to the people on the 'Other Side of the Water', also known as 'The Wirral'. As far as they were concerned, we were unsavoury, spoke

DOI: 10.4324/9781003281313-4

in a shocking 'Scouse' way, and clearly were beneath them because the four of us had 'NO DAD'.

You would be surprised in this modern and enlightened world, where gender reassignment, same sex marriages, adoptions by same sex couples or even single people and equal rights for all are accepted as standard in our society, to learn that only a few short years ago, this was not the case, and simply being from a single parent home with 'a story' was a scandal. So naturally, we were picked on. We were different. What the children and adults who judged us could not have known was that their insults and physically threatening behaviour were water off a duck's back for a veteran (albeit of junior school age) of violence such as me.

When they threatened my siblings, my superhero mask would slam down over my face, my cape would be out with a flourish and I would be ready to crack skulls and make sure everyone stayed back (even if only verbally, I've never cracked more than an egg!). Everyone was afraid of me, to my eternal shame, because I told them that I had eight big brothers who were all older and lived in Liverpool and would be prepared to come and break kneecaps unless the bullies left us alone. When they picked on us and said we were trash because we didn't have a dad, I told them my dad was a war hero who had died in the Falklands (I watched the news and read stuff, handy really when a quick fabrication was required), and I brought his family medals (a Dead Man's Penny from the First World War!) and Glengarry (provenance unknown) to 'prove it'.

My only brother was actually four years younger than me, and my dad was dead because he chose to be, and he was as far from a hero as it was possible to be. The lies worked, though. They were a bridge between being new and being accepted. I was tall and strong, and very fast. Eventually everyone forgot I was from Liverpool and became quite pleased with the fact I could run 80m like the wind and jump like I had springs for legs (although unacceptable now, my nickname bestowed upon me by the inimitable man who was such a father figure in primary school was 'legs').

Integrity – how might it look?

Safe to say that integrity hasn't always been at the forefront of my personality. When I was ruminating about this topic, several thoughts came to mind. The first time I had to enact my *leadership* integrity was when I was leading a school in Kenya, only two years into my teaching career, when I had to support a Teaching Assistant (TA) who had AIDS. As what may have been referred to as a recently qualified teacher (RQT until 2021), yet someone entrusted by the spouses of ex-patriate European farmers to teach their children to a UK standard, running a curriculum, organising staffing, meals and procurement, I have to say, I learnt a great deal at the teeth end of life when I ran that school.

Nothing could quite have prepared me for the guilt of telling a very unwell woman, with a child to support, in a poverty-stricken environment with no social infrastructure at all, that she would no longer be able to come to work. It was at this point that I became acutely aware of the duty of care we have as educational leaders (and I was only 24 years old), not just to our colleagues but to several key stakeholders and in myriad ways, most importantly of all, the children we serve. The TA had AIDS, which many people did have (at one point I was told that the statistics were 30% of all adults in our area), but it was my duty to ensure that the environment the children were in was as risk free as possible, and this meant routine testing for HIV and AIDS. Even before the testing began, however, I saw the lesion on her cheek and, despite her being absolutely lovely with the children and a great asset to our Prep School, on the Timau road, in the foothills of Mount Kenya, I asked her to stay at home until she was able to get her results.

It paved the way for how I have dealt with my colleagues ever since – with compassion, empathy and yet always with the children at the heart of what we do – and this has made difficult, upsetting and painful conversations that little bit easier to manage. I have jumped ahead, however; let me rewind the integrity loop again!

Integrity – how might it begin in life?

As a small child, one of my early memories is of being in the chemist on Windsor Street and feeding my baby with a 'bottle of milk' that I had picked up. It was a short walk to our house on Pickwick Street, and I was holding the pram my mum pushed, with my younger sister in it, carrying my 'baby'. We were halfway home from the chemist when my mum noticed that I had the bottle of milk (those over a certain age will recall the small plastic bottle with viscous, opaque fluid in it that appeared to disappear as you upturned it and 'fed' your baby doll). The fact is, I am not sure I understood the concept of *transactions* at that point; I had simply picked up the milk to feed my baby.

My mum saw a perfect opportunity to educate me (also known as traumatise me for life) and marched me back to that chemist, demanding that a shaking, wide-eyed version of me return the bottle to 'the lady' because we could not afford to pay for it, and sternly telling me that taking things without paying for them was stealing. Naturally, I was horrified. My father was, alongside being a violent sexual sadist, a criminal, and I think my mum was determined, even at that early stage, to ensure that the apples would fall as far from the tree as was humanly possible, and her sense of 'tough love' was not only my first taste of integrity, but also the blueprint for my own parenting.

Some four decades later or so, my own son, Thomas, was in high school, and I was called by the (long suffering) Head of Year. It was explained to me that Tom was due to be in detention for pushing some Y7 boys when walking down the corridor. I was scandalised that my son would have done this, it was out of character, but I thanked the teacher for letting me know and assured them that he would be dealt with at home. Upon his return that evening, he tried to tell me that he had done nothing wrong, that he had been at the back of the group and hadn't pushed anyone (nor would he, apparently, not only as an exemplary and model citizen but also as a Year 9!).

I had two choices: call the school and tell them that my son had been unfairly treated and was 'innocent' and have the detention rescinded through employing intelligent argument and persuasive techniques, or accept the punishment and explain to Tom that he was learning a life lesson. I chose the second option, despite it creating an issue for me and a 45-minute round trip to collect him from 'an after school', with the added headache of dealing with an initially disgruntled teenager. The rationale I gave him was simple; had he been in a group of boys out in the street and one had pushed someone, or hurt them, or one had stolen something or damaged property, then the police could have been called, and he would have been arrested as part of the group – with the potential of being found guilty of the crime or misdemeanour through association. I told him it was better to learn this harsh lesson now and think of it as a valuable mistake, through which he would grow and nobody had been hurt, than to learn it in another way. He accepted this with grace, and I am happy to say, it has done him no harm.

Integrity – how might it begin in leadership as an early career teacher?

My first experiences of working with integrity in education, however, were accidental and almost like a black comedy, showing me that children are capable of teaching us, as much as we are of teaching them. As a Newly Qualified Teacher (NQT, although that expression wasn't coined when I had just qualified in 1997 and has been replaced with Early Career Teacher – ECT), I went to work in an *amazing* middle school in Killingworth in Newcastle-upon-Tyne. Although I could probably write a book about what I learned in the four terms I worked there, as a Y5 core subjects teacher and a KS3 girls PE teacher, I will focus on my over-enthusiastic organisation of numerous residentials and fund raisers, fun activities and sports events. Now, those of you who may remember North Shields in the nineties will recall the (now permanently closed) indoor waterpark 'Wet N Wild' in Tyne and Wear. It was the United Kingdom's largest indoor water park when it opened in 1993, and in 1998 was the scene of me almost losing my job!

The name of the place, alone, would strike fear into the heart of any young female teacher accompanying hundreds of teenagers anywhere (we were a five-form entry middle school – five classes in each year group), but particularly where raging teenage hormones, swimsuits and water slides were concerned. In true INFJ style, I planned to the highest degree, and one of those plans was to wear a full Victorian-style bathing costume and a T-shirt. Needless to say, I was mortified when I was told by the attendants on arrival that the T-shirt would have to go. Despite the acute shame of the wardrobe malfunction, the trip was a huge success because, with great relief, we returned everyone back to school in one piece, no injuries or embarrassing episodes, and everyone had fun. If you have ever organised any kind of trip where you are in 'loco parentis', then you will know the pressure faced to make sure nobody comes to any harm – the planning, risk assessing, medical forms, transport, costs, letters . . . but when the children thank you, and the parents do too, then you know it was all worth it. As my first big event, I was delighted, for about 24 hours, and until I was on break duty with Y8.

Alice, one of the girls from the Y8 hockey team I coached, came to tell me that she felt she needed to do the right thing and come and be honest with me because I was 'kind, fun and lovely'; although I like to think that her sense of duty would have extended to those she thought were crabby and strict! She had some difficult information to share. Tim, one of the Y8 boys, had been telling everyone that I had 'been down the Black Hole' with him, and he had, in that dark and noisy place, with both of us wearing very little, touched my bottom. For the purposes of clarity, and to remove any doubt, this was not a euphemism, The 'Black Hole' was a snaking black tube with a figure eight rubber tyre (designed for two people to sit in and hurtle along at pace) as its transportation. It was a 45-second white knuckle event in the darkened almost vertical tube. I was apoplectic. I had not been on the Black Hole, nor would I have been on it. I saw my career dissolve before my eyes and felt physically sick in my blind panic. However, I went to report it to the boss, Mr Todd, then (as now) the most inspirational Headteacher I have known, in a complete state.

Mr Todd, pragmatically (and possibly by today's standards utterly inappropriately) laughed. He asked me if I had been on the ride. I hadn't. He had to explain to the extremely naive and socially inept 21-year-old 'me' that this could be easily rectified and that this was a simple fix. Upon asking Tim to come to his office, Mr Todd quickly established, from the highly intelligent and articulate Tim, that he had made the whole thing up after seeing me in a bathing costume (!) and was more than apologetic, not realising the impact that unfounded allegations such as this could have on the career of anyone, but especially a young female teacher in this case. No lives lost, as they say. Mr Todd showed leadership purpose; Tim, I am sure, will have learned a valuable lesson; Alice did the right thing; and I was lucky not to go grey. School is, after all, the place where education for citizenship takes place just as much as developing mathematical and literacy ability! The story of the Black Hole was talked about for some time afterwards in the staff room . . .

Some time later, the whole school went to the cinema for a Christmas treat. Different year groups meant that we were all separated out across various screens, but what a brilliant idea for all concerned. Remembering that this was a completely different era in teaching, and some of these things were just 'the norm', helps to understand the following story and also for us to see just how far we have all come in just a few short years, but this was then.

Each Friday a hard core group of staff would head to the pub for a pub lunch. Some of these guys were self-confessed 'old school' teachers, very anti-establishment, and for a young and impressionable teacher, they were like rebel superstars. I would hang out with them, the young 'wanna be' hanger on, very keen to 'fit in', but not that keen that I would drink! Drinking has always been my most lamentable non-skill, and to do so mid-day would have been catastrophe.

Anyway, this motley crew hatched a plan that during the film, when it was dark, they would sneak out and head over to the pub and have a pint, rather than remain in the cinema and watch children's Christmas movies. I knew that I could not do this. From the minute they were discussing it, I was already thinking of an exit strategy. Situation normal for me.

What I didn't know was, right up to the moment I needed to, how I could get out of it. So here is what I did: I pretended to fall asleep and did not go at 'H Hour', the agreed time of departure from the cinema. I had to come up with something convincing as an excuse for afterwards; I knew this even as I sat there with my best 'fake sleeping' look effected despite the negligible lighting. Looking back, they needed us newbies 'complicit' so our idealistic selves would not 'tell' on them, but I was not familiar with telling lies, especially given my lessons learned from the 'Falklands' lies of my primary school years, and thus my mind was blank. So I stuck as close to the truth as I could, and when challenged by the crew on the bus back to school, I claimed that I was so hard core, that even though it was mid-week, after a particularly heavy night out for my birthday, I was so hung over I had nodded off. I was the only one of the NQTs who I started with not to have gone, and when the ubiquitous Mr Todd 'set to' and commenced a full-scale investigation into this sorry state of affairs, he asked me why I had chosen not to go. I told him the truth – including how I had lied to my colleagues – and the shame was temporarily all-consuming.

What I learned from that day was that *integrity isn't a dirty secret*. That at times, not only would I have to act with integrity, I would be compelled to, but also that I would have to demonstrate this to others – even if it made me unpopular.

Integrity – how might it develop in leadership as a mid-career teacher?

Some time later, when working abroad and supporting the school where I worked as it was closing down, I made a mistake. The children in my KS3 Science class were all doing an assessment so that I could check their retention of knowledge on a topic. The lab was quiet, and I was marking papers when I panicked as I realised I had forgotten to check the address of a job application I was sending that day. I quickly logged onto the website and was in the process of jotting down the address when the Headteacher walked in. Noticing the large screen behind me, and the downed heads of the children, the Head said nothing, fixed me with a glare, and then left.

I knew the Head would be angry, despite the logical part of me knowing that checking that address was simply an example of concurrent activity and efficiency – I would be marking the assessment papers of one class whilst another class were completing their assessment. There would not be enough time for me to mark all of the papers; this was something that would spill into the evening and the weekend and I was okay with that, the address I needed was time sensitive and I was a professional who could multitask and organise my time effectively. The website was not inappropriate and was only on the screen for a matter of moments. The irony was that had I not been connected to the big screen with my laptop, the head would never have known, yet they did. Cringe.

So, I sent off the application and marked the papers that night, not all of them obviously, and the next day I was called into the office by a very irritated Head-teacher, accompanied by one of the young assistants, who interrogated me about my activity. I simply told the truth. I am not sure whether this was what the two leaders challenging me expected, actually, because with telling the truth, there could be no real issue. I apologised and said that it would not happen again, and naturally it did not.

This taught me that even when I had done something my superiors perceived as wrong, a genuine and heartfelt apology could take the heat and anger out of a situation – after all, where can people go if you tell the truth? It stops any further investigation or cross-examination, and all that is needed is a decision on the sanctions to be applied. I now encourage this kind of 'owning' with any member of staff who messes up or makes a mistake, as I know that people do. I am one of them, and I understand that lessons can be learned and also that your leadership style can be brought to life in doing so.

Integrity – how might it be enhanced in early leadership?

I once had an unexpected flash point of a situation to deal with when, as a school, we were nearing the time of year when every year group was planning to deliver the week-long 'Relationships and Sex Education' (RSE) lessons. As the head of a school with a large proportion of Gypsy, Romany Traveller (GRT) children, I was always extremely conscious of the cultural issues around this sensitive topic and also around the communication barriers that existed, often involving us reading letters to our GRT parents, or supporting them in form filling. I always asked class teachers to contact by telephone the parents who would struggle to read the letters we sent out *en masse*, which duly happened. What I suppose was not made clear in either letters or phone calls was that RSE week was a whole week and involved the whole school, all year groups. Thus, if you had a call about RSE week and had children in several years, you would be ticked off a list (we love a tick on a list us teachers) rather than receive a separate call for each child.

It usually transpired that in RSE week the GRT children would all 'go travelling'; some years they even developed a mystery illness, which meant the children could not attend, but by and large we all bumped along okay. Periodically I got into hot water, for example, when I invited a fabulous theatre company in to do a presentation of *The Happy Ever After* (I kept getting the name of that wrong, but thankfully for the purposes of the book, I have managed to ensure that it is correct!). So what? You would be right in asking, it is a pantomime, you run a school . . . yes, however what I loved about this panto was that the handsome prince (principal protagonist) did not want to find and marry a beautiful princess, no no no, he wanted another gorgeous prince to marry (the second principle protagonist), and they actually shared a quick kiss at the end of the play. I only had death threats for about six months that time, but this time was a little more frightening.

We had a Y3 child in school this particular RSE week, who we did not expect to see, but by the time we came to question it, she had already seen cats delivering kittens, and the cat was most definitely out of the bag. Within moments of the child being waved goodbye at the end of the day, a mob had assembled outside school baying for my blood, and it became quite a serious and potentially very physical situation. For the majority of our non-GRT families, including me as a mum, I felt that seven and eight year olds learning that boys have boy parts and girls have girl parts was tolerable, as was learning that cats have kittens (I have to say now, some years on, I am a bit perplexed by the binary aspect of this whole boy/girl concept, and this is a huge topic where I absolutely must learn more to be able to understand more, but at the time it was fairly simple and age-appropriate stuff). For our GRT families, their children had been 'spoiled' – a *very* serious situation indeed and one that horrified me.

Aside from seeing a mum, who I had personally helped and actually visited in her trailer a few times, in a state of apoplexy, spittle flying from her mouth, eyes wide and wild, and dragging her child by the scruff of the neck, I was also worried for the recently qualified teacher whose class the child was in – death threats were being bandied around like throwing confetti. She was bundled out of school via a different entrance and escorted home by another member of staff. I had to get quite loud to ask the numerous angry people to leave, and I had an escort to the car for that day (and quite a number of months afterwards) to make sure I was not jumped and the threats enacted on me. Police were informed. My front door at home was locked and remains so (much to the absolute frustration of my children), and I check as I leave and arrive every day.

We arranged a meeting with several representatives of the community and my stalwart Chair of Governors (Andy) plus the well-known Mrs W, and we tried to sooth fractious relations. I protected the teacher both physically and emotionally, taking responsibility for the situation myself. To no avail. The child was removed to a different school, and I was blacklisted as someone who poisoned children's minds, who was not fit to be a mother, who should have her children removed from her, and who should essentially burn in the fiery pit of Hell. Lesson learned, assume nothing, ever. Make sure you communicate everything in a range of ways, layering it so that there can be no confusion, and then check again.

Integrity – bringing together the life and leadership lessons

What does this eclectic range of anecdotes mean to you, in terms of leadership and leading with love? I needed to find my inner strength and my voice. I needed to find and own courage. For someone like me, this was terrifying, and yet eventually the most empowering thing to experience.

Find it I did, through many such incidents and events as those I have recalled. I never dreamed as a child, whose voice was silenced and lost for years through fear, oppression and the weight of responsibility beyond my age, that I could ever be in the influential and privileged position that I find myself in now. I have, as I have already alluded to in the earlier chapters of this book and publicly acknowledged in my TEDx talk, battled with imposter syndrome for all of my life, and the performance anxieties it creates.

I have delved into my cultural reference points and, with maximal effort and the generosity of so many people's support, have managed to mitigate for its effects. Now, as a well-respected leader, as someone who is listened to, it is a moral imperative that I not only create a culture in which everyone feels that their voice is valued and heard, but also one in which those who need it can have their voice developed and their confidence enhanced. But I get it wrong – in trying to get it right, there will be times that this is inevitable. Failure is just part of success.

It is really tricky to think of yourself as an inspirational person, or to accept that you are considered an inspirational person by others – however, I often think that it is genuinely a pleasure and a privilege to be raising one or two (as awkward as it feels for me to admit this).

Integrity is the bedrock that has facilitated my success as a leader and parent, layered upon knowing myself and developing resilience. But that integrity did not come from reading a book about how to learn to tell the truth, or how to turn around a failing school, or how to frame tricky conversations.

Integrity grew within me from positions where I had to make a decision and back myself following each until I realised the outcome. To accept when I had done something morally wrong and reflect on why, ensuring that where possible the lesson was learned – once. Then paying this awareness forward to others who, like me, were fallible.

What has all of this to do with leading with love, with you as a leader?

Everything!

You know the 'drill' by now, but the point of this chapter is:

- Don't hide from doing the right thing, celebrate it (which means that you can . . .)

- Lead by example both creating and sustaining a lived culture in your setting (because . . .)

- Integrity is everything in transactional institutions such as schools (because . . .)

- Relationships are built on trust and trust comes from all stakeholders knowing that you, as the leader, will do the right thing, with the expectation that they will too (also . . .)

■ If you know how it feels to do the right thing, even if this may make you nervous, anxious or unpopular, you can explain to others how it might feel, and give them agency and licence to talk through their own dilemmas and learn from them (to make the best team you can be).

Further reading/listening

If you like a podcast and 'integrity' is something you want to know more about in terms of leadership:

1. Steve Ingham (you can find him on Twitter as @ingham_steve) Has Recorded a Super Podcast with Dr Eva Carneiro (no.66), on 'Doing What Is Right'. https://tinyurl.com/Doing-What-Is-Right.
2. The High Performance Podcast. Toto Wolff: Empathy Over Engineering. https://tinyurl.com/empathy-over-all

If you like a book and want to get the best potential out of your team in a number of levels:

1. Kerr, James (2013). *Legacy*. Hachette, Australia. ISBN: 9781472103536.
2. Scott, Kim (2019). *Radical Candor: How to Get What You Want by Saying What You Mean*. Macmillan. ISBN: 978-1509845354.
3. Lencioni, Patrick (2009). *The Five Dysfunctions of a Team*. Jossey-Bass. ISBN: 9780 7879 60759.
4. Ryan, Will and Ian Gilbert (2008). *Leadership with a Moral Purpose: Turning Your School Inside Out*. Crown House. ISBN: 978-1845900847.

Words can lift us up or tear us down

Be careful with your words. Once they are said, they can be only forgiven, not forgotten.

Unknown

Taking personal responsibility for what we say

My mum always says that it isn't 'what' is said but 'how' that matters – to a degree, she is right. I think that the power of language is immeasurable. We know, as there is a large body of research that proves it, the impact of both the language and behaviour of adults on outcomes for children, in other words that both *what* is said and *how* really does matter. I am living proof of this, as many of you will be.

As random as statistics can appear (sorry mathematicians and statisticians), they do help at times to appreciate quantities of scale, for example, on average, research suggests that we use at least 7000 words a day. 7000. How many of us are aware of the words we use, their power and their potential? In how many different media do we use our words? To what ends? Some people can make lifetimes out of sentences such as, 'Would you like some water?' Others can make words like 'Education' sound like a death knell – so what?

If each of us committed to singularly taking responsibility for each word we say or write, if we put our words through filters as well as we do our 'selfies', imagine what the constructive impact could be on our fellow humans? My belief is that we should say what we mean and always mean what we say. As with most things, I don't just preach this, I also actively practice it (although by my own confession earlier, this hasn't always been the case). After a committed period of implementing my own understanding of conscious gratitude and kindness, I no longer have to think about doing it; this attitude is so ingrained in my subconscious behaviour patterns, hard wired now, that for the majority of the time I am completely unaware that I am paying compliments, offering to help, or simply being kind to people – in every walk of life. We are what we consistently do, as leaders and humans. The cognitive 'muscle memory', for want of a better expression, is such that it becomes a default setting.

 DOI: 10.4324/9781003281313-5

As perceptive humans (theoretically) with our heightened awareness, we 'should know better' as my nan would say. We know so much, yet we exist in an age of collectively acceptable voyeurism through social media and reality TV and ill-informed decision making because of fake news; an age where it is common-place and almost acceptable to be publicly aggressive, narcissistic or intimidating, whether we are young or old, using professional or private avatars waving banners of 'freedom of speech'. What appears lacking as we exercise our rights is a collec-tive admission that there is an absolute responsibility and necessity wedded to them regarding self-regulation and ownership of our language and behaviour in order to prevent unseen harm. The lack of this heightened expectation means that, increasingly, negative behaviour pervades throughout every aspect of our society, and as it becomes normalised, its potential for influence extends not just through today's society but long into the future.

What if each of us made a conscious decision to harness the power of language in a positive sense and engaged in interactions, not just on social media but in real life, not just with our loved ones, but with everyone, that perform like random acts of kindness, helping others to be the best version of themselves? In this instance, I think we may not utilise *social media* as much as we would utilise and propagate a collective *social conscience*. Whilst social media *can* be a transformational inter-face between us, so can every single human interaction that we each have. This is the place where leadership can really make a difference. Not just in schools, but in life, through example.

Harnessing the power of our language in schools

I have said this before so forgive me for repeating it if you have heard it, but for those not familiar with the story, I am indebted to my first primary school because of one young teacher and the power of a single sentence that she uttered, which maybe held little value to her, yet I genuinely believe altered the course of my life. I have often looked back and reflected on whether that school saved me, and the extent to which that comment literally created a 'sliding doors' moment in my life. The truth is I will never know.

Statistically, based on today's reductionist narrative of deficiency, I should never have been the success I feel that I have become. If I were in primary school now, my siblings and I would have been at the highest level of Child Protection (CP), and my mum and her family classed as the safeguarding adults, only permitted supervised access with my dad due to his rapidly deteriorating mental health and his repetitive threats of murder-suicide. Yet, I believe that I am a success in a large part because of words – words uttered to my mum and my nan at a parents' evening in that school, which incidentally still exists on Admiral Street in Toxteth, 40 years ago.

I can't really talk about the enforced isolation that my father subjected my mother to without explaining that I grew up in a home with a father who was a violent, paranoid schizophrenic and a lovely, yet vulnerable young mum. Her limited social life meant that we, her infant children (I am the oldest of four), were her only companions. I was immersed in language as my mum chatted incessantly. We were too poor for TV, and as my mum was a talented pianist and singer, there was always, always music and singing (when my dad was not around). As such, at a very early age I had a wide vocabulary and could read well before I ever entered a classroom. This potentially catastrophic start in life actually facilitated the inordinate amount of parental input that I received from mum, despite the enormity of what she faced on a daily basis, and as such, I know that I was blessed.

The first book I read as a child was *Tess of the d'Urbervilles*, by Thomas Hardy. The copy we had was green leather with gold inlay, a Reader's Digest version, I think. I could read it; I wasn't mature enough for the concepts back then, but I did know that Tess, as a heroine of sorts (albeit a tragic one), was a wonderful and caring girl who would do anything for her family. She was young, innocent and beautiful. This of course was her downfall because inevitably, as the female protagonist in novels of that era, she was sexually exploited – illustrative of a gross lack of agency of women at that time. She was a survivor of manipulation and physical abuse, and I loved her for it – not hard to see why! It remains one of my all-time favourite books, and thus began a lifelong love of literature, and let's be honest here, the myriad alternate worlds that stories offer readers as refuge. Many people who have watched the TEDx talk have said that me talking of this early relationship with words resonated with them, so I know I will not be alone – many of us take sanctuary in reading as an escape (and, incidentally, it is far healthier than doing so in alcohol or drugs).

Encouraging a love for language and a passion in reading is the greatest gift any of us can give our young people, and so many amazing Edu-Twitter friends are advocating for this on a daily basis (two oy my favourites are Rich and Simon: @Richreadalot and @Smithsm) that it is incredibly empowering, particularly for young teachers and students, to be able to access the most diverse range of texts with a mere tweet. There is very little excuse for children not to have access to the language diet they need today, in my view. Reading, supporting all children to engage with and develop joy in story, is a driver for me in school, and I never accept that some children cannot access text content because of ability – there is always a way.

The advent of the audiobook, for example, saved my own dyslexic son from a life of literary privation! Besides, nobody would have believed, in a reductionist society, that a child of infant age in a place like Liverpool 8, with the home life we had, could have not only read Thomas Hardy, but also that it would fuel a desire to read anything and everything they could get their hands on that has spanned decades. I do not limit my diet to one genre, and I advocate that nobody else should either, as those of you who received a random text from me in the #AVicCarrCalls book recycle will know. I digress . . . Unusually!

At the end of my first year in school my teacher said that I was 'University Material', and who could have known that those words would act as a magic key and would unlock the door to my potential? Even at my age now, and given my substantial experience in academia and education, I remain confused about what that expression meant in relation to my observed or perceived prospects, but what I do know is that no one in any generation of my working class family had ever been to university before, and therefore nobody really knew what it meant! Conceptually, though, it was an indicator that I had huge potential, and from that point on, I was treated as such at home.

Just for a moment, pause and consider how your family have talked about you since your childhood; think about how you talk to your children, nieces, nephews, grandchildren, if you have any. Think about how you talk to the children you may work with. Think about the messages you give from what you say and how you say it, and also the messages conveyed with what is unspoken. Do you say the kinds of things you really want someone in the future to tell you have lasted 40 years and still affect them in the most positively profound of ways? If not, what can you do to change this? Today.

Make no mistake, by accident rather than design, I absorbed this extremely positive narrative, and I came to understand that I *was* university material (*whatever that was*) because of the encouraging affirmations that became the discourse that surrounded me. The idea that there was an escape, to an educational institution where I could read books and be studious, was like a beacon flashing to me from down a tunnel in the middle distance. That there was *light*, regardless of the daily chaos our family struggled through, was a lifeline. In my mind as a small child grew a belief that evolved with my advancing years and exposure to life: university was an extension of school. School, which was actually a total revelation for me, was a place where I felt safe and where I knew and understood 'the rules' without having to perpetually second guess the atmosphere, the emotions and potential responses of every adult in the room.

Both of my primary schools were places where there was always someone pleased to see me with a hug and some kind words, which mattered because the chaos did not quite stop with the final, and successful, suicide attempt of my father when I was almost eight, and our subsequent move to the Wirral. My secondary school, however, truly did build on this because the rhetoric of success was relentless. The wonderful building that smelled of floor polish, and achievement, has hardly changed in 35 years: it smells the same, the language used with the girls is the same, the expectations are the same – I know this because my daughter has just left. But what a place for the academic and scholarly to stretch their brains and their ability to be resilient in the face of stress!

How we can absorb words from influential people and they can become part of our internal narrative

As an ugly duckling who had been told by a boy (in that hinterland between primary and secondary school, when your legs are too long for your body and you cannot co-ordinate, in the mid-80s when fashion was, at best, questionable), a boy whose name I have never forgotten, that I was the *'ugliest thing'* he had ever seen, I was quite glad to avoid boys.

In secondary school I felt so inadequate next to the laughing, glossy haired, happy girls that it is hard to put into words even now, these many years later. But school, the place where the teachers talked to us of this mythical paradise 'university' where we would all eventually go, and all things were possible, made me realise that I was *surviving*. I was getting closer to my goal. Whenever anyone questions my resilience and determination, I often think back to those days and smile quietly to myself. Let them question. Whenever I wonder if I can continue, I now have an abundance of examples where I *have* continued, and I think about those times and simply tell myself that I can. I really have survived all of my 'worst' days to date.

Secondary school, as it happens, was also the point at which the world properly opened up to me in a way that a child from an inner city, who experienced the terror of riots first hand on their doorstep, could never have imagined. If you are lucky enough to work in a secondary school and you are reading this book, I must urge you to reflect on your legacy, the one you are creating this very day. You wonderful people are in the business of working with those possibly in their most malleable and formative years, when peer pressure is potentially at its highest. The influence you can wield is simply astonishing. There are so many stories that people have shared with me personally or that I have read of celebrities who have been told things in secondary school by an adult that have remained in their minds and partially dictated the way they operate as adults – both shockingly bad and also wonderful.

I was encouraged by adults in secondary school to do both the Duke of Edinburgh (DofE) awards and also join the Air Cadets (ATC) in my teenage years – again things my family had no experience of and therefore could not have signposted me towards. It is important to acknowledge that, at that point, my life was lived in the narrow, socially and emotionally restrictive parameters of my home, unless I was doing sport, with the ATC, or doing DofE – but genuinely, these things were the making of me and forged my character and social interests for life. The elements of teamwork, healthy challenge and competition, alongside learning about the world, and the opportunity for endless sport and adventurous activities enabled me to begin to find mental calm, and a sense of physical harmony, in a way that city living and academia had never offered me.

You could be the person who makes the sliding doors comment to a child, or young person, to their caregiver – *you* could be talked about in years to come. You may not work in a secondary school, I don't, but when I was asked by the DofE leader of the local secondary school if I could help out, giving up a week of my summer holiday, I jumped at the chance. Although the trip did not take place in the end, I approached it as I do with all things – if you *can* help out, and it is not materially detrimental to your life or ability to support your own family, then pay it forward. I am not suggesting everyone rush out and volunteer, just that none of us switch off to the fact that opportunities may arise where we can do actual good, in word or deed, and it is worth reflecting on our ability to do so.

Harnessing the power of our language in life and leadership

University became a place where so much frightening change took place for me, and I had to cross so much unfamiliar territory, that it was only navigable as an absolute result of the love and devotion of two great men, father figures, and people that I love, trust with my life, and treasure to this day.

Johnny Lockley, my beloved friend and proprietor of The Golden Rule, in Ambleside, taught me to climb, to kayak, to canoe, to paraglide and, most importantly, that it was possible to feel safe. He gave me a job, through which I enjoyed a social life of sorts (I was utterly socially inept, as I remain) as I pulled pints. The bar was the physical and emotional distance that I needed then from other people in order to cope with crowds, and I knew that behind it I could begin to be someone who was happy, who knew what they were doing and who people found likeable.

I knew the locals, what they drank and in what receptacle; I knew the regular holiday makers and what they drank. I invested in people and made them feel special. I now translate this as a leader to investing in staff. I met each of the almost 90 staff in my current school on arrival and simply talked with them. I talked with them about their families, hopes, dreams, career goals and more besides. Around the busy day job, in a school considered 'failing', this was a large proportion of my time initially, but time well worth investing. I knew the way Johnny has 'seen' people, talked with them, accepted them warts and all, so they felt loved and valued in his pub made a difference to them and how they saw themselves. I knew he helped people regardless of who they were or where they were from. This is my take away from him and his investment in me, and I use it across all walks of life, most notably as a leader but also as a friend. For example, like all Headteachers I am emailed on a regular basis by a range of professional bodies in need of a variety of skills, or offering courses or support for people in various positions. From information gathered during the conversations I have had with staff, I am then able to assess opportunities and present relevant ones to people as I know what interests them, and where they are keen to grow. This means they automatically feel valued and their careers (and our workplace) are enhanced directly, not to mention spin off opportunities.

As a larger than life character, one of the most magnanimous, kind, caring and wise people I know, I was blessed that Johnny chose to invest time in me, and we talked about everything on our roaming trips around the Lakes. We were always off on an adventure, and never once paused to consider our physical safety – but those stories are for another day. He once said to me I had a 'brain the size of the universe', and said one day I would write a book – how right he was (about the book anyway). These days we continue to challenge and champion one another. We both had Covid at the same time and were poorly for weeks together, and we are both in the process of writing books – his is a colourful and hilarious autobi-ography which he calls me up and reads excerpts from (which make me blush!). What makes it so wonderful is having lost touch for a few years, a random twist of fate which brought my lovely mate Paul (who named me Vicki Scouse in Univer-sity – a name which still endures) and Dev, the 'Twit' to my 'Twoo', back into my life, subsequently brought Lockley back into it also. All the old crowd still pass through the doors of 'The Rule' periodically; Paul, Dev and I are no different. The Lake District has that effect on you – The Rule at its epicentre is like gravity, with Lockley at its heart.

Richard Lemmey, my lecturer and most cherished champion and friend, showed me more than the pure joy of sailing, Boursin cheese and lapsang souchong tea, he showed me books where I could find the wisdom I needed to begin to understand myself and heal from within. He inadvertently showed me the art of Kintsugi, and through our time in the Picos de Europa, walking with him through the Lakeland fells, sailing on Lake Windermere, and sharing my love of music, I began to metamor-phose. I babysat for his children, who have all grown into stellar men; he shared with me the pain of losing his first wife to Motor Neurone Disease, and the joy of finding his second wife, Jo, on a sailing trip. He has traversed my highs and lows alongside me, as I have his alongside him. The ebb and flow of life has inevitably brought us closer at times and placed miles between us equally, but we are always there.

When we talk now, it remains intellectually challenging and full of rigour as ever it was. We laugh and 'spin dits' (tell random stories), talk of the lectures and where those foundations in experiential learning, environmental science and out-door education have taken me – and it warms my heart. I tell him that he is still having the same impact on young minds now as he did then, and I know that I am right. Recently our paths have become intertwined professionally, and, to my great surprise, I have been working back where it all began in a small capacity, which is both an honour and a privilege.

Throughout my life I have been genuinely lucky and always met people who wanted to help me, and who talked to me about, and facilitated, my thirst for knowledge and drive for achievement. I now aspire to be that kind of person in all of my own interactions, particularly with young people because I genuinely believe that it is crucial to try to be proactive rather than reactive, to signpost and inspire early rather than try to signpost and fix later.

We know our responsibilities, as educators, as decent human beings invested in society, to ensure that every word we say to children is effective and appro-priate. This is particularly important in the current age of social media, austerity and financial pressures because simultaneously there is a diminishing capacity for good mental health and increased suicide rates in children (as they compare them-selves unrealistically to media-driven standards). Sadly, all of this is set against the backdrop of a deteriorating welfare state, and as a result, the formal support networks for the vulnerable in our society. This reality has been exposed in the aftermath of the Pandemic response, but it has been there, nevertheless.

Harnessing the power of our language to create legacy

We know the power of our words in building resilience and encouraging children in a school setting, and how modelling our behaviour is vital as children may not have the role models they need at home to do this with (and for) them. However, what I may perhaps *not* have realised until a few years ago, when for the first time in a decade I was off work (recovering from a double mastectomy and reconstruction surgery), was the power of words on adults!

This may seem naïve, because of course I know that over the centuries words have given us, as humans, armour – had the ability to break us and build us back up again. Powerful prose has *always* influenced and inspired generations, but I realised that ordinary people, like me, *like you*, could also have similar influence. What was incredible to me at this time was the outpouring of love and thanks, respect and care that I received – not from my family and my loved ones, but from people outside of that very small and tight circle whose lives I had briefly touched.

I was forced to reflect on my life, myself, what I had overcome, my career and the people that I had met, who have all had a part in my journey, and me theirs, and throughout it all were woven, like golden thread, words that created key moments of realisation and self-actualisation. I came to understand that never allowing any spare minute of unoccupied time had done what I wanted it to – prevented me thinking about what I thought was my dark and shameful history – but it had only been temporary. The minute I was forced to stop, I had it all to deal with. Two things emerged which may be worth sharing.

Firstly, if you have a lot of stored up 'stuff', talk about it with someone. I can promise you, if you let it out, verbalise it, it can no longer damage you from the inside, and you can sleep much better.

Secondly, it became apparent that I have not just been influenced at times, but that I had been influential: not just to children, who I have obviously nurtured and cared for in my job, as I was cared for and nurtured in my own schools, but also adults from all aspects of my life – many of whom wanted to tell me this fact when I was at my lowest.

It was both incredibly humbling and heart-warming to hear of how even very small incidents (many of which I had all but forgotten) where a throw away comment I had made, or a specific piece of advice I had given, had actually had enormous ramifications in the lives of the recipients. From nail technicians to strangers in coffee shops, mums in a running club to acquaintances on Twitter whom I had never met. Simple things, like saying 'You're not going to stop there, are you?' to a volunteer for example. I am very proud to have been part of her journey, incidentally, and I told her so when, after a few years of hard work, she didn't just have a Level 2 TA qualification but was a specialist HLTA for dyslexia. But when I reflected on this, I became aware that this is actually a statement that I say to a *lot* of people – particularly as a school leader or an MA lecturer, when people I am working with are progressing and achieving, but isn't a sentiment exclusive to those roles – I also think and say it in other walks of life. Which means we all can.

I heard from a young man who had been my 'star' pupil when I taught GCSE maths and English in the Army Education Centre years ago, Dan. He left as my most successful student, with both qualifications and an ability to interact effectively with people in the educational establishment. It broke my heart that an able and warm young man had been failed by both the social and educational systems and I was thrilled for him. He told me of the lasting impact of me having faith in him and giving him attention and time. I also heard from a parent from a previous school who contacted me to say that as I had shared the surgery, she had forced herself to get checked out and discovered, early, that she had breast cancer. I was astounded that 'throw away' comments, or simply how I am with people, had a lasting impact on them. It nailed home the fact that I needed to be SO careful with what I said in the future and actually take ownership of it to become more effective at doing this. We can influence people without knowing it.

Equally, three years ago I attended a formal dinner during which I talked with two lovely men that I had never met before, both of whom unwittingly inspired me in different ways; one even motivated me to take on a change in career! Between them, they changed my self-perception: my TEDx talk, this book, the podcasts I have done, the invitations to talk at things like the Army Foundation College, and the First Sea Lord's Leadership Conference recently, amongst many other things, and connections, are products of that night. Without their conversation, which ostensibly was about what I had always considered my 'boring' self and boring life, I would never have considered the prospect of becoming a reservist soldier, nor that someone like me could be considered an interesting person with so much to give! I might have said that, if asked, they would possibly not even remember me, never mind our conversation, when actually this isn't the case as we are still very much in touch, but the impact of their connection, for me, was a second 'sliding doors' moment – only this time I was completely aware of it and seized the initiative. You can inspire and be inspired in any setting, at any time and at any stage in life, to do anything. Fact.

As an educator, it is inherent in my DNA almost to help bring what is for me the true sense of education to life wherever possible, through formal and informal means, and in a range of contexts, from working out in the gym, to social media to teaching the national curriculum. I am therefore fortunate that I have, in the past, been able to not just coach my peers on MA courses in leadership, but also influence the academic journey of people such as Mike B from my circuit training class, spending many evenings after my youngsters were in bed going over his assignments and supporting him (he calls me 'Inspiration'). My neighbour at the time accused me of having an affair with him, painful and mean spirited, and also totally untrue! I just knew that I could help him, and help him I did. He has gone on to do an MA (and I think there was a first somewhere or the other . . .) and is thriving in his career and life. I was chuffed to be invited to his wedding and to have really felt that I left a legacy when his beautiful wife said she knew all about my part in his development.

Charlotte, a perfect stranger, was sitting working (and looking sad) in the coffee shop one day. The only free seat was next to her, and, noticing a pile of academic papers next to her, I just struck up conversation with her whilst awaiting my friend to grab our coffees and join me. Ten seconds in and all I wanted to do was assist her because she said she was going to resign from her post as a secondary English teacher and remove herself from the MA course she was doing, the research for which was beside her on the bench and the main reason I struck up conversation. My friend Rebecca joined us, amused that I was chatting to another 'stranger' and let on to Charlotte that if anyone could help her, I could. . . . By the end of our chat, I had given her my contact details, and we were corresponding. She didn't leave teaching, did get another job and also attained her MA! She is now influencing young women in the school where she works and advising on future pathways. Incidentally, she always leaves a parcel on my doorstep at Christmas and often asks to have a walk and usually runs career options past me when we are out. She educated me in the fact that random life-changing conversations like this are called 'Bus Stop Moments', which was in fact the subject header of our first email exchange.

From my own most recent MA research, I was able to connect several inspirational speakers with some of my secondary friends and colleagues in order to support their endeavours in school in relation to careers. These seemingly insignificant connections matter to people and alter outcomes in ways we cannot see at the time. It is only when people bump into you, or seek you out years later, that you become aware. One of those people recently visited me and, over coffee, asked if I would do some work with them to add another dimension to the outreach activity they occupy themselves with; of course I said yes. I am contacted on Twitter regularly by people asking for help – with applications, mental health, how to resolve personal issues and so on – and I give help willingly because in helping one person, you are helping all of those people that they in turn will help further down the chain. If you pause for a second, that is actually a simple, yet mind boggling fact.

In my 25-year career, I have been able to challenge the stereotype that teachers carry, not just through the words that I say, but through my behaviour – and this realisation took a lot of reflecting and honesty, not to mention imposter syndrome quashing. Teaching does not stop during the 13 weeks holiday we have or at 3 PM. Not one educational practitioner that I have worked alongside goes home and stops wanting to positively impact friends, family, colleagues, children or parents. Not one educator that I personally know is anything other than a lovely human being. Therefore, I believe that if I treat my colleagues well, if I coach them effectively, then the ripples will be felt by everyone that they interact with in their lives and so on.

In each interaction I have with other people, I endeavour to make a positive difference through what I say and what I do, whether I ever see it manifested or not; it can happen spontaneously, but it can also be planned carefully. Whilst the unique combination of attributes and traits I have developed as a result of my life challenges and experiences makes me who I am, there are elements of my beliefs and how I behave that are not unique to me, and I have been extremely lucky that I have been influenced in the same way by people who clearly share my values. I could list hundreds of people who have made my life bearable, tolerable, wonderful, full of hope, hoofing, glittering, amazing and all things in between – I hope I tell those people at the time, and afterwards, I hope that they know. The truth is, we all have the capacity to be that person who can make the life of someone else awful, bearable or amazing. We all have a choice.

I joined a networking group a while ago that involved simply walking around a local lake early on a Sunday morning. Christina, the lady who encouraged me to join, having seen my posts about authenticity and leadership on social media, shared my philosophy on how we each have a responsibility to improve outcomes for others and to live with integrity through human interaction and reached out. She simply wanted to help others who have aspirations, where this is possible. Christina and Kate, the third person in our trio and someone else I have forged lasting links with from that group, won't be the only people who do, but they actively do it – coaching young people and taking the vulnerable under their wing. For some of us, it is about knowing *how* to encourage others, for which I would suggest that there are many books on leadership and coaching that can help if you are in your workplace in a leadership role, but there is an even easier place to begin for everyone regardless of their job, and that is from the next moment, with the next word you say to someone, the next tweet or Facebook post, the next Insta or TikTok.

Harnessing the power of our language to model how we can succeed

People looking at my substantial CV and list of accolades may be tempted to think that this has all come easy to me, that in some way I have led a charmed and perfect life, when nothing could be further from the truth – although I am undoubtedly lucky, blessed even. I have learned the hard way, I have been badly hurt and let down when people have said things to me they did not mean, when people have overpromised and under delivered or simply lacked any kind of moral integrity. I have made it my mission to try never to behave like that because I know how it feels to be on the receiving end. I always talk from the heart, as a leader in work, the leader of my home, a young leader in ATC, and as a potential leader now, in a very small way, in the Army Reserves.

Being open and vulnerable, being honest about the hurdles I have been forced to overcome, and not being afraid to share my strategies for survival and resilience, even on my weakest days, may well have given people hope. What drives me, and has created my success, however, is living each day and relentlessly focusing on being my best self, and by association anyone encouraging the same in anyone with whom I come into contact – conversation by conversation, word by word, message by message. There are no quick wins, or easy fixes. Like losing weight, where a diet can only get you so far, it is the small and sustainable changes you make that become routine and habitual that will ensure that the weight stays off, and you are healthier for it, the relentless attention to detail.

I am a mum, headteacher and officer in the Army reserves – as a publicly recognised leader, I believe that I have an absolute moral imperative to take care with what I say to everyone. Those of us privileged enough in our roles as we move up the leadership ladder perhaps have a working knowledge of this in the workplace, but for all of us in our roles in society as parents, family members, colleagues and friends, we need to ensure that we take responsibility for our words and our language because it matters. Children follow what they see, but so do grownups. We have leaders amongst us, those aspiring to it and living it.

What we say matters; the best leaders know this and *actively* seek opportunities to say meaningful things to anyone and everyone they come across. It is this concerted effort that distinguishes the good from the great as it enables 'reach' and influence to extend far beyond the immediate group of individuals because people recreate what they see modelled and enact it in their circles of interaction, a ripple effect.

What has all of this to do with leading with love, with you?

You will be familiar with the layout of the summary by now, but the point is:

- Language and what we say matters; words are valuable currency (which means that you can . . .)

- Invest heavily in others in all walks of your life, from the staff room to the coffee shop, a governor's meeting to a beach walk (because . . .)

- You never know the impact of your words or a single conversation on someone, the impact may take decades to be realised (because . . .)

- We only ever see a fraction of someone's life and what they are dealing with, the demons they battle, the goals they aspire to (also . . .)

- We know that if you can empower others to be and do better, then it is your moral obligation to do so (to make the best team you can).

Further reading/listening

If you like a podcast and 'language' is something you want to know more about in terms of leadership:

1. Greg Clowminzer: Episode 30: The Language of Success. https://tinyurl.com/defining-success

2. The Shine Show: 103. Unlock the Secret Language of Success. https://tinyurl.com/Success-language
3. Kelly Holmes: One Person Can Change Your Life. https://tinyurl.com/Kelly-Holmes
4. TED Conferences. https://tinyurl.com/TED-for-Time

If you like a book and want to get the best potential out of your team in a number of levels:

1. Sant, Tom (2008). *The Language of Success.* Amacom. ISBN: 978-0814474730.
2. Burnett, Dannella (2021). *VISIBILITY: Success Stories from Elite Leaders Making an Impact from the Stage.* Hybrid Global Publishing. ISBN: 1951943449.

5 Influencers are dreamers

Dreaming big – so what?

One of my earliest memories is one of dreaming big, I just didn't know it at the time. We all allow ourselves to dream; a lot of us strive to accomplish our dreams, whilst some spend lifetimes lamenting not doing so. One of my perpetual conundrums is, as leaders, how can we support others to reach for and realise their dreams? How can we show people their potential and enable them to create the steps towards reaching it? If you haven't grown up seeing it, or working amongst it, how can you dream of attaining it?

When I grew up in the 70s, children in impoverished families in lots of schools in deprived areas were given free milk! At the time this was shrouded in controversy because I recall the slogan 'Thatcher, Thatcher the Milk Snatcher' commonly bandied around after the Secretary of State for Education at the time, who became future Prime Minister Margaret Thatcher, authorised the end to free school milk for children older than seven in 1971. Interestingly, I came across a report recently that suggests she actually opposed this decision and was forced to announce it by someone else. The poor lady was a scape goat (Spence, I know she is your hero, so I hope you are happy that I have defended her!), but nevertheless, our school must have decided to divert funds to ensure that we had it, and I am grateful! I digress, again!

At the time, it was just a 'thing', milk, and when I have asked people about this since (people of a similar age!), they tell me that theirs came in bottles – but some inspired individual (or logistical genius) made sure ours came in cartons. Those cartons were like a trail of breadcrumbs to the world beyond the realm of our tiny little corner of Liverpool, because on the outside of those cartons were countries. Admittedly, they were quite stylised, stereotypical images representing countries, but they were a psychological hook. At first I wanted to have the full set, and I tried to be methodical about ensuring this happened, keeping little notes in my mind of the ones I already had (my personality!), but in the end, I was always trying to get the one that had Kenya on it. Kenya. Land of the unusual. Land of dreams.

DOI: 10.4324/9781003281313-6

I was obsessed with that Kenya carton and swigged the milk, warm or cold, in 'quick time' just to be able to flatten and enjoy looking at it! Who knows why or how they chose the countries to put on the cartons, but Kenya was eminently intriguing to me. It had a whole host of wild animals, unusual looking trees and wonderful savannah, and I began to dream about going there even when I was only five and had never travelled beyond the boundaries of Towyn in North Wales.

Now, my auntie was a prolific traveller and storyteller. She would tell us stories about the smells and sounds in souks and bazaars of Marakesh and other wonderful exotic things she had experienced, like waking up to see the sun reflecting off the majestic pyramids in Cairo and so on. I asked her about Kenya, and she told me about this place where animals roamed, and people on safari could sleep in tents and watch them at waterholes. In my childish and fanciful mind (and if you can picture something similar to that of a hybrid *Out of Africa* meets David Attenborough), I hung off her every word. I was there!

What I know now is that at that time, even as described by my aunt, colonial rich (and often but not exclusively white) people were cutting around and exploiting the land and the people. It was more creamy pith helmets and mass slaughter for ivory, with afternoon tea served to memsahibs on the veranda and sundowners served at the Safari Club and less human rights and equality than it should have been. Nevertheless, I was determined to visit Kenya one day, and my dreams came true, quite unexpectedly, when I was 20. Not only did I visit, but I was even blessed to live there.

My love of Kenya was unimaginable: from the smell of the red earth when it rained, to the sounds of the insects at night, the beauty of the Acacia trees, to the incomparable majesty of seeing animals in real life. I was hooked from my first Christmas holiday visit. When the chance came, after I had graduated and had some experience under my belt, to move there permanently and run a prep school, I jumped at it.

Our home, a modest wooden house with views of Mount Kenya from the windows and a 45-minute drive between us and the next nearest neighbours, no internet or TV, no phone for a year, but filled with books that I bought from the little shop in town and some that I had posted to me on account by Fred Holdsworth, the bookshop owner in Ambleside, was perfect. Even then I knew the wonder of dreams coming true. Even then, the life-changing influence of what we see in school was evident. The power of influences in the classroom is not to be overlooked.

As a leader now, reflecting on the current national pressures imposed through an Ofsted inspection system, of a 'diverse broad and balanced curriculum', I actually see dreams being made, not inspection reports being written. I think back, 'All of that from a carton of milk?' Imagine then what seeds we as educators can plant in the minds of children these days, with virtual reality platforms, interactive web resources, 5G video clips and movies, books and TV documentaries embedded as part of your wider curriculum offer?

If a carton can inspire a traumatised young mind to dream big, dream beyond the borders of her post code, city and country, then each of us, each of you can do so in your classrooms if you are guiding learning and creating magic. Imagine your range of influence on pupils alone?

How our dreams can influence the environment we create for ourselves and others

What this story illustrates to me as a reflective adult is that our environment, where we live and work, filled with the overt and also the subliminal, can be influential, just as much as our families and the people who formally educate us. Of course, marketing executives will be laughing at my naivety, it is those messages that help them 'sell', but for those of us not well versed in marketing strategy and psychology, there are stimuli everywhere – so, let's maximise the impact of it as leaders.

Our human influences are largely those people that we grow up with, who nurture and care for us, but not everyone is lucky enough to have a bard for an aunt to tell them stories, or to travel, or listen to music or read books. Right now in the UK, after more than a decade of enforced austerity, particularly post-2008 financial crash, and especially since Covid, poverty is rapidly on the increase, and families are under so much pressure that even those invested in their children may struggle to give them the time and stimuli to help them grow dreams. This is what makes our jobs so vital. We have to be in the business of generating dreams!

A leader, an influencer, is someone who motivates and inspires others through the sharing of knowledge, philosophy or vision. We, as educators, can influence the minds of young people, especially as leaders in schools, but we can also influence the minds and attitudes of adults – an absolute passion of mine.

What about when we achieve our dreams?

I have achieved my dreams to date. Bar one. My dreams have been varied, and once I have realised a dream, I begin to think about the next one. Although I have always had help with my dreams, nobody has actually come along and handed them to me on a plate. I have been a lifelong learner. That is evident, I know, and I am often asked about how I squeeze my study into my busy work schedules and family life. The secret here for me is prioritising. If I commit to study, be that the National Special Educational Needs Coordinator (SENDCo) course in England, the National Professional Qualification for Headteachers (NPQH), or an MA, I simply acknowledge in my own head the time frame that I will need to sacrifice other things in my life, or marginalise them, as I focus on achieving the qualification. This balancing act sometimes gets 'out of kilter', and my social life has taken a back seat, or my love of exercise, but it can quickly be brought back into line with careful compartmentalising of my diary, and the support of my family. It is possible, if you were wondering . . .

I know that achieving dreams is sometimes about luck, as my Kenya story was; sometimes hard, hard work, dedication and sacrifice as my doctorate was; sometimes being in the right place at the right time to even know there was a possibility open to you, like joining the ATC after seeing Air Cadets in Liverpool one day collecting money for charity; and sometimes a combination of all of these things, like this book. Dreams need work to be achieved, but not all work feels like hard graft or manual labour. Sometimes we actively help others realise their dreams, and at other times we are oblivious, and it happens because they see our example – this is why we can never let our standards drop. We can never allow ourselves to lose our integrity, and we must always be aware that adults and children are looking to us for the standard we expect.

Leadership dreams

When I moved back from Germany, my dream of working as a deputy head was realised, but moreover, I found in one of the governors who interviewed me for the post, my very best friend. We essentially raised our children together and supported one another to be able to work. Her self-less commitment to supporting me was irreplaceable, and I am forever grateful for it.

At my last school, in my first week of my first Headship, my path crossed with someone who has become my firm friend ever since, but hilariously, the first few times we met it was not pretty! Five days in and her son thumped another child in the face. Horrified, but with righteous indignation on my side, I rang her and said how disappointed I was. She responded quite aggressively and told me that she had instructed her son to take matters (that she insisted were not being dealt with) into his own hands. I was equally forceful when I explained that I had only been there a week, that she needed to give me time and information and have some faith in me to do the job before writing me off as ineffective and prepared to turn a blind eye to child-on-child aggression. She agreed.

The following week, she and another parent had an altercation in the car park, and, again horrified, I called the police to send a clear message to all parents that this was unacceptable behaviour. I received a written apology. I had been warned not to allow this parent into school, under any circumstances, and it was evident that she felt alienated, yet she was passionate, committed, dedicated to children and a very prominent member of the community. So I pondered during my circuits class about how to engage her in productive and meaningful dialogue and a fruitful relationship, and thankfully hit on an idea. That idea planted a seed in her mind that she could achieve in her own right, and it grew.

I asked her to head up the PTA, which had been run by the Teaching Assistants in school to that point, all of whom I was asking to do more and more during their day job, and who I wanted to ensure were not over-taxed by also doing fund raising. I have to say, she not only headed it up and raised a lot of money for school (with bells and whistles on!), but she went to the next level of being a 'good egg' and supported the vulnerable in our community. She brought the elderly and the school together, worked with companies and charities to generate income to self-perpetuate the good work she was doing, cared for the children, put on events for staff, did night shifts for us when we decided to do sleepovers in school – she was, and is, amazing. She ran in local elections as a counsellor and was successful, doing something similar in her village that she had done in our school. She also ran a non-profit-making summer club for children in three villages to support a government initiative and became an active member of the school Governing Body. She travelled to London with me, twice, and shared my dream of running the marathon there, twice, as my unofficial support crew. She brought me a welfare package the night before my first breast surgery and was there not long after I woke up after the 12-hour ordeal to check I was okay.

She acknowledges that partly as a result of my belief in her, she has accomplished so much since we first met. She has found dreams, and these have led to more. I think all I did was help her fill in a few forms. She had the dreams – I fanned the flames and gave the psychological crutches for her to find her feet and realise them. She has no sisters, her mum died some years ago and having that strong female role model, despite us being the same age, has perhaps helped her to find her calling. We are both lucky that the third spoke in our wheel also got stuck into school development in that school, and although we have all moved on now, our friendship is as strong as ever, probably based on the difficulties we faced whilst there.

Each of us can do that, invest in people, be creative and supportive and make our own minds up about people based on what we know of them, not what others tell us. Incidentally, her son, who I excluded for half a day for thumping another child, recently became a title winning professional boxer and is extremely talented . . .

Influencing others is more than being 'an influencer'

Each of us as people in any capacity can influence others in any and every conversation we have, as discussed in the previous chapter, and repeated by me often in most things. In our modern world, however, this does not just involve influencing (as leaders) within our schools and those we 'reach' every day in person. As members of a functioning society that relies more heavily on social media interaction, now it can involve careful social media behaviours to accomplish this *externally*.

Therefore, a huge leadership responsibility is, if you can influence, then influence with grace and for the greater good. If you can help people dream and visualise what they are capable of, scaffold them as they begin to believe in themselves and their capabilities, then there is a moral imperative to do this. Leaders exist among us; whether as a Teaching Assistant, friend, teacher, union rep, Headteacher or gym instructor, leaders are simply people with followers (virtual or literal) or people prepared to listen.

If people are listening to you, what you say and what you communicate with your behaviour, then say something meaningful, transformative and positive. As a human being, if you do things with the intent to spread love and gratitude, with the desire to uplift people and hold a mirror to them so that they can see their good qualities whilst supporting them with the aspects of themselves that they struggle with, then you are a leader; you need to acknowledge and demonstrate leadership.

At the start of 2021, I saw a tweet from a regular Twitter personality, @Censoredhead. He had, in the past, undergone some difficult issues that had necessitated his anonymity, and in so doing, he was able to be honest in ways that those of us with public accounts could never be. I read his tweets for some time, not knowing his name, gender, age, location etc., as anonymous as it gets. Shortly after the third great lockdown for our country was announced, he posted over the weekend that he had faced such a difficult two days due to the inappropriate behaviour of a group of parents at his school that actually he did not want to go to work the next day.

Having been bullied in work by a colleague once, and parents more than once in my career, having experienced the acute, brain freezing effect of anxiety around going to work, I decided to overcome my own issues with 'telephoning' and offer privately to call the next day to discuss the issues he was facing. I was surprised when he jumped at the chance, and the next day, a Monday, I called him. Thus began a mission to offer, randomly, to call at least one person a day to raise their spirits, listen to them, support them and offer practical help – coined #AVicCarrCalls. This endeavour was so successful that I now have several excellent, like-minded supportive, professional friends and associates whom I have reached out to, who have then gone on to reach out to others (like Paul who wrote the foreword to this book), and others whom I have since met in real life.

I have coached women whom I randomly connected with who wanted to apply for a leadership post and lacked confidence, who then went on to apply, some successfully, and some not (the first time). I have sent SIM cards to others who have had their faith in humanity restored at the same time as being able to help their families and students access education. I have talked to foster carers who have been without foster children and isolated as a result of lockdown and had no conversation in weeks. I have listened to people's marital issues, shared my own personal sorrows and shared so many learning and leadership resources that I have lost count. All respectfully, confidentially and with love – all it cost me was TIME.

I will never know the influence I have had, if any; I know that people tell me, publicly and through direct messages, emails and gifts, that they are thankful, but we never know the long-term impact of supporting someone to achieve. My take on this is that I don't need to know; what I do know is that everyone I help out is more likely to then help others, and who wouldn't like the idea of that?

All of us face obstacles of time constraints in our daily lives as we are increasingly asked to do more with less; some leaders may be unfamiliar with social media platforms and may be uncertain about what to say on them, but you can say influential things every day to anyone, and it doesn't have to involve a great deal of time or technical knowledge. You can start with each conversation you have within your schools or workplaces, today.

Social media – what it is and isn't

Social media is not real life. I knew very little of social media until the last few years, I am not sure I know much more now. Until recently, for example, I had no idea how to work out who you follow once you had followed them! Much of what I post is simple observation about my life, school experiences to show others that they are not alone, and parenting – all very relatable topics, and all show I am not a superstar and have the same angst as everyone else. I have talked about the pressures and joys, trials and tribulations of parenthood, and I have been explicit about how this makes me feel.

The inbox messages and public replies speak for themselves, but I know this level of honesty has been invaluable to people (particularly during lockdown) when they feel like they are on their own and perhaps not doing as well as they would hope, or when they compare themselves to people who *look like* they are winning at life on social media. I have shared my leadership highs and lows, some of the constraints and limits, some of the freedoms, and this has helped others to broaden horizons and gain confidence. I share and retweet, and I don't worry about 'follower counting'. Largely, I leave the views of others and their desire to either 'follow' me or 'unfollow' me to them; I just focus on being me and sharing the parts of me I feel able to in such a public way.

Another way to use social media effectively is to reach out and ask for what you need. There is always someone with a huge following prepared to retweet, and in a matter of minutes you find yourself signposted to what you wanted. Equally, you can reach out and approach people whom you think may influence and support your mission in school.

A couple of years ago I saw a post from @ForceAtlantic, an Army rowing team, who were sharing their story with a school. I approached the man in charge and simply asked if he could visit us and inspire our children. To my surprise, the team came, and not only were the children inspired by the stories of the rowers, but also they were inspired to row themselves that winter, on a rowing machine in our hall, and raise money for the @ForceAtlantic charity, which was The Army Benevolent Fund. They petitioned the staff and got the rowing machine from one of the student teachers, put it in the hall so that the rowing could be a public event, established how many miles a day we would need to row in maths lessons, gave us all a slot, and as a school, we set off! They raised £300, which I deposited into the charity coffers, but more importantly it brought our community together and inspired our children. Who knows where that may lead in years to come? Perhaps one of the 300 children who were desperate for them to bring back their boat will end up as Olympian rowers, or will row the Atlantic themselves one day – certainly three of them told me afterwards that they were determined to take it up as a sport and have since left school, so I cannot ask if they ever did (but my eyes will be trained on the rowing teams of the future)! As a complete aside, at the time of writing, I applied for and am astonished to have made the cut for the next stage in selection to become part of the first all-female team to row the Atlantic, in the same boat, in 2024 . . .

Similarly, I invited amputee Andy Reid MBE (@andyreid2506) into school, having seen a post on Twitter, and he did a talk with our Y6 children, some of whom were struggling engagement-wise. They were mesmerised by him: not just the source of his physical impairment, which was in itself a topic of conversation, so too was the way in which he had overcome this and other issues in his life. This had a dramatic impact on a number of children and really supported both our inclusivity agenda and behaviour expectations that we had in school.

So what – dreams and concrete experiences

A critical first step in having successful outcomes in your life is to dream, or more practically, if the idea of 'dreaming' is off putting, then to *visualise*. When you are young, you are not able to dream about things you don't know about; you need concrete experiences or something visual that shows you what is possible. In addition to visualising and dreaming, you must also mean what you say, and say what you mean, and to refer back to Chapter 1, you must know yourself. If you don't 'dream big' about the future *you* want, the person *you* want to be and so on, then how can you influence others to do so? How will they have faith in the integrity of the advice you may give? You must live your reality and create a reality in which others can learn to visualise and dream, also.

When helping others achieve their dreams, I know I am not enough on my own. I therefore actively look for other people to come and support that endeavour. I am always scouting for talent and inspiration for myself and for members of my community. This can sometimes drive my team mad, but that is another story!

One of the things I will post regularly about, and talk about in the majority of the podcast interviews I do, is in the domain of stretching yourself and how possible it is, of not allowing the imposter in you to talk you out of achievement, and striving for it. Essentially, I am talking about dreaming! If you verbalise your dreams to others, it gives them the opportunity to try to help and signpost you towards steps to achieving them. It becomes like a contract with yourself and the universe. It is here that performance management meetings sit in my own leadership discourse.

Bringing dreams to life as a school leader – a culture of reaching

I have ensured that we budget for, and encourage staff across school (in a range of roles) to challenge themselves and learn – I ask them to think about this ahead of their meetings with me. We discuss logistics and practicalities and how I can support their endeavours, coaching, mentoring, emotional support and counselling, Master's degrees etc. This means for me, I have a motivated and committed staff. Some of them are actively engaged in their additional research or study, and this can simultaneously positively impact on, and benefit, both them and school.

They see me doing it, they hear me talk about how I manage it, and then they can enact it in their own lives. Then they see their colleagues doing the same thing, and before you know it, this is the culture of your school. TAs, early career teachers (ECTs), senior leaders and admin members are all part of a big learning community working towards being their best selves because they see how it can be done and know how it feels to achieve as an adult and what it means for children to see this.

So many people talk themselves out of *reaching*, shut down their dreams, deflect positive influence, preferring the safety of their comfort zone, and believe that others are far better qualified than they are to strive. If you dream big, and others see you applying for challenging roles, or roles in challenging settings, and stretching the boundaries of your comfort zone, then they will be increasingly more likely to do so. Learning how to develop self-belief and courage is not only impressive and inspirational, it is also contagious and self-perpetuating – this means it is well worth the undertaking.

I don't think anything – age, gender, socio-economic background, faith or sexuality – should hinder you from dreaming big. I may at times think 'I am too female' or 'too old', but I never truly believe it once I have had a word with myself. I get ideas, and then ask myself the steps necessary to make those ideas real. I am convinced there are books out there that help you break down big ideas into small steps, but I think we are all capable of doing this ourselves, if we are given time and the support we need.

Recently I decided, after telling myself that I was done with research and study following the 'joys' of doing a doctorate, to do a third Master's. Some may consider that after two, you would know what you were doing – note to self and sharing with others (as it is 'caring'), this is nonsense. My current MA is in military history, with a focus on leadership, and this is a whole different ball game to any sociology post-graduate study I have done to date!

Firstly, a 'Literature Review' is now a 'Historiography' . . . bibliographies must be separated into a range of primary and secondary sources rather than lumped in a list of alphabetical references, and dates really MATTER! Imagine for a moment (you are five chapters in so it won't take much to see where I may struggle) someone like me having to write with clarity, brevity and be succinct?

I am way out of my comfort zone, learning a new methodology, style, referencing guide (as an INFJ who is not really detail crazy!) and grappling with a whole new language. I went through what anyone going through this for the first time would, as in, I considered giving up! However, I did not give up, despite writing a book and doing MA research concurrently, running a school through a pandemic and participating in ongoing training with the Army. I did not and will not. I compartmentalise and tell myself that it is possible, despite the potential barriers to success. I feel no shame in asking for help from more knowledgeable and detail-oriented minds, such as my good friend and partner in academic crime SJ (who nearly disowned me for writing a 97-word sentence once as I jotted down a stream of consciousness, regularly pulls out his hair when he reads my work and puts it through the sieve of brevity when necessary – in other words, always).

In dreaming big, and challenging myself to work outside my comfort zone, it is not a vanity project I am after – but something to make my brain work. The multiple benefits of doing this of course, for those who (like some of my friends) think I am nuts, are evident. Doing something that occupies your mind and distracts you from stress inherent in your day job as an educator can prevent 'burn out' and minimise the negative physical manifestations of stress. Doing something that makes you think differently, or which can actively engage all structures in your brain at the same time (e.g., your prefrontal cortex, hippocampus, neurons, neurotransmitters), in turn can stimulate new connections between nerve cells (possibly even supporting the generation of new ones). What you are doing, then, is developing neurological 'plasticity' and building up a functional reserve of brain cells (like having a big savings account or insurance policy providing a hedge fund against future cell loss!).

Doing a course that results in a qualification may help you stand out when applying for a job, not least because of the nature and level of qualification, but also because it signifies to employers that you have 'staying power' (endurance) and the ability to synthesise a range of information into a coherent product – who wouldn't like an employee with those skills? Most importantly though, it is fun to learn about new things at a deeper level and be challenged on your understanding, thoughts and awareness in an area that you are not familiar with. You meet new and fascinating people, and life is all about the journey and the relationships forged along the way.

Breaking down dreams into achievable markers

Your dreams, and the dreams you support others with, don't have to be academic, incidentally. In recent years I decided I wanted to pass my motorbike test – I was asked if it was a mid-life crisis (it wasn't), and my mum is still only half speaking to me for even contemplating doing it, but in dreaming of travelling the North Coast 500, on a motorbike, wild camping and enjoying the elements, I had to break down the dream into manageable chunks in order to achieve it.

Step one was passing the Compulsory Basic Training (CBT), which I did in Chester. When driving a car for almost 30 years, you become accustomed to the controls, and as we have said, muscle memory kicks in so that you can be driving miles before you are even aware that you have been driving! Riding a pushbike is similar, and I have been riding one of those in excess of 40 years, the controls are different to driving a car, but when mastered, then you are physically able. A motorbike is different again, and involves a whole new skill set, applying knowledge gained to new methods – as with all things, once the basics are mastered, you can develop the confidence required to ride comfortably and pass the full test in order to be able to ride a bigger bike. Needless to say, I was pretty rubbish for the first hour trying to co-ordinate hands feet, new controls, keep an eye on the road and also keep my balance . . . but then I remembered taking my son out to drive for the first time (only weeks before), and I laughed at the irony.

A painful lesson I learned in differentiating dreams from hopes was this: a dream is something achievable with hard work, determination, desire and a smattering of luck because you are in total control of it – like running a successful café, or running a marathon. A hope is nebulous, existential and never in your control – like avoiding the family history of breast cancer in order to see your children grow up, or enjoying a lifetime of love and contentment with your soul mate, or winning the lottery.

If we are committed to dreaming, to striving, to learning and never stopping learning, then these feelings of initial inadequacy will be standard – situation normal! Everyone feels them, whether they are 17 and learning to drive a car, 23 and learning to horse ride on huge polo ponies from Mount Kenya Polo Club, 45 and learning to ride a motorbike, or 46 and learning to sea kayak, unless we are undiscovered geniuses, then we all start from a place of little skill and aptitude and learn by doing, or from observing people who have excelled. Giving ourselves a coaching talk (self-talk is later in the book), acknowledging explicitly that we have developed similar skills, that these can be applied in slightly different contexts, to great success, can really help rationalise any negative feelings – if you then have people you can talk to who reinforce the understanding that you can apply skills to new situations, then you are already onto a winner.

The final step, naturally, in achieving my latest 'Big Dream' is to find confidence on the motorway and to ride safely in bad weather – one cannot guarantee the Scottish weather, after all – and then I will have all the necessary skills to fulfil my dream. So, when dreaming big, remember that in order to achieve them, there may be several steps that you need to undertake, often with friends or experts, and although time is a constraint (along with money), age and gender are not!

What has all of this to do with leading with love, with you?

Lead by example. Open your mind to new experiences and dream of what you could do and be. Visualise yourself living your dream, and work out what the steps are in order to be successful, approaching each element with your full attention. Let others see your journey, your determination and what it means to have the endurance and resilience to overcome any setbacks. Ask others about their dreams and facilitate their realisation, or part of it, if you can.

You will be familiar with the summary by now, but the point is:

- We need to dream big and have high aspirations for ourselves; as leaders, people look to us for how to behave (which means that you can . . .)

- Lead by example, influencing others, showing how we have overcome barriers (because . . .)

- If people see it, then they know that they can do and be it (because . . .)

- Influencing others takes many forms, one of which is lived reality (also . . .)

- Your team need you to be the best version of yourself so they can follow in your influential footsteps, which helps you (to make the best team you can).

Further reading/listening

If you like a podcast and 'influencing, visualising and putting your dreams into reality' is something you want to know more about in terms of leadership:

1. The father and son duo, Tim and Brian Kight, host podcasts that constantly deliver a system of leadership principles that are timeless. https://tinyurl.com/Leadership-across-the-board
2. John Eades leads Learn Loft podcasts. https://tinyurl.com/Pursuit-of-Leadership
3. Visualisation for Success: 10 Guided Imagery Scripts (PDF). https://tinyurl.com/Visualisation-of-Success

If you like a book and want to get the best potential out of your team in a number of levels:

1. Grenny, Joseph (2013). *Influencer: The New Science of Leading Change.* McGraw Hill. ISBN: 9780071808866.
2. Green, George (2021). *The Art of Influencing People.* Independently Published. ISBN: 979-8713346232.
3. Priestley, Daniel (2014). *Key Person of Influence.* Jaico Publishing House. ISBN: 9788184954753.

6 It's not what you are, but what you are afraid you are *not* that holds you back

What have you got to lose?

We are a third of the way through my book of 'secrets of great leadership', and I think you will agree, so far there have been very few 'secrets' and a lot of self-reflection and an understanding of how one experience leads to another and each one builds within us until it shapes who and how we are, and therefore our 'lived experience' of the world.

Building on from visualisation and dreaming big, as discussed in the previous chapter, I think that the best leaders apply for anything they feel could be right for them – no matter if they hit all of the job specifications and criteria. There is empirical evidence and research out there that tells us men do this as a matter of course, women much less so. The best leaders not only do it, but encourage their colleagues to follow suit, imbuing the same enthusiasm and confidence into their tribe. They will actively say, when asked for advice, 'Give it a go!'

I am often asked for advice about job hunting, job applications, at what point one should apply for this or that role, at what age one should think about promoted posts; sometimes it just randomly comes up in conversation with people, and usually I repeat the same message that I give to myself when staring at potential and possibility, which is – what have you got to lose? The only reason I am where I am career-wise is because I have replied to myself: nothing.

I know, like other experienced leaders, that for everyone, the next step (sideways into a different field or up the career framework) is always a 'reach' – because I have done it, and I know that each individual, me included, learns to fill the role even if they have been way out of their comfort zone to begin with, and actually pretty terrified. I articulate this feeling as I coach people and offer guidance and support to anyone who takes this (sometimes giant!) step. Then they end up paying it forward.

DOI: 10.4324/9781003281313-7

How to feel fear and do it anyway

Coaching others, bringing experiences to life and providing an emotional and professional handrail to others underpins much of my leadership and is core to my leadership belief. It is that 'love' for my fellow 'strivers', for my kindred determined souls intent on continuous life-long improvement and those allies in learning and self-development, that gives me purpose.

Fear of the unknown, limiting self-beliefs and 'what if?' scenarios will always prevent people from challenging themselves, and this chapter is about how to *feel the fear* and do whatever it is anyway – be that apply for the promotion, take on the challenge you may be offered, or purposefully place yourself in a challenging situation.

I have felt fear on quite a few occasions and, like with most things I will talk about, it is never one event that teaches you how best to deal with situations, but a number of them, overlaid and deepening your understanding of yourself and how you react to situations. If you have read the book from the start, you will have seen that I have not just posited opinions and moved on, nor have I framed my views with academic research – I have illustrated how with life comes experience, with understanding of that experience comes understanding of yourself and with that comes the ability to bring the authentic 'you' to your leadership. There are any number of robust academically referenced models and formulae for leadership from change management to creating culture, from having difficult conversations to financial practice – each must be interpreted and enacted by the reader (or leader) and only through the transaction, the implementation of what you have read, comes your style. That interpretation and leadership style are unlikely to ever fit neatly into a pigeon hole or box; you will never be the same leader in all situations, but you will be the same human being, and if your leadership is based on integrity, a sense of service to and love for others, then the minutiae will take care of itself.

To coach others, learn to coach yourself

If you look back at your own life, you will be able to track through and make sense of what I have just said. As a rudimentary example, the first time I left home, for University, I was quite literally terrified. I had chosen a small campus college in order to try to manage my fears, but nevertheless, I was wide-eyed and full of dread. The unknown scared me and made me feel vulnerable. I did not feel safe outsides the strict confines of my home life, and despite being keen to leave, I was integrating this desire with a complex set of emotions that I now know to be separation anxiety and post-traumatic stress. In fact, this separation anxiety stopped me from completing a degree in English and Geography and directly led to me staying in Ambleside and switching courses from that combination to Outdoor Education and Environmental Science (this is for a different day, and a different book, but am I EVER glad that I changed courses).

How did I manage this scary first step into the unknown? How did I learn how to take ownership of 'adulting' – establish my new address with a range of agencies, pay bills, organise my own time, do washing, ironing and so on (also known as 'personal admin') around working to pay for my accommodation and also my studies?

I realised that there was nothing to be afraid of. I made lists and methodically went through them in order of priority (something I do as a leader on a daily basis – I am a consummate list maker). I had been doing the washing and ironing for my whole family for many years, so it wasn't that. The Sunday Top 40 was the backdrop to my four-hour Sunday ironing sessions, and I was not allowed out of the house unless the ironing was done. I actually was legendary – I even got ironing a shirt down to five minutes (always target driven!). I am wandering off again. I had been cooking dinner for my whole family and making lunches for four children every night, been in charge of the house (a large German Shepherd and three siblings) overnight, whilst working my part-time job, doing my school work, and playing sport – it was no different. I just had less of it to do, and I only had to worry for myself!

Very quickly I was in a routine – the outcome of which was that I was calm. I learned something perhaps quite obvious now, with the benefit of hindsight, but at the time that did not feel obvious at all. With routine and habit comes a sense of serenity (it is the same for children). Doing the simple, routine and perhaps boring tasks that do not tax the brain yet get the body moving really do help. That is it! My secret to change management, learned when I was 18, has never failed me in any situation.

With a list (that you work your way through) comes sense of purpose and achievement. Combine the two (routine and a list) and you are able to tackle pretty much anything – I have used exactly the same methodology for taking on a large, and very troubled school, successfully turning around its fortunes after only two terms, for managing a divorce, even for recovering from surgery.

The next time I moved, from the Lake District to Newcastle, when there was no choice as my course was over, I felt the same anxiety. I recalled how nervous I had been about meeting new people, locating key resources, finding my way from one place to the next in unknown surroundings, and I felt a little better – I had a benchmark from which to work, therefore it took me less time to settle. Each successive move, Kenya to Northumberland, Northumberland to Germany, Germany to the Wirral, has been less anxiety inducing and much less troublesome.

Own the fear

It is exactly the same with moving to a new school – you know you will be nervous, but each time you move to a new job the anxiety becomes more 'known' and therefore more manageable. The pathway is created in your brain, and your neurones remember what to do. You can actually say out loud to yourself,

I have felt this before. I know that I will have flutters in my chest, I know my heart will race, I know I will not sleep well, but I also know that if I make a list and go through it systematically, I can minimise these feelings in a matter of days. I am not alone. I can call people and tell them this is how I feel and why. Most people feel like this with something new.

If you apply the same logic to any workplace, then suddenly logistical fears become almost negligible. Very early on in a new role, establish some simple routines that give you a handrail to the day, be that the journey in, coffee making, the greetings you give to people, the route through your workplace or the way you organise your kit the night before. Simple, basic, physical tasks – see how much they improve your mindset. The professional fears take a little longer (as we know, imposter syndrome can be quite irritatingly resilient against simple mantras, as I am ready to admit), but with increased experience and support of those around you, fears about your performance can really begin to diminish. This is why the setting is more important than the role, in my view. You can apply for a challenging role in a place where you feel that you will be able to flourish, that 'feels' like your kind of place and has a similar ethos and value set as your own, and really thrive. Equally, you can apply for a role which you could do standing on your head in a toxic environment and fail miserably as the environment is simply not conducive to success.

This is the sad reality that I share with people when they ask me about promotion, or tell me their confidence has all but evaporated as they have been unsupported or even actively bullied in their professional lives. In fact, it differs little from the advice I give to people in relation to their home lives. You are you and can be the same version of yourself in two different environments, one where you thrive and make the lives of those closest to you a joy to experience; however the converse is true – if you are not thriving at work or at home, then you and all closest to you will suffer. There are some eventualities: it is true to say that with honest dialogue and a shared desire to rectify a toxic environment, then it can be successfully addressed and the outcome an absolute miracle, but if this is not possible then the only course of action open (other than to stay in the toxic soup) is to move on.

I feel sure that in reading this you will have a tickertape running through your own mind where you could list off times when you have not been supported or valued and moved on to pastures new where life has taken off and blossomed. I am not advocating a butterfly or helicopter type of mindset here, where you flutter about and alight or descend into different roles and places on a whim or an ad hoc basis. On the contrary, I am suggesting that you take a long hard look at your own behaviour, how it manifests, what the outcomes of your behaviour on any given situation are, and evaluate whether changing your own responses and reactions can alter your reality. This may involve a conversation with another adult, and on that basis you can then make informed decisions to move on with purpose and few regrets. The caveat to this is that this is my approach and has worked for me – I have no regrets about my life or how I have lived it. I accept that at each decision point there have been options and that I chose the option I felt best suited the current and future terrain at that point in time. Hindsight is what has given me the wisdom to reflect on and evaluate those decisions and to try not to make erroneous repeat decisions as a result.

How does this look as a leader?

When I took over my previous two schools, they both needed a tonne of love, a little emotional intelligence and a lot of drive, fair and equitable treatment (not to mention someone not prone to histrionics and who is quite calm in a crisis, of which there have been many!). There were people in both environments who just needed 'a break', someone to look at them differently, someone to give them the opportunity to change and reinvent themselves, to rewrite their story from that point in time.

A fresh pair of eyes is always beneficial and can provide that change in step or pace that someone in a rut needs. By having frank and empathetic conversations, I was able to establish the barriers to success for some of the staff and support them on a journey out of the situations they found themselves in. Some went to promoted posts (one teacher, for example, had been in the same school more than 20 years and applied unsuccessfully for scores of promotions until I spoke to her, and then simultaneously and randomly got an email about a secondment in a school up the road – she successfully undertook the leadership secondment and never came back!). Some went to schools closer to their home, others still took sideways moves into Special Education and so on. I did nothing magical or arcane, I just invested my time in them, asked them what they wanted to do if they could do anything (see the previous chapter) and found ways to facilitate this. Working creatively and outside the box is a little maverick, but where all parties benefit, and within the constraints of the budget, employment law, and Human Resource (HR) policy, what isn't to love? They thought big, or dreamed, I took time to get to know their dreams and aspirations and made time to try to create favourable conditions for them to realise those dreams.

Remember, everyone must begin somewhere – even the most successful leaders will have started out feeling exactly same fears. You may be sitting with those fears right now, and I am here to tell you that those who have success, those you can see in the public domain and judge as successful, have had those fears – what is most important, though, is that they have overcome them, and the likelihood is that they will have commenced overcoming those fears at some point during their childhood or early adulthood without even being aware that they were doing so. Anyone considering the next step in their job, or sideways move, or academic challenge knows that it could be a great career move, but it takes bravery to step forward and do it. If you don't, how else will you ever broaden your professional expertise and ability?

Bring to life what learning from experience can look like

Equally important to anyone working with young people and children is the concept that those children will be learning from experience. If you can articulate some of the learning, give them the vocabulary and licence to discuss them, then you are actively assisting them in the most important journey of all – that of self-awareness and discovery at the point of learning, not 20 or 30 years later when they begin questioning how they ended up where they are (in either a positive or negative sense, although it is perhaps more critical to avoid a negative one).

Again, I can speak about this from my own life. If I look back now, at my age, on the first time I experienced leadership and leading through hardship, of fearing I was not enough, it isn't as a Headteacher, it isn't even as a teacher, it isn't as a member of a successful netball team as a teenager, or on modules in MA programmes that I have led. I genuinely believe that it was either the Duke of Edinburgh Scheme or my experiences in the Air Training Corps (ATC) that gave me my first taste of staring at imposter syndrome, of overcoming fears of failure and inadequacy, of wondering if I was good enough to pass *this* or achieve *that*. I was lucky that alongside feeling normal fear, both organisations had the added value of giving me tangible opportunities to both support others and raise morale, showing me visceral evidence of the unequivocal importance of teamwork – all key elements of leading, as I am sure you will agree.

The fact that DofE has stood the test of time and managed to ride out the societal changes in the last 70 years, branching out to more than 140 countries around the world, speaks for itself in terms of the appeal it has to young people, but it saddens me that those most in need of engagement with a programme such as this may not be able to access it indefinitely. Locally to me I know of very established providers no longer being required as more commercial and more expensive providers take over and make it less socially inclusive perhaps, but I digress.

Back in the day I recall my Gold DofE expedition through the iconic, and internationally renowned, Snowdonia National Park in North Wales. I was in a group of five girls from school, a late addition to the group, best of friends with one of the members and barely knowing the names of the other three. For those unfamiliar with the DofE expeditions, you need to be fully self-sufficient, wild camping for the duration and therefore carrying all kit and food from the outset (this was to be distributed through the group). For teenage girls, this was a tall enough order, we were carrying upwards of 35 kg.

You may also be surprised to know, reader, that it rains in Snowdonia, and rain it did during the five days we were in the field; it was rain of biblical proportions and utterly morale sapping. Not to mention that at that time, the lightweight and ultra 'high-performance' equipment that I now furnish myself with for a day in the hills was yet to be invented (it wasn't quite hob-nailed boots and tweed coats, but you can picture the scene), and frankly, nor had Haribo.

I had not grown up in a family of outdoor enthusiasts. This is an understatement. I had never challenged myself in the way that the expedition section of the award challenged me, and although I had progressively built up the ability to complete them with each award, nothing prepared me for the final Gold challenge. The weather, the time away from home when things were particularly tricky there, having to be in close proximity to people that I did not know, the list did not stop there. The fear of failure was paralysing, and even putting on the heavy rucksack on day one lent a physical dimension to the weight I was already carrying in my mind. And yet, I refused to give in to it. I tried to swallow down the lump of anxiety in my throat. I focused on the practical, packing the backpack (I would call it a bergen these days, but you know what I mean), ticking off the kit list as I went, planning and re-planning the route, checking the menu and the distribution of items. I feigned high spirits ('fake it until you make it' hadn't been invented at that time as a bumper sticker, but I was definitely faking it).

Both my friend and I were sportswomen, and as became apparent, the physical aspect of the hike was not a problem for us, as it was for the other team members, who became more affected by the weather and the steep climbs of the Glyders as the hours passed by. As for the challenges of Tryfan on the last day – it tested every ounce of my own determination to not just carry my own ruck sack, considerably lighter for the food we had already eaten, but taking turns with my friend to carry that of another group member who was struggling to place a foot ahead of the other.

I recall mentally counting off the hours and the days, of playing tricks with my mind to get to the next check point and to get the camp established in order to get us all warm and fed, which became the sole focus of both me and my friend, and we took it in turns to rally the team. I realised then the power of collaboration and of endurance, of planning and preparation, and how reaching for something that seemed beyond you was possible with all of these factors. There were times I wanted to give up, when the weight of moving the team forward just felt too much, but there were two of us, and together we managed it. On Exercise *Wavells Warrior* as part of 41 Platoon recently, I reminisced about this experience when on 'stag' sentry duty – it is as clear in my mind now as it was 30 years ago.

We were the group leaders, unofficially, and we had to behave as such, even if we did not have the first inclination that we were, or any overt training in order to be. Of course, that is the whole point, and it is easy in retrospect to see that, but at the time it was hard, hard labour. This first toe-dip of leadership, as I now look back, was a perfect age and stage-appropriate rehearsal for my second headship, but moreover for both London marathons, for parenthood and for life in general! The irony of this is that shortly afterwards I was away at college and the ATC unit I was in, through which I was also doing part of my DofE, lost the book . . . I was never awarded the award despite completing every gritty and agonising part of it! Anyway, I am not bitter at all about that . . .

I know these feelings now: they are not my friends, but they are acquaintances. I have shared on occasion that I still battle them, and I do. Only recently I was in a sea kayak off Llanddwyn Beach with a very experienced and much-loved friend. He is an instructor, and I am a novice (a 'baby-paddler' as he calls me). We had made the plan the week before that we would meet in the car park and take the boats out for the day. On the sea. The actual sea. I fought my childhood memories of *Jaws* (there are no Great Whites off the coast of Anglesey, for those with similar childhood emotional scars or flights of imagination), the fact I hadn't done an 'Eskimo Roll' for more than 25 years and the fact I had forgotten more than I knew. I panicked that I would not manage to even get out of the bay and the day would be ruined, potentially by me drowning, but at the bare minimum being rescued by the coast guard. I decided I would not go – that I should cancel because I wouldn't manage it. I wasn't capable.

As it was, my desire to see and spend the day with my friend overcame my fear of drowning or death by killer shark, and I turned up at the beach. His training as an instructor was so effective that he took me through the entire safety brief, and we were out on the water before I had time to panic. I paddled for six miles and swam off a deserted beach on the headland off Bodorgan, where we had lunch, chatted and sunbathed. If I had let my fear of failure rule, I would not have seen fish leap from the sea or seals moult on rocky outcrops, or eaten avocado and feta salad with my new 'spork'. Fear would have stopped me from creating memories and enjoying the simplest of pleasures being outside. I know that each person reading this will have a time springing into the forefront of their mind, when they did not do something for one fear or another. You should tell yourself right now that you won't let fear hamstring you again.

Imposter syndrome

Many people are afraid to do something new because they don't want to appear foolish or incompetent, they don't want to lose face, they carry the weight of the expectations of other people on their shoulders and are living their lives for other people, their identity is too closely tied to their current role, they take refuge in their title and the quasi respect it may gain them, or their identity is with their school or workplace, or what they know, and they link one or more of these to identifying their own self-worth – they can't step away from this, even if they are unhappy. Fear of failure can be the single most debilitating emotion any of us have and can seriously hinder our ability to lead well.

The converse, however, is just as self-defeating: the fear of success, often referred to as 'imposter syndrome', can curb the desire to reach for the next rung. What I find so incomprehensible about imposter syndrome is that it disproportionately affects 'high achievers', those who find it difficult to accept their accomplishments, questioning whether they deserve any respect or congratulations. What will our family or our peers say if we look like we are doing well for ourselves? What will people say if I try and fail? Will they think we are getting too big for our boots?

Who do I think I am? I can't possibly tell people I have won this award, published that paper, achieved this qualification, been offered a job with that company, they will be waiting for me to fail . . . what if I fail? What will I be? What will I become?

Sound familiar?

This is not a modern phenomenon. It was highlighted by psychologists Pauline Rose Clance and Suzanne Imes in 1978 when they conducted research which focused on high-achieving women, although in 2021, I feel certain that this is an all-encompassing issue that has no gender barrier. Clance and Imes theorised that 'despite outstanding academic and professional accomplishments, women who experience the imposter phenomenon persist in believing that they are really not bright and have fooled anyone who thinks otherwise'. More than 40 years have passed, and despite decades of initiatives, research, books and theories to tackle imposter syndrome on a practical level, it still exists.

Perhaps what we could explore and discuss further, now that there is a large body of research in this area, is the role systems in our societies and workplaces play in creating, fostering and worsening it. I wonder if my own self-beliefs were influenced by classism experienced as a child, but then I am also sure that there will be people who would argue against this, believing that in thinking this is about me, rather than the environment I live and work in, I am focusing on the wrong thing! There is something to be said about this.

I can only talk as a woman; I identify as such and have always identified as heterosexual. I have white skin and am British, so whilst I try to, it is hard for me to truly understand the 'additionally' of race, sexual fluidity and a deviation from gender binary norms on someone and how these things make them feel inferior. What I can do is to try to ensure that I rewrite the narrative for myself and those with whom I work – tricky but not impossible when you look at things from a slightly different perspective. If I refute the pathologised concept of anxiety in my workplace, deny the syndrome, and simply attempt to create positive role models who demonstrate professional competence for others to emulate, from a range of historically marginalised demographics, then I will create an environment that fosters diversity. I may not have the range of people on my permanent team, but this is the beauty of connectivity and reaching out to embrace that diversity and try to educate ourselves on the impact of it on how we feel. I think this could be key – it is not who we are that might hold us back, but who we think we are not – and this could be based on who we deemed 'professional' in our childhoods and why: an internal assessment process affected by cultural bias and therefore potentially skewed. One thing that levels us all, however, is the finite nature of life.

Steve Jobs described his thoughts on fear and decision-making when he was extremely unwell:

> Remembering that I'll be dead soon is the most important tool I've ever encountered to help me make the big choices in life. Because almost everything – all external expectations, all pride, all fear of embarrassment or failure – these things just fall away in the face of death, leaving only what is truly important.

What has all of this to do with leading with love, with you?

Learn to understand and then master your fears and what they are telling you. This is possible only if you know yourself and can really dig beneath the superficial to understand the root causes of your feelings. As a leader, you are leading yourself first and foremost, and others will look to you for implicit and explicit guidance. What are you demonstrating? How can you guide and support others and create a healthy environment where excellence is the way things are done on a daily basis if there exists fear of failure – your own included?

It is not who we are, what we are capable of, or our determination and passion that might hold us back, but who and what we think that we are not. Thus, it should be a personal and professional mission to remove systemic glass ceilings and limitations, and also those we impose upon ourselves.

You will be familiar with the chapter summary format by now if you have been reading through each one in order, but the point is:

- You need to master your fear and reach beyond your comfort zones (which means that you can . . .)

- Enhance your own self-esteem, self-worth and efficacy (because . . .)

- In learning how to fill a role you were not 100% confident in or qualified for, you raise your own bar, through collaboration, training and assimilation (because . . .)

- You chose to remove your own glass ceiling; plus, success begets success (also . . .)

- If others see you doing it, they will gain the confidence to do it, and everyone striving to be better and develop skills is excellent for your main effort as a leader (to make the best team you can).

Further reading/listening

If you like a podcast and 'fear' is something you want to know more about in terms of leadership:

1. Yours Truly Podcast with Naomi: Feel the Fear and Do It Anyway. https://tinyurl.com/Feel-Fear-and-do-it
2. Living Your Truth Podcast: Ep. 19 Feeling the Fear and Doing It Anyway. https://tinyurl.com/Live-Your-Truth
3. TED Conferences. https://tinyurl.com/TED-I-dont-know-what-I-want

If you like a book and want to get the best potential out of your team in a number of levels:

1. Jeffers, Susan (2017). *Feel the Fear and Do It Anyway: How to Turn Your Fear and Indecision into Confidence and Action.* Vermillion. ISBN: 978-0091907075.
2. April, Craig (2020). *The Anxiety Getaway: How to Outsmart Your Brain's False Fear Messages and Claim Your Calm Using CBT Techniques.* Mango. ISBN: 978-1642502169.

7 Nothing is more expensive than a missed opportunity

Scanning the horizon – what can you see?

The weirdest thing about being a school leader, and I have no reason to doubt it is different in any other leadership role, is that you must constantly balance a range of competing priorities – sometimes even in your sleep. Maybe I am wrong, and others would disagree, but balancing financial stability (including 'future proofing' your organisation's finances and insuring yourself against a number of potential losses), balancing the criteria for judgement on efficacy of the school and how best to achieve progress in this regard, balancing perception of your organisation from a range of stakeholders, and balancing morale of staff and their career pathways against the needs of the organisation can be quite the tight rope exercise. When factoring in complaints and the management of them, improvement and moving with the times (which involves a lot of change management!) and thinking outside the box, plus behaviour, special needs and constantly changing curricular, really, it is amazing any educational leader knows top from bottom. What does this mean then, in terms of how you lead from the heart and do so with love?

I think that the best leaders take any ethical opportunity they are presented with. *Any*. They don't just stop there; they are not passive, awaiting things that drop in their laps. They are constantly scanning the horizon for opportunity (and simultaneously, threat), both consciously and subconsciously, both for themselves and for members of their community.

My take on this is the following: who knows the benefits in the long run, in personal/professional life/character development/mental health, of any appropriate opportunity that presents itself unless it is seized? The best leaders have a *Nike* attitude to life, taking calculated risks and nevertheless thinking: 'Just Do It' ©. They know that the worst that can happen is that their pride may be dented if it doesn't work out; they don't let ego stop them and always place the needs of others at the forefront of their decision making. Equally, they don't throw money and energy, like shooting buckshot, at every fad or new idea, hoping that something is on target and will 'stick' – they appraise and assess the needs of their setting

DOI: 10.4324/9781003281313-8

alongside the opportunities presented and evaluate cost versus reward. I do this really well, but only because I work in part of a brilliant team!

As a leader, I operate within a process of effectuation (best explained as the opposite of causation). In tune with my personality type and strengths, I am always trying to find and create entrepreneurial opportunities for myself, the wider school community and team members. I do this also in my military role, and, I have to say, in my personal life, and some things I take on or involve myself with I don't even see the potential of realised for decades. I usually just look at something, and if it is interesting and manageable, then I do it.

As I have been writing each chapter for this book, I have been reflecting, and I can't help but think that my school leadership style is simply my life leadership style, and I would be hard pushed to separate the two. That makes me a very untechnical and largely talentless leader, in many ways, but a very altruistic and authentic one – I will leave it to you, the reader, to decide if that resonates or is valuable, but I have made no secret of the fact that much of my leadership has been intuitive.

I have arrived at having the time to read more academically around leadership as a result of post-graduate study that I have done or taught – only then did I become aware that what I do intuitively, as a component of my personality and character, has been codified in several ways, by several seminal thinkers in the leadership field. I have had many moments of thinking as I have read a book or a paper, 'aha – that is actually a "thing" not just what I do!' which is affirming and also quite amusing.

The 'BLUF' – bottom line up front

The 'so what' from this is that each of us arrives at leadership in our own unique way, and we each bring to the challenges and demands of leadership our own style and understanding which in turn crafts the dynamics for the transactional relationships that we have as part of our role. There is no 'one-size-fits-all' to being a good leader, an effective one, or a transformational one, so reading technical and academic books on leadership is good, but take from them what you choose rather than use them as a doctrinal guide to exactly how *you* should do it. You will find your own way.

I suppose it is like finding the perfect Bakewell tart recipe for me. I love Bakewell tart – it is one of my all-time favourites, as is lemon torte if we are on the topic of desert – but a few years ago I happened on a recipe from none other than Mary Berry. Now some of you know that I have taken fashion inspiration from Mrs B (I have a hat very similar to hers which I utterly love), but for me, the Bakewell was the gold standard in inspiration, and I set to making it. Don't tell her, but I think my incompetence may have affected the quality of the pastry, which was a bit too oily for my liking (not that it stopped the whole thing being scoffed in an instant), and to that end, the next time I made it I reduced the amount of butter I made it with.

I also added a little more almond essence than the recipe suggested and a lot more jam. The third time I made it I added a little more ground almonds and kept the jam to pastry ratio the same et voila! For my tastes, the perfect Bakewell had been created. I am now able to replicate this, and each time it works a treat.

Leadership in a nutshell. Take inspiration from experts in the field, make it your own through trial and error, adjusting and refining, and then you will be confident. There are only so many ingredients and combinations in any good Bakewell – the cook, oven, quality of ingredients, time and effort taken at each stage of preparation and the flourish at the end can all be adjusted – it isn't that different in leading an organisation.

Take the opportunity now, reap potential benefits later

Anyway, as much as I can talk pastry 'for time', back to the subject in hand! When I was at university I did a course in my spare time, a 'niche' course back then, called Philosophy for Children (sometimes abbreviated to P4C). I actually really enjoyed the inquiry and language element of it (unsurprisingly), but had no real clue if I would ever put it into practice. I didn't do it for that purpose but because it looked interesting. For the uninitiated, it is a programme that aims to develop both reasoning and effective discursive skills in children. To me, it felt like it could be a vehicle for teaching just about any contentious or contested ideology or concept in a way that children could explore bias whilst simultaneously broadening their vocabulary and ability to analyse and assimilate their views. What was not to love about this programme?

I know that at the time in college we were studying the work of developmental psychologist Jean Piaget, and he was of the impression that children were not capable of critical thinking until approximately 11 or 12. I questioned this because my understanding (even then, before I was qualified as a teacher and before I became a parent myself and had any first-hand experience) was that children would surely benefit from being taught reasoning skills through philosophical inquiry, even in early primary school? I did the course, however I didn't use it for more than two decades. I had all but forgotten its charms and possibilities until one day, as I am known to do, I was on a run, and I had a 'Eureka!' moment!

I had been a head for almost a year in a challenging school, a school where there was a clear racial divide, in a non-traditional sense some may say, between the Gypsy, Romany and Traveller (GRT) community we served and the non-GRT community whom we also served and who co-existed in the village where the school was situated. I had been wracking my brain for a way to bridge the gap of understanding and acceptance between the children, and I had come up with several unsuccessful approaches until I recalled (in the annals of my withered and pressurised brain) the P4C model. In many ways the views of their parents were set, so although resolute in my inclusive approach with them, I focused energies, time and money on the ability of the children to embrace difference and celebrate diversity, thus hopefully enacting the change in their generation in the hopes that it would make a difference. What better methodology than P4C?

I invested in staff training, which randomly was facilitated by one of the people who had been on the course with me more than 20 years before, and everyone agreed to use the approach in both discrete weekly P4C lessons that were crafted around teaching children about social, emotional, moral, cultural and spiritual aspects of life and also to teach humanities subjects.

The pedagogy underpinning P4C is pretty diverse, the use of a 'community of inquiry' method (rooted in the work of philosopher John Dewey) places the emphasis on the class or group talking and then inquiring together into questions that they may generate – with the teacher as a facilitator – I kid you not, this actually *does* work. Long before Ofsted decided that schools should adapt their curricular to ensure relevance and 'sticky' learning, our children were focused on topics that created empathy and social conscience founded in diversity through constructs such as poverty, wealth, family, happiness, freedom, pollution, justice, equality and so on.

I am biased, but it was brilliant. I found all the resources and essentially wrote the syllabus for our school, and our staff followed it and implemented the sessions. In time we found that respectful debate and discussion were commonplace. There was a progressive commonality of language, and children of all ages were utilising it to communicate their views, to have them challenged and then to reassess what they originally thought. Registered in 1994 (only a year before I did the course, just shows that Charlotte Mason College was ahead of the curve!) SAPHERE, the charity behind P4C, has trained thousands of educators over the years. Their focus is the social development of children and young people, particularly those facing disadvantage, which evidently works as the Education Endowment Foundation discovered in their research in 2015.

It changed how *we* worked, more to the point, and was a really beneficial way of us operating in that school. Naturally, I don't believe in a one size fits all approach, so I am not on commission for the programme, I just believe that it had a positively transformational impact on my leadership and our school's development. Had I not taken the opportunity to do something a little differently, even as a university student, then who knows how long I would have grappled with the issues we faced as a school decades later, and who knows what alternative I could have found to support our learners?

Now, I realise that a programme such as this really isn't as life changing perhaps as finding the vaccine for Covid-19, but genuinely, that was an opportunity I took for my own development, and then years later I successfully employed it as a school leader.

Regretting the opportunities we don't take . . .

Most people, if you ask them, when reflecting on the opportunities they have seized and the amazing outcomes that have resulted, will say they have no regrets.

Opportunities provide growth that helps them evolve as people and supports progress in the organisation, often creating other spin-off prospects. This has certainly been the case for me: in saying 'yes' to projects that require investment of time and resources, I have then been approached to do two or three more, and before you know it, opportunities just keep presenting themselves without much effort for me to look for them.

I suspect that what prevents many people from taking opportunity is that they cannot see the immediate or the long-term value of doing so; 'value' itself is a loaded concept because each of us sees 'value' as part of our world view, which is affected by our childhoods, social situations and our general expectations in life. Others do not take opportunity through a misplaced perception of guilt. That, or they are stuck in a rut of their design and unable to break out of it through fear, lack of resources, lack of faith in themselves and so on.

I remember my aunty coming to stay with me when I lived in Kenya; through a series of circumstances that machinated to prevent her taking a holiday to Cairo for her 50th birthday, she elected on a whim to take the opportunity to come to me. She had a three-week holiday of a lifetime, and I made sure she left saturated with experience and memories. Twenty-two years on, and she still remembers the night we were in the tented camp and heard the grunt of lion, the night we saw the Maasai warriors dance by firelight, and her visit to the Mount Kenya Safari Club – she does not regret not going to Cairo.

For reasons best explored elsewhere, my mum did not join her on the visit to me, to her eternal regret. It took a decade for my mum to find the opportunity to visit Kenya, with my aunt actually, and her life was changed there under the same azure sky that I fell in love with, through a random chain of events, and since her mind was opened, there has been no going back. Her advice to anyone now, although it has taken her most of her lifetime to think this, is don't wait, life does not wait for you. She is right, and I am glad it did not take me until I was 66 to work it out. Maybe this is a chance for you to pause and consider what opportunities you have right now that you could take advantage of? What will you regret not doing in a year, five years, a decade?

The first time I realised the 'opportunity game' mattered was when I was at the 'decision point' that all school leavers arrive at in the UK at 18. What after A Level exams? I knew it was either university, a well-trodden path for my school to advise me on, or the RAF to be a Chinook pilot (my dream). I dithered and prevaricated and could not decide what to do for the best. In the end, I decided to let 'fate' choose (AKA Royal Mail). In today's digital world this would never happen, everything pops neatly into your email inbox, but back then, it was snail mail or no mail. The University offer came first and that was it, decision made. But the opportunity to do something totally different, to be maverick and take the chance, to be the first woman to fly Chinooks, it burned inside me, and as an opportunity missed has always quietly played in the back of my mind, what if?

I had no confidence to do anything different of my own volition, unlike the confidence I have instilled in my own children now. My son recently rejected his choice of a career in the army, did not complete his basic training at the Army Foundation College, despite it being his dream from the age of two, and did a complete u-turn into doing an engineering apprenticeship. I supported his decision: at 17 he did not need to commit to the rest of his life. I haven't committed to one single career. I have done lecturing, charity work or study alongside my day job, and now I choose to do reservist work. In our modern world people do not work in the same place for 40 years and retire – they have options, retraining, revising their professional alignment as they grow. My daughter equally went to a very high-achieving selective school, which did not suit her. Whilst some parents may have insisted she stayed, for the kudos and prestige, I wanted her to be happy, so she left and now attends a sixth form college where she is challenging herself with three very academic subjects that she was unable to select in the school and doing brilliantly. They co-create their own future; we discuss options all of the time and potential outcomes of any decisions they make, or we make as a team.

Remember in the last chapter when I changed my degree course to enable me to stay in the location where I felt safe and settled? My children do not have those hang-ups, drivers or motivators, they have me – they are free to choose, the options are limitless. My daughter talks of a gap year after A Levels. I would no more have considered 'a gap year' after A Levels than I would have considered running naked through the streets of Liverpool. It would never have entered my head to do something that there was no clear outcome for, that offered me no security, no way of definitely self-funding, and no safety net.

For me, much of that was tied up in being able to fund myself and not have years of debt like a ball and chain around my neck. The government was in the process of changing the 'grant' system as I attended university, and although I did not need to pay for tuition, the eventual outcome of the Dearing Report, I had to take a loan or get to work because my mum and my step-dad simply did not have the money to pay for my food and accommodation. I worked (at times) five jobs, did teaching practice and also academic study whilst at university. My stepdad was a policeman, and it was deemed by the government that his salary was more than enough to provide for him, my mum, my three siblings, his daughter, plus also fund me.

Public sector workers do not have the advantage of accountants who can take advantage of aspects of 'self-employed' tax laws as many of my contemporaries had at the time, and therefore, if I wanted to develop myself, then I had to go it alone, something that prepared me well for adult life as I have explained to my children. It does, on reflection, make me a little sad because it really does highlight in even a small way that disadvantaged members of society have a glass ceiling imposed if they want to further study academically, simply because education is commodified and has been now for about 40 years. This is a whole debate of its own, so we won't digress about neoliberalism and what our successive governments choose to spend taxpayer's money on, but suffice it to say, it is my firm belief that education is seen as a ticket to social mobility, and limiting access to education of quality, in any way, limits access to that mobility if it is something that an individual wants to explore. When you consider how educational funding has been eroded in the last decade in the UK, then you can appreciate the frustrations of all school leaders who know that their capacity to enrich lives is diminished.

Nevertheless, despite this backdrop, I still managed to actually save and go to Kenya and save and go to Thailand whilst a student – the dichotomy isn't lost on me! I lived a safe and happy life working hard and looking for opportunity to experience new things – within my means. No different to how I am now as a Headteacher, no different to the road map I created for myself that has facilitated my academic study and acquisition of qualifications, no different to my blueprint for life and parenthood. I earned money and made decisions accordingly, living within my means and putting in the hard labour to see the outcomes – the aspect of life that is adversely affected, my social life (then, as now), is fairly limited.

I remember another pivotal moment, again that indicates the way our minds are wired to take risk based on our predispositions and early wiring (or not), when I was in Thailand as a student. I was there six weeks, and on Koh Phi Phi, before 'The Beach' was filmed off the coast there and long before the tragic tsunami of 2004. Walking through the coconut groves to the shack I was calling home I saw, nailed to a tree, the opportunity to join a yacht crew and sail from Thailand to Australia. I stood and looked at that advert for ages, I am not kidding. I ran through the scenarios in my head. Outcomes and possibilities. And I once again stood at a crossroads in life, a decision point. I had lived off grid for weeks, survived on fried rice, lassis, and watermelon. I read all day, walked by the sea, contemplated life. I visited Buddhist temples, considered life in all its glory. I didn't apply, despite yearning to do so.

My fears of funding, of managing to put 'pause' on life back in the UK, of not really having the support network to do this effectively, just put a lid on that adventurous spirit, and whilst I enjoyed and loved the holiday, I went home and thought about how different life would be for me if only I was brave enough to grasp it. I have often thought of that moment, in the baking sunshine, when life was simple and I had few responsibilities. What was it that stopped me? It can only have been fear, programming from childhood about self-sufficiency, the knowledge that if I didn't make a living for myself then I could rely on nobody else. I wonder what would have unfolded had I taken a different turn at either of those points?

How can you develop a growth mindset in your team and yourself?

What those moments taught me, and how they affect my life and therefore my leadership, is that when an opportunity presents itself, accepting and rationalising the fact that it may not come back in the same form (if ever again) creates a level of awareness about whether you want to reject or take it. Often, an opportunity will arise that involves us travelling outside of our comfort zone, and this presents issues discussed in the previous two chapters. If you can overcome those issues, and part of that is about knowing yourself and having a 'growth mindset', then a world of choice opens up.

But here is the thing: you don't necessarily develop either self-awareness or an ability to operate a 'growth mindset' all on your own. It didn't happen for me overnight, and it certainly wasn't natural. It took real work and lots of fortuitous meetings with influential people before I was able, and even then, blinking imposter syndrome (I dislike this expression as it is reminiscent of a Victorian kind of female hysteria of sorts, and it definitely isn't that!) would not disappear!

I try hard to simply accept the decisions I have made in the past – they were based on what I knew at the time and on my ability and circumstances. I try to tell myself that I was a different person then and did my best. I try not to live with regret, mainly because I look at my fabulous life, but I do know of people all but consumed by regret and sorrow, and I feel terrible on their behalf. If it can be avoided, therefore, then it is better not to enter a situation where regret is potentially a real outcome in the first place.

It is therefore imperative as a leader in any field to be actively aware of limitations and barriers that people will place on themselves because of their background, innate lack of confidence or lack of self-belief. Once aware, and that comes from knowing our teams and investing time in them, we can support, guide and signpost effectively so that ceilings can be smashed and everyone can seize opportunity, even if they are a little scared. I am in the business of doing this. Over time as a leader, I became increasingly interested in creating environments that supported others, as I had been supported. I became committed to being the change I wanted to see – more inclusivity, more equality, more advocates for the vulnerable and struggling, more compassion, more ethics, more glass ceiling smashing, more removing barriers to success for myself and others. This drive and passion is what reinforces my leadership narrative.

In my last job, not long after I took over as Headteacher, the rumblings at governmental level were quite worrisome about Teaching Assistants (TAs) and their 'value' in terms of how many months of learning they could increase a child's progress by (please do not ask me to try to justify these arbitrary statistics that are often bandied around in education in relation to learning, a distinctly individual transactional activity and immeasurable in many respects). Concerned for the jobs of the TAs I had recently inherited at the school, and on the back of individual conversations I'd had, I decided to upskill as many as I possibly could to ensure that not only were they able to enhance the lives of the children we served, but also enhance their professional profiles and ensure that if the government made any changes, they would be really 'employable'.

First up was GCSE maths and English. I searched for an opportunity for adult education, contacted the provider, and managed to arrange it on site, during the school day. I thought two of the TAs were either going to gang up and batter me or have nervous breakdowns when I suggested it. I reassured them that I would help them every step of the way, happily I had taught soldiers and their dependents at this level in Germany so I knew I was capable, and I had a 100% success rate there so I foresaw no reason why I wouldn't be successful with the dedicated individuals I wanted to support in school.

Perhaps I should explain here that it was not a three-line whip, there was no management instruction, I just explained the benefits to seizing the opportunity that I was presenting. We overcame fear, anxiety, panic, skill fade, lack of self-confidence and lack of knowledge, and I am delighted to say both passed (as did others)! They have never forgotten this, and to this day they talk about the investment made into them as human beings and also professionals. They retained their jobs in the end, the government must have realised that what they were advocating was somewhat nonsense (often the case), and in fact one now works for me in my current school!

I believe that it is a truism that if you are habitually pursuing positive opportunities, you develop deeper understanding about what you really want and how you can achieve it with each one that you embrace and immerse yourself in.

My most recent MA in military history, specifically 'Modern War Studies', is another case in point about seeking opportunity that unknowingly has multiple benefits. On completion of my doctorate, I was determined no more study. I took on the inspiration of the inimitable and totally gorgeous AW and his sidekick SH, and off I went bumbling into the reserves to share my skills in a sideways, and frankly crazy, move.

We then suffered lockdown, however, and with that came cessation of activity that I was used to. All life seemed to grind to a halt, and I decided to look into research again. Never having done a history qualification, but always a super keen historian on the back of my secondary school teacher and his wondrous lessons at secondary school about WWII, I approached the professor in charge of the programme and asked if I needed to start at the bottom with an A Level in history and an undergrad. Everyone I shared this notion with thought me mad. I pursued it, however, and I was reassured by the professor that this would not be necessary as my academic record supported the study level, and I could choose the topic that most interested me.

As I felt a little unsure (or a *lot* unsure in reality), I kept pestering the professor, and after several conversations, we set upon the idea of combining areas of interest and making the research about leadership in the British Army. Many of the things that I had lectured in at MA level, practiced in my day job, and inherent within the Army codes of practice were synonymous – it made sense. During the refinement process, we settled upon something slightly different, but as I was going through the initial stages of the research and information gathering, some interesting things evolved.

Firstly, I was invited to observe at several recruitment locations in different Services, and from that I was able to link up some of my secondary colleagues with outreach and engagement teams in both the Royal Marines and also the British Army for some pretty amazing and enriching events. In conversation with influential individuals, they sought to sigh post me to opportunity. It took effort for me to both speak to the outreach teams to see if there was any relevance, almost to filter whether I thought their programmes could be implemented, and then to follow up in a busy schedule with my friends and colleagues in order to facilitate their uptake.

How one opportunity leads to another . . .

My research, and making contact with people that I otherwise would not have done, lent itself through careful curating of opportunities and ability to exploit them, to hundreds of children and young people in my neck of the woods having their lives enhanced. In me seizing what could be considered 'random opportunity', this has become a force multiplier. Therefore, young men and women, many from deprived areas, young women from girls' schools, and young children from specialist provision who would not routinely have accessed military outreach work (because they were unaware of it) have been able to, In making connections, and sharing links, I have supported many useful endeavours. The aims of these programmes are not to indoctrinate the young into joining the forces – they are not recruitment aims, but engagement and social development aims, supporting growth of values, self-belief, nutrition and mental health. Of all of the outcomes so far in my own research, this has been the most rewarding.

Having said that, as a direct result of both the TEDx talk I did and my research, I have been asked to also do several talks (brief) in a range of military facilities, and who knows where those opportunities may lead and how much value I may add – even to the life of one person.

As a leader and a parent, as a friend and a child, it is crucial to remember that what you do and say influences others. How you behave and how your behaviour influences others will become your legacy. There are always people, often impressionable ones, watching you, and if you allow yourself to stagnate, through fear or fixed mindset, then this is the legacy you will leave others. If you are a parent (or leader of your family), then you have a duty to work on yourself so that you do not pass on your own hang-ups to your children; as a leader, you will have influence over far more people than as a parent, but they have equal importance. You are shaping the thinking, the lived experience, the neural connections of other people – you are creating stress or minimising it, you are creating opportunity and support or removing it. With a deep breath, commitment to your community, a lot of faith in yourself and your mission to change lives as a leader, you can make a difference.

All of the above will enable you to look for, grab, make the most of, and pay forward opportunity. When I prepared the talk for Women in Defence at The Army Foundation College, Harrogate, I said the following to the Junior Soldiers:

> Each decision you make in the next few decades, every chance and opportunity you grab, every person who supports and champions you, is building and creating your legacy – what you will eventually leave behind

for and with others. Your decisions, even now at your age, are not meaningless, they will be like keys, opening doors that you didn't even know
existed with endless opportunities on offer to you, so you need to be aware
and ready to seize those opportunities as they crop up, and the Army will
be bursting with them.

I meant every word, but this could be applied to each person I come across, and
indeed that you come across.

What has all of this to do with leading with love, with you?

The point of this chapter is:

- Life is full of opportunity, created and spontaneous (which means that you can . . .)

- Change the course of your life with one simple decision (because . . .)

- You never know where an opportunity will lead you (because . . .)

- Regret is an unhealthy emotion and can undermine good mental health (also . . .)

- As a leader you can horizon scan, and the more you do, the more opportunity
arises for your team, supporting your main effort as a leader (to make the best
team you can).

Further reading/listening

If you like a podcast and 'opportunity' is something you want to know more about
in terms of leadership:

1. Siya Kolisi: Always Be Ready for an Opportunity. https://tinyurl.com/Always-be-ready

If you like a book and want to get the best potential out of your team in a number
of levels:

1. Tadevosyan, Hayk (2019). *The Power of Mindset: The Manual to Why Most Successful People Feel Unfulfilled and What to Do About It.* Firebrand Publishing. ISBN:
978-1941907115.
2. Clear, James (2018). *Atomic Habits.* Random House. ISBN: 978-1847941831.

Life never stops teaching, so you don't stop learning

Life has a way of teaching you painful lessons – if you can take the learning from them

I will often be quoted as saying that I learn all of my lessons the hard way, and it is so true! My life lessons are always powerful, usually painful, and occasionally attached to deeply profound feelings; this is what gives them their influence and ability to send a jolt of adrenaline to my heart each time I am brought within touching distance of remembering and repeating them. The difference between life lessons and actively pursuing learning is that conscious endeavour is something we can all be engaged with, for ourselves and others, in a routine way. Life lessons have a nasty habit of rocking up and giving us a bit of an unexpected slap in the face – the learning that takes place from that is from reflecting on what it taught you rather than dwelling on the potential nightmare that you need to sort out in the aftermath!

In the UK each August we see the furore of media reporting on exam results. For the UK it is GCSE and A Levels, one a gateway to post-16 study, and one a set of tickets to post–school life. I totally 'marmalised' my A Levels and still managed a good career and financial stability. I had been going out with a boy for a while, can't recall his name now, and a few weeks before my A Levels were due to commence, his best friend's mum knocked on the door to tell me they had been 'seeing one another'. I don't suppose I need to develop this anecdote further. Needless to say, I was pretty devastated, and the outcome was that I did no revision for A Levels and completely tanked them – in my memory I think I only graded because of the coursework I had done over the two years. I earned three C's and an E. I got what I needed, the little educational passport, and off I set to the university college of choice, as you do. Based on predicted grades, I had been offered an unconditional place – thanks be!

I never forgot the valuable lessons I was taught through that experience, which I am happy to share right here, as I did with my niece recently, and which I think are key to life and leadership! We are responsible for ourselves and what is in our control; revision and effort are within our remit. How we choose to respond to a stimulus is in our power to control. I had nobody to blame but myself. I could have blamed the boy, his lover for her timing, or both of them for their behaviour in general, but it wasn't their fault. The fault was mine. I learned that I should put the work into what I am doing all of the time, each piece of work I create, and never assume that the quality doesn't matter because it really does. Other 'takeaways' were don't believe all you are told and if something doesn't feel 'right' then usually it isn't, no matter how uncomfortable the cognitive dissonance is to acknowledge. You can survive humiliation, heartbreak and sorrow.

Exam results are not definitive – at other times in life, when I was not juggling multiple complex issues on many levels in many aspects of life, I have even been known to pick up a distinction or two. I neither let the highs or the lows define me, rather simply enjoy the work that went into the achievement as much as I can along the way.

Seeing exam results as anything other than a representative letter or number, graded against sometimes subjective nuance on any given day, is futile. You are much more than the sum of your achievements. This keeps me, as a teacher and school leader, quite focused on what really matters, and that is the whole person, not SATs scores for children, or grades for adults I am thinking of employing, or for myself. I think you can force people to learn just about any topic and perform to just about any measurable degree if that is what your focus is. What matters more to me is that the children, young people and adults that I engage with see their own potential and seek out learning for themselves. With self-motivation comes a new level of investment.

And all of that from failing my A Levels!

When in university, I was working multiple jobs, keen to explore formal learning and also understand how the world worked, whilst learning to live 'life'. Hilariously, I was described by one lecturer as having 'little potential' – clearly someone who did not look beyond the person in the lecture and try to understand their lived experience, but I digress. One of the most vivid memories that I have from that time is of placing my faith in a so-called 'subject matter expert', namely, The Balloonist.

I have introduced Johnny Lockley in an earlier chapter, he was (and is) the owner of The Golden Rule, my boss at the time, but moreover my dearest friend. He is renowned and pretty famous in outdoor circles around the world for the mad-cap things he has done (and survived), but at the time, I was just under his wing and went everywhere with him as his not-so-glamourous assistant (please remember that this period of the 90s was one of fashion paucity, before contouring, hair products, fake lashes and 3-D brows were a thing!).

One fine, Lakeland autumn day, he rang the house early and in true Lockley style said, 'V, get your warm kit on, we are going on an adventure!' Without question I was ready, and off we went to rendezvous at the carpark beside Thirlmere. It was a bright, cold and windless day with beautiful blue sky, the reflection of which was almost blinding on the water in the morning sun. Early in the morning, nothing was moving, and it was very quiet. I had no idea what the adventure was (I often believe that blissful ignorance is preferable at times such as this) and simply waited, enjoying the moment and basking in the glory of nature.

A long wheel based Landover pulled up, complete with trailer, and the trailer disgorged its contents, a rainbow coloured hot air balloon (envelope). My heart skipped a beat. A balloon? In my inexperience I had no idea how huge the baskets (gondolas) were on a balloon; I had never seen anything like it. The lines, the burner and the scale of it were all immense, and I was mesmerised. Anyway, quickly and efficiently the balloon was rigged, and the burner on full and roaring until the huge rainbow orb was levitating above us, straining at her stays. We were ensconced in the gondola and The Balloonist, or aeronaut, a very good mate of Lockley's, was chatting away with him about the weather, the direction of the very gentle wind and the perfect nature of the atmospherics for my first ever balloon ride as we cast off.

My nerves disappeared as we rose with confidence, silently, above the majesty that is the English Lake District on that faultless day, no need for the burner to be on constantly, just a quick burst from time to time which had the effect of us lurching upwards momentarily until we steadied off. The russet colour of the leaves, the vibrancy of the grass, the image of grazing livestock seen from above, are etched onto memory – it was so serene and peaceful.

We rose steadily and were suddenly moving across the landscape much more quickly than I had expected that we would in the direction of Grizedale Forrest. I looked at first to Lockley for reassurance, and as he seemed unperturbed, I remained so. Until we began a very sudden, strange and soundless decent, which was akin to the sensation of being on a silent roller coaster as it plummeted. I panicked and shouted to Lockley 'We are going to crash!' as The Balloonist began to furiously pump the burner and try to heat the (by now) cold air in the envelope.

Now, I am no physicist, but I do know now that the thermals created that day had lifted us in a gentle ascent, in a rising mass of buoyant air, from our take off to the point where we were spewed out of the top of the thermal column. A form of atmospheric updraft, the convective current that is a thermal transfers heat energy vertically – naturally, this is invaluable information to anyone who participates in an aerial pastime and one would assume it would be critical knowledge for a successful balloon aeronaut! On this day, however, the day I was in the gondola, the knowledge had slipped his mind for some reason, and we were hurtling towards the earth at a stomach-churning rate, and for probably the fourth time in the space of a few months (whole other stories!), I was convinced I was staring death in the face. Which I was.

As the aeronaut fought with the burner, the envelope had begun to droop to one side, so the air being heated and the direction of travel of the wind meant that we were being pushed across the land, as well as rocketing towards the ground. Lockley shouted at me to brace myself into the bottom of the gondola and I literally did just that. Trying to breathe through my panic as we hit the tops of the trees, and were dragged through the canopy of the forest, I suddenly became very calm indeed. There was a lot of noise, and chaos, branches whipping, and a kind of tumbling, and then the impact. The gondola was pressed up against a deer fence and the envelope was the other side of it. As we all emerged, dazed, staggering, shaken up, cut and bruised from the disaster and checked ourselves for significant physical injury and damage, I could not believe what had happened.

We were stuck, without radio or phone, it was back in the day (BMP – before mobile phones) in the middle of the forest. The issues we now faced were not survival but logistical. I have no recollection of how we got out, of how they retrieved the balloon, or even our injuries – I think I may have been concussed as I do recall blood trickling into my eyes at one point. True to form, we were back out adventuring the following week, however. In the days before my sister's cancer diagnosis, I had no fear for my own life and no concept that life could literally be extinguished in the blink of an eye, just a quest for adventure, so very little stopped me.

What did that experience teach me about life and leadership? On an existential level it reinforced the idea that even the most knowledgeable and experienced people can make mistakes that can be disastrous if they are not paying attention to their immediate surroundings and the changing situation. That taking your eye off the ball, losing concentration even for a second, can cost dearly. It taught me that knowledge and skill do not make a person invincible. It taught me that nature is powerful and despite what we know of it, it can bring us to our senses very sharply. It taught me that arrogance is expensive. It taught me that even when, to the out-side world, there is only perfection, when things are looking faultless and going swimmingly one should always check behind the façade, on the basics, and make sure the contingency plan is there for when you may get thrown unexpectedly out into the cold. On a personal level, it also taught me that there is a deathly calm that settles within me when a catastrophe is about to take place, which gives me almost superhero aptitude for speed and clarity of thought, which has been put to the test many times since.

Incidentally, I never saw the aeronaut again (Lockley tells me he is absolutely fine!) and wondered periodically if he ever had such a mishap repeated, or if he had also learned a very scary lesson that day. None of us were killed or seriously injured, which, when you consider what had happened, is miraculous. I think his envelope and gondola were badly damaged though. Maybe humans learn best when something hits us in the purse!

How can we apply life lessons to our educational leadership practice?

How I apply this to my workplace is quite simple. We are always contingency planning, not to excess – I am not an obsessive – but in order to ensure that unex-pected disaster is mitigated for as far as is possible. We plan ahead for Ofsted inspection so that the information we will require is to hand, and we are not last minute scrabbling around for it. This helps us plan laterally and create systematic actions from those plans. We plan for capital improvements and staff training; we plan for enrichment and enhancement in the lives of children, and always in the background is the work done for us to be able respond efficiently in any eventuality. This is eminently transferable to the military role I have, and the transition between the two is seamless.

How can we apply life lessons to educational leadership development of colleagues?

In effect, that incident and how it transposes onto my day job also informs the future work of my early stage school leaders, those junior members of the leadership team who are learning their trade and how the mistakes of others can help us not to make the same ones. We accept that we will make others, of course – mistakes mean we are operating at a creative level!

One lesson that my senior leaders learned at my current school fairly recently was in relation to professional credibility. I had taken over the school when it was in a terribly tricky situation. The size of the school and the range and depth of the problems we needed to tackle were quite overwhelming for a moment, but I broke them down and was lucky enough to work alongside the most amazing and talented professional leaders who managed to help me turn the fortunes around very rapidly in that first (pre-Covid) year.

Our initial priority and main effort for the year was the rationalisation of how and what was being taught across the school in core subjects of reading, writing and maths. I had to get these three things sorted, and rapidly, and a member of the senior leadership team (SLT) was each assigned one. We had other SLT members assigned Early Years and foundation Stage (EYFS) and Safeguarding, plus Special Educational Needs and Disability (SEND) because every aspect of school needed immediate action.

Again, in terms of prioritising, Year 6 became our focus year – not for SATs scores, but because they had been disrupted for at least four consecutive years, and there were significant gaps in learning that would have a huge impact on their ability to access secondary level education that I believed was a travesty. The three Year 6 teachers at the time were a new team and had a lot to do in a short space of time, but they also had allocated to them a member of the SLT to sit each week and support them to plan, sequence lessons, differentiate, spot gaps, analyse data, feedback to children and manage pastoral issues and behaviour plus barriers to learning – they were well supported to do the job they needed to. This support came from investment of funds from the Local Authority (LA) who were keen to see the school right herself and become the learning environment it should be, and me deploying human resource in the areas I needed coordinated action.

As the year progressed, having commenced the plate spinning, I checked period-ically behind the façade to ensure that the foundations were being laid and I wasn't just getting the positive feedback loop I was hoping for. We worked transparently and efficiently, at pace and with great rigor (it was unsustainable but it needed to happen, particularly for the Year 6 children). As we began the process of debt recovery, we were able to support other year groups, and I was happy that we were making a difference. I asked not just children and parents, staff and governors what they thought of our progress, but also other professionals to come and triangulate my views on the work being done, including friends, colleagues and external pro-viders. All were in agreement – we were making rapid and sustained improvements for our children. My thanks MUST go to my then Chair of Governors, Rev Jackie, one of the most inspired and inspirational women I have ever met and the person who took a chance on me as Headteacher when she interviewed me. She gave me a chance despite me rocking up in red Birkenstocks because I didn't know it was an interview and looking rather frazzled as I had been dealing with some very sig-nificant problems in my other school. Hopefully she feels vindicated for recruiting me on a permanent basis! I was committed. A lot of people were watching. A lot of people were waiting to judge. Ofsted came and went, validating our work.

The summer of that year we were told, as we are each year, if we would be part of the LA moderation of assessments. We, surprisingly, were not due to be. I was not happy about this. I knew that it would create extra work for staff to be part of the process – not only would they have to assess the work of the children as they would routinely do, but they would also have to conduct a whole lengthy process outside of that if they were part of the moderation. They had worked extremely hard for two whole terms at a relentless pace, and I knew that it would not make me popular if I were to insist with the LA that we were moderated.

I asked to be moderated, anyway. I felt it would quality assure what I already knew was happening, evidence 'bang for buck' for the LA in terms of their mon-etary investment in improvement for school, and give credibility to the teachers for their work, the SLT for their work, and Ofsted when they came to check on the progress of the school in their monitoring visit (we had received the Requires Improvement judgement at the end of the second term – thank goodness we had all put that work in; when I first arrived I knew without doubt it would be deemed Special Measures).

Needless to say, two of the three teachers struggled to talk to me for a good few weeks until the day of the moderation took place. I had spent the morning in a particularly challenging Human Resources (HR) meeting and was exhausted and fractious by lunchtime; given the year we had also had, I was pretty 'thread-ers' (threadbare and empty). I was called by the team to join them in the room where the writing books of 90 children had been assembled and the three teachers, three moderators and SLT representative had been busy. Adjusting my demean-our accordingly, I walked in to wide-eyed and emotional faces, and I confess, my heart sank. I thought I had royally messed up and that our judgements on learning progress were not as wonderful as I had expected. I was blunt, as only the utterly depleted can be, 'Hit me with it, what is the headline?' I said.

The moderator, who had done a similar exercise two years before when not one Year 6 child was due to leave the school for high school at the 'expected standard' – not one – was actually crying. In September when I took over, it had looked like a similar picture to that of the two years previous. We had worked our socks off, and not only were 81% of the children at the standard (and of them, 20% above the standard), with a few weeks to go before the results needed to be submitted, we expected that to rise, meaning that the vast majority of our children would arrive in high school ready to access all learning. I could hardly think straight, but I found that moment of superhuman clarity and sharp thinking and saw a learning opportunity. I asked the moderator to explain to the three teachers, to articulate for them, what going through the process meant for them as individuals and our school as an organisation. I asked her to verbalise the impact of them validating our internal judgements so thoroughly.

Looking confused, she explained that the two who were leaving for posts in other schools could use the experience and evidence in their letters and CVs and, more importantly, to actually improve practice in their new school, if that was required, as they had been part of the team that had systematically reversed the fortunes of the children in our school, not through some sort of arcane magic, but just relentless and purposeful pursuit of excellence. She explained that anybody doubting the integrity of our data, which on paper looked miraculous, could not challenge it as we had been externally moderated, and the (widely accepted) suspicion levelled at schools where no moderation had taken place and data was 'high' could not, therefore, be levelled at us. She explained that sometimes the best thing to do was not always the easy thing, and that we had done the very best thing for our reputation, their careers, the children, the parents and our professional pride, for all stakeholders. I could hardly talk without emotion at this point and thanked them all for the work done that morning before leaving for the quiet sanctuary of my office.

The best leaders take lessons from every experience they have – be they positive or negative ones. I knew what the outcome would be for the children and what the moderators would see. I knew the legitimacy and credibility that would be earned by the teachers and the SLT. I may have spent some nights lying awake and wondering if I was doing the right thing, with a couple of the staff unable to meet my eye and clearly very angry, but I knew in my heart that it was and just dug deep into my reserves of resilience. Tough love isn't always obviously love, but it comes from the same place.

Deciding how not to lead is as important as deciding how you want to lead!

The best leaders take time to think about and reflect on the outcomes of an experience and therefore learn how they *don't* want to be and evolve naturally into how they *do* want to be. The best leaders never stop learning: academically or practically. They see lessons in everything and absorb them to create a nuanced and bespoke approach to their role, and a repertoire of approaches to apply to situations that arise. This is why there really is no 'one-size-fits-all' kind of leadership manual. Leaders need to understand theory, understand themselves, and overlay both to create their unique style.

I think we have certainly shared life lessons and how they can transfer to our workplaces, creating professional lessons, in the first part of this chapter. Now we must give some consideration to planned and 'badged' learning and qualifications (I may know a little about this)!

The best leaders I know actively want to develop through reading and listening to podcasts, having discussions which also enhance their ability to read situations and people socially, and challenging themselves. These leaders recognise that the diet they feed themselves is more than just the food they eat: it is the people they surround themselves with, what they allow into their minds, what influences their thinking, the culture they create. They are never complacent. As I said in the previous chapter, the best leaders are horizon scanning for opportunity, for them and those they serve, and this may well be academic qualification.

To study or not to study – this is the question

Many of you will consider doing additional study whilst you are also working. There are hundreds of online and face-to-face courses that you can do, and although there may be many battles to overcome before you even sign up, as discussed in the previous three chapters, creating time and making time for this valuable self and professional development is not only helping shape your career, but also the way you think, day to day, about life itself.

My first foray into officially badged post-graduate study was when I was four months pregnant with my daughter. My son was not even six months old, and I knew that I would be at home for the foreseeable future and not able to pursue my full-time teaching career. I was alone a lot of the time, in Germany, as my then-husband was deployed overseas. I needed something to occupy me, and it was study. I chose a subject area that I thought would interest me, and the Master's degree was in 'Diversity and Equality' where, over three years, I looked at literacy and barriers to learning to read and write, which gave me valuable insight into dyslexia; behaviour, which gave me valuable insight into a range of challenges where behaviour is communication; and leadership, which was an excellent academic introduction to things that I had been doing anyway. I did not think about the three years it would take me to complete my first MA, the hours of reading and assimilating information I would need to do, the writing and re-drafting I would need to do, and the possibility of failure. I simply decided I was doing it. I based my decision on the fact that whilst at school I had completed GCSE and A Levels whilst working part time, being in the ATC, playing netball for five different teams, playing hockey, running orienteering and doing DofE. When at university,

I had achieved a 2:1 pass whilst also doing teaching practices, working five jobs, running the netball team, climbing, sailing, walking, canoeing, kayaking and paragliding (and being a student who had little potential). I felt that being at home with two children under one, whilst my husband was away and I was not being paid to work, meant that I could apply my usual discipline and simply crack on. So I did. Routine was my friend, as was self-discipline. If I didn't feel like writing on the night I had set aside for my MA, then I would read for it. If I felt like doing neither, then I would do things I felt up to and swap out those activities for MA work on another day. I never left a minute unfilled. I have never been a 'drink coffee and pull an all-nighter before submitting an essay' kind of person! This also helped me combat the terrible loneliness I felt when my husband was away and stopped me becoming melancholy.

Now, some would think this is ridiculous, and for them, it would be. For me, it worked. I like this mode of working as it helps me organise my week, sometimes my month or my term, and I feel calm that I know I can achieve my goals in a timely way. I am goal-oriented, and I do like to keep myself busy. In the past, this has been for less healthy reasons (mainly to distract myself from looking within and battling demons), but these days I like to keep busy because I have so many worthy and enjoyable projects that I want to see to fruition, and they keep my mind fresh and prevent burnout.

After three years, I attained my first MA and attended the Bridgewater Hall in Manchester to receive my award. I wore a cornflower blue robe with yellow edging on it (which I didn't know until I got there would be this colour) and looked very 'put together'. For those who know me, I was extremely excited that this was the case as it happens so rarely! I was wearing yellow sling backs with intricate ivory butterflies on the front, and a yellow cardi over white trousers and a white vest. It was sweltering; my daughter wore a beautiful 'broderie anglaise' white smock, and my son a short-sleeved shirt and shorts. I remember it like it was yesterday. They watched me walk across the stage and shake hands with the Dean, whilst sitting with my uncle and aunt, mum and dad (their dad was still away), and they were so proud! The speech was for the audience, for the families who had supported their post-graduate recipient through their study. It was about the work and time and commitment it took for someone to complete a post-graduate course. I felt quite emotional as she was saying it, mainly because I had done it alone, and it felt like nobody would understand the work that had gone into it all, but it was being said out loud, and all of the families, as you could see just by looking around, really did know.

Many outcomes emerged from that day. Amongst other things, I thought about how I could congratulate my colleagues to reflect my sincere understanding of the energy, commitment and impact they brought to their work as the Dean had to me. This led to me doing things like writing to the families of the SLT in my last two schools, especially when I have been working them hard to overcome hurdles and make a difference to children.

I thanked my mum and my aunt for investing in me as a child, for doing their best to support me and champion me as an adult – I can never, ever thank them enough. I was glad for them that their investment was being realised. Although they would never ever think like that, I kind of did frame it that way initially for myself. I couldn't bring myself to be proud of my own achievements, it felt too self-obsessed and awkward, so I made it about other people – being a role model to my children, being a source of quiet pride for my mum, being a living representation of my grandfather's rescue mission the day he arrived with a shot gun to take us to a safe haven decades before.

What I now know is that this is not healthy. In order to authentically congratulate others and share their joy and achievement, you need to give yourself permission to feel the same. It is not something I am good at, but like most things for me, I am a work in progress! I am trying to learn to take the time between one achievement and launching myself into the next to appreciate what I have accomplished and all of the sacrifices that have been made, alongside practicing gratitude towards the people who have helped me. I think it is called 'practicing gratitude', but I am happy to be corrected.

As many of you will know already, in addition to the first MA I did, I completed a Level 2 adult education certificate; the National Professional Qualification for Headteachers (NPQH); the faith school equivalent of the NPQH, the 'Christian Leadership' award; the National SENDCo Award; another Master's in Leadership, where my dissertation was about attachment theory and trauma in children; a Doctorate in leadership, with my thesis being in politics and how it affects leadership of schools; and I am completing another MA in Modern War Studies, with my dissertation in recruitment of British Army Officers. The point I make here is that I chose subject areas that interested me, some of which were relevant to my job, some were in an area of weakness that I wanted to expand upon and know more about, and some 'just because'!

Overcoming barriers to studying part time

There is nothing to stop any of you doing the same; languages, creative topics, professional study – you can be and do what you like and should not let age, job title, fear or anything else stop you pursuing something. Logistics can largely be overcome, with help, and you should ask for that because good people always want to ensure that others succeed.

Part of the battle of thinking about engaging with additional study lies in both creating the time alongside running homes, raising children and enjoying fulfilling relationships, plus the demands of a day job, but also in having the support from your own line manager who sees the holistic value in encouraging you to learn. Part of it is financial consideration that must be reconciled, alongside the academic underpinning you may have from your youth.

As a direct result of having had that support myself from two successive and inspirational Chair of Governors', and the natural way in which I work, I am a huge advocate for lifelong learning. As the Head, I am now in a position to support colleagues from every aspect of school in order to complete courses that enhance their thinking, well-being, professional ability or future career. I love talking to staff about their career aspirations and how they may achieve them (encouraging them to dream big!). It is one of the many pleasures of my diverse and demanding job.

As a leader who continues to learn, you will have to juggle the constraints that are incumbent in your job, and family, and demonstrate to others *how* it can be done, whilst also managing the organisational implications of other staff who are doing further study. These implications can be both positive and negative, and weighing them up against the desire of the individual is critical to ensuring the balance is kept between organisational integrity and also the staff member feeling valued. If this balance can be successfully struck, you end up with an empowered and enthused workforce, keen to develop themselves and their practice, and that can only be a good thing, surely?

For me, I do this as part of the School Development Plan (where possible) and the individual Performance Management process, if it is appropriate. This means that the work of the individual is celebrated, and its impact can be verbalised by colleagues and school leaders alike. I also love to celebrate the achievement of staff on the weekly/monthly blog so that parents know what a fantastic body of committed and forward-thinking adults they have working with their children.

What has all of this to do with leading with love, with you?

The point of this chapter is:

- Learning whilst 'doing' enhances what you do because you learn to question what has always been done (which means that you can . . .)

- Think differently and seek improvements without accusation (because . . .)

- As society changes, so may some of our attitudes towards the way things are done and why (because . . .)

- Leadership should reflect the society it serves and strive to take it into the future for inclusivity and sustainability (also . . .)

- As a leader you can facilitate career enhancing learning for your team, supporting your main effort as a leader (to make the best team you can).

Further reading/listening

If you like a podcast and 'lifelong learning' is something you want to know more about in terms of leadership:

1. The High Performance Podcast: Frank Lampard: Have a Conviction and a Willingness to Learn. https://tinyurl.com/Frank-Lampard

If you like a book and want to get the best potential out of your team in a number of levels:

1. Pennelle, Palmer (2021). *Maturity Brings Happiness: The Many Benefits of Lifelong Learning*. Independently Published. ISBN: 9798730740198.
2. Vanderbilt, Tom (2021). *Beginners: The Curious Power of Lifelong Learning*. Atlantic. ISBN 978-1786493118.

9 People may forget what you said, but never how you made them feel

Hero leadership is so passe

I perhaps shouldn't admit to this, but we are more than halfway through now, and with each chapter (that I decided to write in the order you are reading them – if you are going through chronologically!), I have not known what I would exactly write until I have sat down with the chapter title in front of me and thought about it! It makes book writing quite a scary experience, but also a rewarding one. I am forcing my mind to really look back on pivotal moments, those that can be shared without landing me with a lawsuit, to support my views on leadership and try to bring my philosophy to life.

If you have stuck with it this far, then you will hopefully not have been too bored, and you will see how difficult it is to extract your human self from the leadership persona you have. In fact, it is perhaps much more healthy to align the two, integrating the lessons learned in both to gain deeper understanding of yourself and how you can improve. I have said throughout the book, and will continue to say, I was born with none of the innate leadership skills and abilities that some would argue are essential components to inspirational leadership. I have learned lessons along the way, tried to make sense of life and learning as I have gone, and somewhere in there I have found my own pathway and what I am comfortable doing in terms of leadership. Not all of the things that I believe will have resonance with every one of you who is reading, and that is okay. You are free to substitute your experiences with mine or even add your own interpretation onto the personal experiences I describe here.

A common leadership theme for me is that the best leaders are not heroes, they don't want to be, and therefore they do not operate in isolation. The best leaders work hard to create an environment where other people feel valued – with this actually being of paramount importance. They work in healthy and high-functioning teams, usually of their design, and usually created to match the environment and to ensure that their weaknesses are well complemented.

The role of the leader in this configuration becomes more about absorbing the blows, the negativity, the pressures from outside, and radiating the joys created

DOI: 10.4324/9781003281313-10

by success, good feedback and positivity outwards to their team and the wider community.

This is the work, the 'graft', of living *anyway*. The work of life. It is hard, but worth it. The team can then focus without their minds in 'fight or flight', but co-regulated, in a community of practice, with their brains fully connected to their bodies, on the areas the team is dedicated to improving. This happens because the leader has inculcated a culture of healthy and supported risk taking, reflection and learning from all outcomes, and a desire to place ego to one side and learn from every experience. It is usual in schools such as this that when you visit them there is a nebulous sense of inclusivity and respect that is hard to describe and even harder to replicate. It is more than the displays, the curriculum, the quality of the work in books, the lunchtime hubbub – it is intangible. It is the essence of the community of practice.

Clarity of thought, communication and deed

As leaders we must be clear in our own minds what *we* are expected to do and what we are expecting *others* to do – our intent. We must delegate to others more suited to certain tasks in order to secure success for everyone, and we must never overpromise and under deliver. I have come across many situations where staff have been over-promoted without support and training and are therefore unhappy in their role as they cannot function in the way they want to or should. I have come across fractious staff who are isolated, out of their depth and miserable, which undermines their mental and physical health and also the culture of the school. I have come across people who have made demands of me that I have not under-stood, and they have been angry with me at times for not delivering. The disso-nance between misunderstood expectation and poor outcome is so unhealthy, but when the opposite is true, it can be transformational.

I remember when I was about to complete my second MA; although in leader-ship, I wanted to focus the dissertation on attachment disorder and trauma in chil-dren. I had been implementing a programme for children who were suffering with some kind of catastrophic change in their lives (divorce, death, relocation and so on) for about two years in school. I really felt invested in this programme on two levels: first and foremost we had a large number of children who had sadly lost a parent, been adopted or were struggling to deal with the divorce of parents; and on a deeper level, this was the kind of programme that I knew I could have benefitted from as a child, but in the very early 80s just wasn't available.

So I approached the university with my research proposal, and it was accepted, ethics included. I was excited to be able to read far more deeply into the subject area than I had ever ventured before, and as I immersed myself in it, I underwent quite a profound cathartic personal experience. I travelled to places in my head that I had not ventured prior to this, and it was healing. The academic experience, however, did not quite live up to the personal one initially!

For months I would leave work early to drive 45 minutes to the university, find a parking space, walk to the tutor's office through the construction site that the building had become, and wait for inspiration, guidance, suggestion and challenge from the tutor. My tutor, Paul, I would describe as a fiery socialist disruptor, absorbed and preoccupied with politics and political affairs, the scourge of capitalism and 'man's struggles'. He was not a man predisposed to talking about feelings, emotions, developmental psychology, therapy etc. You can imagine that this was not a recipe for success – I am not exactly sure who, in their wisdom, had paired us up in the first place . . .

I have to say (and there is a very happy outcome to this story, so don't panic) that after a year, I arrived at the point of not having written a single word of my dissertation and having had all the enthusiasm for the project completely eradicated. I arranged to see my tutor one last time, and I told him I was throwing the towel in. I had an MA, I didn't need another one, trying to make sense of the project seemed impossible, and although disappointed, and completely going against the grain, I was not going to complete this course as I couldn't make headway on the research piece and just had no more mental energy or emotional bandwidth to try.

At that point, he took a brave move, I think, and suggested that I pop down the corridor to speak to his friend, Anne Marie, as a last-ditch attempt to salvage the situation before me jettisoning it. Dejected and completely disillusioned, I did so, and once again I met someone who utterly transformed my life and has since become one of my most treasured friends.

I told her the parameters of the research, the back story and what I was trying to do, and she smiled and said it would be easy. She talked to me about a concept that I had never heard of before, as I had done quantitative study previously, rather than qualitative, so I was entranced when she explained about ethnography, reflexivity and the fact that what I was doing was obviously linked to what had happened to me as a child. That conversation became an emotionally illuminating moment in time that I can recall to this day, and she was absolutely right. I just didn't have the language or the vocabulary to explain or understand it until then. I was in my mid-30s!!!

Needless to say, having discussed each chapter there and then and how it would fit together, I left, and within a week had drafted the literature review and rapidly completed the dissertation in a couple of months which, when marked, earned me a first. A first at MA level. Me. I almost want to call myself 'Vicki From the Block', here but I don't like to be called Vicki!

Remember the girl from Liverpool who didn't feel that she fit in anywhere, who had only paid half the attention to her GCSEs that she should have whilst navigating a tricky home life, work, sport, the ATC and DofE? The girl who had ruined her A Levels through a broken heart and only scraped the necessary grades to head off to university? The girl who had worked five jobs and left university with a 2:1, and a reputation with one of her lecturers as having limited potential, had earned herself an unequivocal first at MA level. It blew my mind. I am not sure I have ever mentioned that grade to anyone until now, maybe one or two people if I have tried to illustrate the point I will make shortly, but this is a very public unveiling of a defining moment for me both as a person and as a leader.

With the right set of conditions, we can achieve anything

I realised several things on reflection in the freezing cathedral when I received my degree. I wore head-to-toe black, by the way, and flat black shoes (in case of a wardrobe malfunction which could lead to a trip on the stage!). The robe was black and had grey, white and red stripes on the hood. My mum, aunty and children all cried, and I realised that my restrained tears were about the fact that firstly, with the optimal conditions, anyone could achieve anything. Even me.

For me, those conditions were both access to the repository of knowledge from someone more experienced, the connection of one human to another and the understanding that flows from that invisible connection, and the time/space/resources in order to be able to devote to the work. At my age then, I had my own warm, safe and comfortable home; my children were in a settled routine and once in bed I had several quiet hours with which to work in terms of study and writing; I had the academic skills to be able to assimilate information and write (although Anne Marie would say that my early stream-of-consciousness stuff is always painful to sift through, I am sure!). In a way that I had never had when at school, or through my undergraduate degree, even when completing my first MA remotely, I had all of the components required to be able to create something that I was truly proud of. Moreover, I had found, purely by accident, the right person to supervise me, who was interested in that kind of work, understood it and could advise me. I also had the raw materials to make the work authentic – my experiences, and my passion for the children I was working with.

How can we create optimal conditions for our team members?

As a leader, this translates for me into simple strategies that I can easily employ. I always make sure that the right person, with the right skills and knowledge, is doing the right job. I have often wondered why, arbitrarily, people are told to co-ordinate or lead on things if they have little knowledge, enthusiasm or skill in that subject or area. I have worked in small schools and very large schools, and what I know is that even in primary schools where subject specialisms are not a requirement in the same way that they are in secondary school, it is possible to simply ask if there is anyone interested or keen in the first instance, competent and keen to learn in the second, when looking to allocate subject oversight to someone. I am not oversimplifying this point – I do genuinely understand the constraints in very small schools where the Headteacher does not just teach but also co-ordinates all of the subjects (I have a teeny bit of advice for this – to be covered in later chapters, incidentally, and involving networking), but I think the right people in the right job is so important!

I also think that connections and how we relate to people matters. In a school we may have internal relationship issues between members of staff, or between particular parents and members of staff, or children and members of staff and finally governors and members of staff. All of these need careful management and delicate treatment if they are not to undermine the integrity of the school, but they require a degree of honesty, self-awareness and reflection, arbitration at times, and also the option for individuals not to be placed in stressful situations but to speak to an alternative person to intervene where possible and appropriate. I see it as no failure to have a parent who cannot connect with me for some reason work with my deputy or another member of the leadership team if they are more comfortable, for example, whilst I work on the long game of building the relationship from scratch over time. Sometimes as school leaders we are faced with the historical feelings of parents who did not have very enjoyable interactions with school staff when they were at school, and therefore, they feel threatened by the 'office' rather than the person. Being able to have sensitive and frank conversations with people is essential to building trust and rapport, but this may take time.

I also realised on far more than a superficial level that there would be children in my school, and future schools where I would work, who may not have the ideal situation to learn in at home, and I wondered about how we could mitigate for that. I realised that there could be parents and staff members who would love to develop themselves, but as a result of their own academic foundations, working many jobs to make ends meet, supporting children at home and so on, may not be able to – not just in terms of time commitment and academic acumen, but also finances to pay for a course in the first place.

It was sobering, to say the least. In some ways it is perhaps what makes me feel a little embarrassed about my own qualifications, I have been lucky that some of them have been funded or part funded as part of my professional development, but others have meant sacrifice of holidays or treats and so on. I wonder what that says about me: am I selfish to have spent the money on my education rather than a holiday for my children? On my education rather than a set of library books for school? Then I think that my deeper knowledge and understanding of humans, of how we work, of how we learn and how we lead, is helping me to change the lives of those I serve, at home and in my work, as a parent and an educator, even in subtle and small ways, in a far more beneficial way than perhaps a single holiday or a book they may read. I then realised that if I can change lives like this, if my staff are also engaged with professional development, then so can they, and the rate of change becomes almost exponential (any mathematicians out there, forgive the hyperbole, don't @me with the technical definition of 'exponential'!).

So, Anne Marie made me feel like a champion, and I lived up to that. She still does, by the way, over a decade later; she makes me believe I am like a modern-day Shield Maiden, or an Amazonian warrior.

The commodification of education

In a neoliberal world such as ours, competition, accountability and the inherent stress associated with this way of living and working (in what is essentially a huge marketplace) is unhealthy if not managed and underlines some of the conflict in the day job of a leader. Leaders in education, as with other corporate environments, have enormous responsibility to try to prevent burnout of their current staff and retain staff with excellent morale and dedication to the organisation, whilst also preventing a staff recruitment crisis in the future. It is complex and relies on the intricacies of relationships, nuanced understanding of need and a great deal of love to counterbalance what is required with managing how people feel about that.

Everyone with a vested interest in education, whether or not they are a parent, regardless of the tier of education they or their child may be in, at any stage, whether they are a part of accountability structures such as Ofsted, whether they are a child or young person, or they are in business/industry and need to recruit for certain skills, everyone is part of the huge educational 'marketplace'. Education is just another social enterprise that has been commodified in the last four decades, and with that comes the expectation of doing more with less, ensuring value for money ('bang for buck') and cutting costs – all whilst maintaining morale and not compromising on quality or exam results. Sound familiar? This environment is not naturally conducive to good relationships and the ability to make people feel like they are invaluable members of the team. Yet in order to thrive, organisations must do this.

In schools where there is a sense of collaboration, the internal manifestations of external accountability inflicted on them don't seem to be detrimental – regardless of the inspection grade the school carries. Often this collaboration and team ethic can be observed and 'measured' by simple qualitative instruments such as good staff morale (laughter!) and highly motivated people working effectively (low sickness absence rates, high engagement in training and consistency of approach through 'buy in'). Where it is lowest, there may be high turnover of staff, poor relationships and erratic quality in things like teaching and learning, which are actually obvious and do not require much formal observation and scrutiny. Where this has happened, and I have actually arrived in schools where this is the lived reality, then the very first job in hand is to build relationships and ensure that each member of the team sees their value and feels their worth. In order to do that, as explored in earlier chapters, it takes investment of time into getting to know staff and a desire to see everyone realise aspirations – as a leader, this means holding your nerve and not jumping immediately to standards and systems, but focusing on people and relationship building.

In schools where morale is highest, leaders actively work as a protective force, almost as 'buffers' between members of their school and external activities and structures: Local Education Authorities, Multi Academy Trust Boards, Regional Schools Commissioners, national government policy and HMI/Ofsted. Those leaders act like a shield, or force field, and absorb the impact of those potential negative or intrusive external agencies. However, even with the most effective leaders acting as buffers, the stress of teaching-associated workload can never be removed – because teaching has become an increasingly demanding vocation where simultaneously respect for the profession in society has decreased. This is a toxic cocktail. Leaders can, however, and should do a great deal to reduce the negative impact by addressing its worst aspects of workload in a holistic way. This can be by rationalising systems and bureaucracy, minimising meetings and modelling work–life balance practices, whilst also offering support systems such as coaching, supervision, mental health training and so on. Each school will have its own unique situational needs, and the job of the leader must be to know them inside and out and create solutions.

When we as leaders address workload and stress, and mitigate as far as possible for external impact, we make people feel safe; that safety enables them to function better, enjoy their personal lives and, in turn, be invaluable members of the team who want to perpetuate that healthy environment. None of us lives and works in isolation; we are not exclusively educationalists – we exist in our families and have lives outside of school that need us to also be the best version of ourselves.

We create the weather

In my current school, one of the easiest wins in the early days, and the first of many significant 'how you make others feel' moments, was before I took on the role. I was part of a group of Headteacher professionals working with our LA to support other schools, Associate School Improvement Advisors (ASIAs), who were invited into the school to do a review of the progress they had made since their last inspection. For a range of reasons, which I won't go into, and despite some fabulous interim leadership, they had struggled. One of the areas I was tasked to look at was maths.

The school had invested heavily in previous years into an eastern mathematics philosophy and the expensive resources to support it. But the training had been sporadic, many people had left since its purchase, and so many other initiatives had been breathlessly adopted at the same time that nobody had been given the chance to get their heads around the pedagogy of the programme. Nobody understood the implications, it was difficult to ensure implementation was consistent, it was not periodically checked for issues and misconceptions for the teachers, or any problems with how it was being taught, recorded, fed back to children, plus a whole list of other contributing factors to the bottom-line up front – it had no positive impact, and standards were still very low.

As part of the review, I observed teachers try to teach this programme and realised they were doing a hybrid of two different programmes, a free one and the very expensive one; there was a huge degree of cutting and sticking learning objectives into books, small tasks also being photocopied and stuck in each day, to varying degrees of usefulness. Essentially, teachers were working for approximately two hours a night to plan, prepare and resource a single maths lesson for the next day that had little coherence, progression or impact on learning and was leaving most staff feeling tired, anxious and overwhelmed.

I fed this back in the most gentle of terms to the staff, and I fed it back in the report to the interim Head and governors succinctly. Then, out of the blue, I was asked to lead the school as Executive Head the following term – into what we knew would be an 'Ofsted year' for certain. The feedback from staff to the leadership team was that I had given difficult messages in a compassionate way and offered helpful suggestions of how they could adapt their working practice and minimise the anxiety being created, and they really appreciated this – and said so. This contributed to my selection and subsequent appointment (at least I think it was this and not my red Birkenstocks). When I was 'interviewed' the following week, I said exactly what I thought, that the school needed 'loving back to life' rather than talking about delegation and standards, my experience and why I was better than anyone else for the job. I had made sure that the staff I observed and spoke to felt 'heard' and 'listened to' rather than judged (which technically could have been perceived as being my role in that situation). This was an excellent foundation upon which to build my subsequent Headteacher relationship with the staff.

In September, one of the first and most immediate priorities was to change the practice in maths and simplify it – to use the free programme exclusively and focus on planning and teaching that well. This caused a little 'tension' with the LA, who had put in specialist support in maths for some time in terms of the expensive programme. The turnover of one-third of the teaching staff and the fact that there had been no improvement in the outcomes for children in the subject area for two years (despite them literally being taught maths and literacy only during this time) lent some strength to my argument. As Head I felt it was incumbent upon me to focus on what the needs of the school were internally, then become the advocate to external agencies, even the most supportive ones, in order to have those needs met. We were allocated different specialist support, well versed in the free programme, and rapidly began to see some real improvement. When I canvassed staff views on this change, it was unanimous – they were all delighted, and from that point on, the majority of the staff were fully invested into the holistic goals of the leadership team as they could see not just impact on their workload, but that I would fight for what was right for the school, and I would provide clarity of expectation and then the training and support to enable the expectations to be met (and exceeded).

This sounds a bit 'braggy' – it isn't meant to. I wasn't at the front on a white charger waving sword aloft and leading this – I was at the back, playing the intricate and complicated game of chess that ensured the right people were in the right role doing the right job – far less glamorous, yet perhaps more important, some could argue! I was also bearing the brunt of some fairly unimpressed male colleagues who felt they were more experienced and capable of doing the job I had been asked to do, who thought I had been hired for the job on the basis of my personality rather than ability; some brutally disappointed parents who wanted to vent, and rightly so, about the past few years; and finally, some very troubled staff who had suffered dreadfully and needed my support.

In the interests of balance, I should say that part of this wasn't really sugar coated. It was quite gritty. With increased expectation (from the third successive Headteacher in three years) comes increased anxiety regardless of the positive outcomes on workload. One or two staff were not suited to the relentless nature of the pace and the work and had all but burnt out in previous years for a variety of reasons. Those people needed watchful care, and most did move to schools which, as they had 'good' Ofsted judgements and far greater stability, had less high stakes pressures and were better suited at that time to their needs, which is always tricky to handle. Done with compassion and from a place of love, these situations can be managed effectively, however, and usually are mutually beneficial.

How I survived bad weather

I have felt very undermined and anxious at times in my own professional journey, and at one point my future in education seemed very uncertain as, for some unknown reason, one of my bosses at the time seemed determined to ruin my career. This person was abhorrent to me at every opportunity and would actively seek out opportunities to be vile. In retrospect, it was bizarre. One October, I applied for and successfully attained a position in a new school, to start in January. Towards the end of December, I got a call from the new Headteacher who asked me to pop over and see him.

My mind went into a tailspin. What could he want? Nothing good, surely? I was catastrophising, sweating, shaking, my heart was racing, and I could barely think straight, such was the impact I allowed my current boss to have on me with the way that they worked and the way I had seen them destroy others over the years. Not only had this individual been awful to me on a daily basis whilst I was in work, when I was offered the new job and accepted, they came to me in the staffroom a few days later as I was making a cup of tea and said, 'Well, that's your life sorted then, isn't it?' before exiting the room in a very dramatic fashion that left me very shaken.

When I arrived at the new school, the Head greeted me warmly and was so pleased to see me. I was on the verge of tears, and he asked me what was wrong. When I told him that I thought he was going to say that he had changed his mind, that my boss must have been in touch and told him I was rubbish and not to employ me, he laughed and said it was nothing to do with that at all! He did tell me that he had received a shocking reference for me from this person but that it was so disconnected from the reference of the other referee, and my interview, and the letter I had written, that he chose to see it for what it was – an attempt at sabotaging someone's career by a very bitter person. Apparently something similar had happened to him, and in his role as Head he was able to see through it and ensure that it didn't happen to people he was working with or for. I couldn't believe it.

He made me feel so valued, and I will never forget that he took such an amazing chance on me after that reference had come through. I endeavoured never to let him down, and although we were poles apart in terms of personality and interests, I sincerely loved working with him.

I am sure that this kind of thing is very rarely seen these days, as we are all so much more enlightened and (dare I say it?) 'woke', but the impact of that toxic situation took many years to overcome. I can still recall the sense of isolation it caused, the divisions in the school, the heightened levels of anxiety and the physical manifestations of that in me. What I realised though, from it, was that one day I wanted to be the kind of school leader, deputy Headteacher, Headteacher who worked ethically and who was people centric, rather than the ego-driven and purposefully damaging kind of human being who can sometimes find themselves in a position of leadership. I have no idea if I have managed that goal, by the way; I try to leave the opinions of others to them and focus on trying to be the best I can be, but I am ever hopeful that I have not and will not allow myself any complacency.

Shield and shine!

As leaders there is a lot that we can do to model the creation and preservation of high morale in a practical, sensitive and collaborative way: finding creative solutions to supporting staff development and career enhancement (as discussed in the previous chapter), reducing bureaucracy and time-consuming practice that does not impact positively on learning or wellbeing (marking and meetings, for example), developing relationships and trust through always working with integrity (see Chapter 3) and coaching and mentoring (see Chapter 10) to name but a few.

As with all things in a school setting, it is the leader and, by extension, their team that is responsible for creating the 'climate' in a school, or the culture, which directly influences all systems, policies and practices that permeate it: including how people treat one another and, therefore, feel. As leaders we can celebrate the work of our staff, parents and pupils, amplifying their successes and thereby adding another layer to the motivation and morale levels in school.

How we treat others, how we interact and speak to them, how we behave towards them is a manifestation of how we feel about ourselves and understand our 'place' in society. My daughter reminded me recently of how good people speak to others in a respectful way, even if they are frustrated or tired, cross or disappointed, because it is the right thing to do.

Whilst none of us knows what someone else is dealing with, the pressures they face and the challenges they overcome to be beside us in our workplace, if each of us is kind, then this should minimise the chances of people feeling terrible and of carrying those feelings around with them even for a day, but sometimes for years. People will forget exactly what you said, unless they are like Cotts in work, who writes down everything that I say (this is the shrugging shoulders emoji because I have no idea why, although she tells me they are pearls of wisdom), but they will always remember how you made them feel – and wouldn't it be amazing if you made them feel good, rather than dreadful?

We can be buffers, and like human shields for our staff, but we can also act as huge amplifiers and encourage their voices. I am loving doing this in my current setting because on the back of the last few years of disruption and difficulty, I am able to sing from the rooftops about my team. They are supporting colleagues from other schools – I am able to share this with governors and parents, and I feel so proud to be working with them all that I can't help but tell people. Shout out to the Woodlands staff!

Between being buffers and being amplifiers lies the nuanced skill of a great leader because if a leader can find the balance between buffering and amplifying, whilst also maintaining ethical and educational standards, and their own marbles, then the school will be a wonderful place!

What has all of this to do with leading with love, with you?

The point of this chapter is:

▪ Life is full of opportunities to celebrate the work and impact of others, created and spontaneous (which means that you can . . .)

▪ Amplify the self-esteem, knowledge or career profile of someone else with a simple deed (because . . .)

▪ You never know what else they are dealing with (because . . .)

▪ Good self-esteem positively impacts on all aspects of life and encourages others to be amplifiers (also . . .)

▪ Filling the cup of one member of your team actually fills the communal cup, and this is what helps you to help your team buffer and repel foes, thus sustaining high levels of 'buy in' and morale (to make the best team you can).

Further reading/listening

If you like a podcast and 'caring for your staff' is something you want to know more about in terms of leadership:

1. High Performance Podcast: James Timpson. https://tinyurl.com/James-Timpson-Success

If you like a book and want to get the best potential out of your team in a number of levels:

1. Carnegie, Dale (2006). *How to Win Friends and Influence People.* Vermillion. ISBN: 978-0091906818.

Invest in yourself – it pays high interest

Time is a finite resource

Time, the most precious resource any human can ever have. None of us know how much we will get, but we all know, with certainty that is absolute, that it will run out. Having time for things, making time for things, spending time with special people, sharing quality time with loved ones, wasting time – we are all well versed in the language of 'time' but perhaps are disassociated from how it pertains specifically to ourselves because we always think we have it.

If we agree that spending time with people that we love is one of the most life-affirming and soul-nourishing things that we can engage in, I wonder what would happen to the way we run our lives if we class ourselves as being in the category of 'people that we love'?

Investment of time in yourself may sound like a bit of an existential and perhaps bohemian concept, but it could make the difference between you being 'good' or 'great' in both your work and also your personal life. What am I going on about, and what on earth has this got to do with leadership? Let me try to explain.

I firmly believe that trying to live your professional life in an alternative style to the way that you live your personal life is not conducive to being a brilliant leader or a brilliant human being. We should all be committed to being both brilliant humans and leaders in whatever context we are in. One of the most powerful things we can do is channel who we really are into our work and therefore allow our best selves to thrive and flourish in both personal and professional contexts. If we work in harmony with our nature and personality, harness the best parts of both for the good of all that we come into contact with, then the benefits are clearly expounded in earlier chapters.

This bit is fairly easy I think, once we lose the ego and focus on learning through mistake making and celebrating the outcomes of those mistakes as scientists do with 'failed' experiments – if they test a theory and it does not work, then they know that it doesn't work and they think of alternatives, constantly refining, reviewing and improving until they find the working, and workable, solution. Who among us regularly looks at life this way, as a series of experiments (failed and otherwise)

 DOI: 10.4324/9781003281313-11

and calculated risks that if they do not work will simply point us in alternative directions?

I digress, whilst it is easier to live altruistically in both personal and professional contexts, because usually we are focused on others and therefore time invested in 'doing' is also time invested in the greater good of others, what is not as easy is to actively spend time and effort on ourselves. Or should I elaborate further and finish the same sentence with 'without guilt'?

Often, the reason a lot of us tell ourselves that we do not exercise or read or cook is because we have no time. I think this is not quite right. My philosophy on this is that there are the same finite number of minutes and hours in a day, days in a week and weeks in a year for everyone – yet some people simply seem to do more with those minutes, hours and days. They are more fulfilled, more productive and achieve greater things.

Through experimentation, trial and error, I have worked out a way of maximising my time, and I am convinced that if time management and 'looking after yourself a little more' is something you need to evaluate, then it is possible for you to go through the exact same process as I have. I can tell you what I have tried so that you can maybe give some of my strategies a go – just because they worked (or didn't!) for me, doesn't mean they will have the same impact on your life, so be open minded.

The caveat here is that if you have been reading the book from the beginning, you will know that filling my time with activity has been an unhealthy coping mechanism for me in the past. It has provided me with a legitimised option for not dealing with the root causes of some of the internalised issues I have, and this actually isn't the best way to deal with them. However, you need to be in a headspace to be able to deal with them before you can do so effectively, so don't beat yourself up too much if you are not there yet. It took me years. Remember the optimal word here is 'yet'. We all hopefully arrive at a point in life where, for whatever reason, we are pulled up short and forced to reflect. It will happen to you if it hasn't already, and sometimes it happens more than once. Time for me, therefore, is a commodity that has been compartmentalised to within an inch of its life (time and distance analogies for the mathematicians to get confused over!).

Invest guilt free time in yourself – physically

I have always struggled with the concept of 'sitting doing nothing' – AKA watching TV for the sake of it, sitting in the garden watching the clouds go by etc. For me to feel good about my time, I always need to feel like I am also being productive. There will be some of you reading this book laughing because you have been my Headteacher, or my academic supervisor, or my friend, and I have had conversations with you from my bath because lying in the lovely hot water and relaxing was not an option – having a professional conversation whilst lying in the hot water was acceptable (perhaps not on anyone else's continuum of either relaxing baths or professional conversations, but I squared it in my mind because both the bathing and the output of the conversation were accomplished concurrently!).

In the past I have trained before work, rushed to shower and dashed into work having exercised but lost some of the intrinsic benefits through the ensuing rushing around. This only provided one benefit, although one is better than none. So, in knowing myself and what triggers and also satisfies me, I have been able to work around the barriers that I place in my own way in relation to investing time in myself. I will now walk, run, or cycle the six miles from my house to my place of work and back. I do it in the pouring rain or the hot sun. It takes me 90, 60, or approximately 30 minutes, respectively, as I am always carrying a day sack on my back, and this usually has approximately 15–25kg of weight. This satisfies the need in me to do something physical each day, to minimise my impact on the environment, and to clear my head.

If I do it in the morning, I arrive in school with the blood flowing around my body, my brain ready to receive information from the day, my equilibrium settled and emotionally regulated. In the past I have been rushing around getting two infants ready, dropping them off at breakfast club, racing to work and flapping about traffic, heart rate and brain racing and not really well set for the day at all. If I had been a child arriving in that state, I would have sent myself to the Learning Support Mentor for Nurture Breakfast and ensured that I was calm and in the proper headspace to learn before even trying to kick the day off. Yet as adults we push ourselves in this way because what choice do we have?

In order to effect this current way of organising my day, and in light of my single-parent status, my teenagers are set up for the morning on the night before. They know I will be out of the house by 6 AM, and I have trained them to lock the door and make the house safe before they leave. The investment of 90, 60 or approximately 30 minutes in the mornings has the unseen and perhaps unquantifiable effect of me being better at my job, not least because of the natural effect of daylight on my skin, but also the expected endorphins released with exercise and their physiological effect on my body. We all know that when we exercise, our body releases endorphins which interact with the receptors in our brains, triggering a positive feeling. That feeling (known as a 'runner's high') in its most basic terms usually then creates a positive and energised outlook on life. So I start my day happier, and this has got to be a good thing for everyone; my body is healthier, which is a good thing for me; and my mind is clear.

I have since modified this simple travelling to work activity, from listening to motivational music on the bike or on the run which I also love, and calling people (multitasking!) on the walk, and have made the very conscious decision to invest further in myself. I now listen to audiobooks sometimes on the way in (I did say that my strategies were very simple and totally manageable, didn't I?). I have listened to some amazing stories and had my thinking about humanity and my understanding of why people behave the way they do completely challenged. I have also travelled through history and really belly laughed! I never thought, as an 'old school' book lover, that I would ever listen to books, but there you go, we can all evolve, even dinosaurs like me!

The general sense of increased self-esteem from these two activities, which satisfy my love of exercise, the operational need to keep fit for my second job and a desire for concurrent activity and productivity, is immeasurable, and I can only recommend trying it before you judge. Six miles is 10 km for those who work in 'modern money' – a lot of people attempt things like couch to 5 km to challenge themselves, so what if you parked 5 km away from school and walked in? What if you got a lift and walked 5 km home? It is worth looking at the logistics to see if you too can reap the same benefits and see if it has a measurable impact on your mental health, home life or workplace productivity.

What I would say though, is this, with no training at all (other than my daily routines), I recently joined my colleagues from the Army Reserves unit I serve, and we did the Yorkshire Three Peaks Challenge – me at the age of almost 47. The mountains of Pen-y-ghent, Whernside and Ingleborough are collectively known as the 'Three Peaks', which in turn form part of the Pennine range, encircling the head of the valley of the River Ribble in the Yorkshire Dales National Park, England. The 25-mile (almost marathon) route is circular, starting in Horton-in-Ribblesdale, and involves a total of 1585 m of ascent, with the idea being that people should complete it in less than 12 hours. Our team did it in just over 10 (discounting loo and tea stops!) in the relentless Yorkshire rain. This isn't a brag, it is a measure, I think, of the physical impact of the almost daily walks I have been doing carrying at least my huge laptop! All those of you who took up walking and running during the Covid-19 restrictions, I think you may be surprised by the positive impact on your fitness and bodies that (until tested in some way) you would have no idea of! Life isn't a series of tests and measures, I know this, but genuinely, I was shocked to have completed it without a single muscular-skeletal issue (save for the two hideous blisters – the military readers amongst you will be rolling eyes now and saying #footadmin), and as the oldest in the team by a long way, I was relieved I was not the 'weakest link' as I kept saying! Sometimes it is only in retrospect that we realise the impact of some behaviours (both good and bad!) on our life, and I would say my daily travel to work is an example of a positive manifestation of my routine behaviour.

The time I give to myself in the reverse journey from school is just as valuable. Sometimes I will cycle into school and leave my bike or get a lift in, walking or running home depending on what I need to carry. This has the additional benefit of my children receiving me home happy (albeit sweaty) and having 'worked the day out of my head'. This is also the time when I may telephone colleagues up and down the country to listen to their stories and try to support them – again, this allows me to be the most productive and help others whilst investing time in my own body and mind. Where some people think, 'where does she get the time?' I have to be honest, I am not a character in a book with a time turning device, nor am I a hero. I am simply adept at compartmentalising. It's not a super power . . .

Where possible, compound investment activities for maximal effect

When thinking about other ways of investing time in myself, one of the things I will do is cook wholesome food from scratch and batch cook. I usually do this with feel-good music playing, and there is something about these two activities that, again, stimulates the happy hormones in me. This is something I know that a lot of people do, but in the interests of oversharing my personal investment, this is 'up there' with the others. I am concerned with being strong and healthy, not thin – this is an important side note, actually. This means nourishing my body on all levels, and food is one of the most basic ways to do this. I am lucky that I can afford to buy food and have the facilities to cook and freeze it, but I think if you are able, then doing this means that at times of pressure, when the temptation is to reach for junk, you are still able to fuel yourself effectively and nurture your body. The added bonus here is of course that my children are also well fed and watered, and even my family (and the old lady over the road) get meals when I am super busy as they can heat up pre-cooked food. Multiple benefits!

I have also ensured, after much trial and error, that in the event of needing to complete an important document or piece of work, I do so from home – free from the inevitable joys and distractions of the lovely people and children with whom I work. The innovative ways of working that took place as a direct result of the measures taken to combat the pandemic may well leave a legacy where more people are able to do this than before, but it really does help when the pressure mounts and you need the mental bandwidth to be able to focus on something for a prolonged period without the phone ringing or emails pinging.

Model what self-investment might look like, and invest time in others

As I have tried to do throughout the book, the reason that I illustrate some of my simple learning and practice with the mundane and every day is so that it makes it explicit to others and also exemplifies how my life impacts on my leadership. This 'self-investment' of time is no different. As a leader I owe it to those I serve to ensure that they know investing in themselves is not only 'okay', it is essential for good physical and mental health, and therefore healthy and productive personal and professional lives. My attitude to life does not just 'happen', divorced and dislocated from how I actually live – it is a product of the way I choose to live. When you consider that there will be many leaders who are also parents, aunts and uncles, scout leaders, counsellors, coaches and so on, this will also involve creating and sustaining capacity for healthy relationships with children who will be looking to all of the adults they come across for the blueprint they will apply to their own lives.

We owe it to those who may look to us to ensure that we are authentically modelling healthy lives so that they can see how to do so in their own lives – adults and children. It is not just incumbent upon me as a leader to model self-investment and care, though, and how it can be absorbed into day-to-day life, but also to create opportunities for it, direct staff to take time for themselves during their working day, and also facilitate them having access to the tools needed around their working day. This is what makes my leadership about love. If I can practice this for and with myself, then I should facilitate the possibility of practicing it for others.

Knowing the virtues of exercise for those under pressure and for those with health or health-related life goals, and acknowledging that exercise and going to the gym or classes can be difficult both financially and logistically, I invested recently in all of my staff in a two-month online fitness app that they could use around their home lives, with their partners and families. Only if they wanted to! I can imagine that some of you reading this are literally horrified, but the app was created by a young dance instructor who had been into school for three successive years to do what we called a 'danceathon' and helped us raise money for charity. She needed to diversify when gyms were closed, and her online membership was relatively inexpensive. All of the staff knew her and enjoyed her danceathons, plus she also did hoola hooping, HIIT and Zumba style classes that she had filmed and which seemed a good laugh. In purchasing this opportunity, it supported a local business, added another layer to the mental health offer that I have for my staff and removed some of the logistical barriers that they may have had to accessing fitness support, whilst also allowing their partners and children to join in at home. I did not, for those who would be aghast, check if the app was used or charge them for it, and it was not instead of a pay rise or as part of Performance Management or anything like that! It was an offer, a layer of an offer for those who wanted it.

I have learned over the years that time invested in me is never time wasted but pays interest because if I am happier, healthier, more resilient and thinking clearly, then both my personal and professional lives are far more harmonious. I am a better mother, friend and sister when all aspects of my life are in sync. The thing is, music and reading, exercise, good food and sleep, drinking 2L of water a day and limiting alcohol intake do not always cut it for helping you to be resilient and mentally healthy.

Even the most positive person would have to agree that at times, life is hard. Our modern world is filled with so much pressure, and many of us have wide-ranging personal and professional obligations that can create a sense of anxiety and a feeling of being overwhelmed at times. It is possible to simply keep going, through sheer force of will and dogged sense of determination, but at times this becomes self-limiting.

Invest guilt-free time in yourself – mentally

There are times when the intervention of an external, independent voice, helping us to see the reasons for us retreating into the comfort zone and confines of a self-created and perpetuated status quo, are invaluable. That intervention can prevent us from allowing life to pass us by when we're so consumed by meaningless tasks, unfulfilling jobs, unrewarding personal relationships and possibly deteriorating health.

Investing in yourself at times of overwhelm (and preferably before you get to that point) is so important. We often get so entrenched that it is almost impossible to see a different perspective, and when personal and professional life combine to make a toxic cocktail of anxieties, it is even more important to seek help. It's difficult to take advantage of the possibilities and opportunities that exist when embattled with daily issues, and almost impossible to create them for ourselves or others when in this frame of mind.

I am not going to lie – I resisted seeking counselling help for many, many years, preferring instead to rely upon my own strategies (!) in order to process, rationalise or even sweat it out of myself rather than allow someone access to my inner-most thoughts, motivations and demons. I worked until the week before my son was born and the day before my daughter was born; I never took a day off due to my divorce, only took what I needed post-mastectomies and worked whilst at home and physically compromised (I actually wrote my doctoral thesis rather than sit and 'go round the bend' as my nan used to say!), so you can appreciate that finally choosing to go and speak to someone took immense effort.

Why and how? Well, heartbreak. Heartbreak. I have had my fair share of this. I know, I know, how can that be, given how lovely I am, right? And yet, I have been eviscerated on more than one occasion. I thought there was something wrong with me, that I was unlovable, so I went and reported myself to the GP with this idea, as I recognised that my thinking was way off, and she referred me to a therapist.

I told my senior leadership team, who were absolutely brilliant, by the way. Firstly, they tried to tell me that there was absolutely nothing wrong with me and told me they thought I was beautiful inside and out. They did say that they thought I was 'driven' and suggested that perhaps a conversation with someone neutral could be helpful as I was doing an incredibly stressful job and may have been losing some sense of perspective and grip. They were, of course, right!

If any of you are reading this and have had therapy, perhaps you can empathise – I was terrified. If any of you are wondering if therapy could help you, then feeling terrified is natural, and lots of people I have spoken to about this since have expressed similar sentiments. If you are a therapist, then thank you for your ability to both contain that terror and also extract the requisite information from people like me to help them process their issues outwardly rather than internalising them – even if it takes them until they are 45 to access your skill set!

Therapy and growth

In my first session, the therapist explained how it would all work. I was hypervigilant, and understandably on edge, but I listened. She explained to me that I could not make it all academic, that at some point I would crack and the emotion and feeling would be revealed, and only then would real growth be able to happen. I felt like I owed it to my children at this point to make sure that I was giving them healthy signals and, as stated earlier, healthy role models so they could create their own blueprint or road map of how to conduct themselves as adults and perhaps one day as parents. I felt that I owed it to myself to lead the healthiest life I could, and if that meant working on aspects of myself that I did not like or that were creating issues in my relationships, then I needed to own what those things were. I felt I owed it to my staff who were looking to me for how to lead in a healthy way to show them what that might look like. So I took the plunge. Not without some bumps in the road, however; some of my avoidance tactics did not go unobserved, and cancelling appointments when the 'need' for me to be in work and doing more important things was not uncommon.

After four sessions of the six you are routinely allocated, the therapist explained that it was within her remit to be able to double this number should she feel she needed to. Given that she usually allocated just the first hour for 'taking the history' (birth–18), and we hadn't covered that by the end of the third session, she felt it was necessary. I agreed. By the end of the fifth session, I had finally cracked. What made me crack was her comment along the lines of 'I am now going to address the 8-year-old girl within you who was afraid, not the powerhouse sports, academic and professional woman and mother you now are, but that scared little girl'. Who knows what that triggered, for another book on another day perhaps, but she got me.

I cried and realised that beating myself harder and harder would not change who I was or where I was from, would not right the wrongs I had done, would not reset the clock or reverse time that had passed so that I could avoid certain mistakes. Nope, I needed to move forward, baby steps as it happened, and begin to love myself for who I was and now am. There will be some of you who will be cringing right now, and I can appreciate that. I never used to talk to myself or about myself in such terms, but that therapy really helped me to see that I was worthy of love, capable of huge amounts of love in fact, when I thought I was neither. It showed me that I was able to create and sustain meaningful relationships and able to set healthy boundaries for my life in order to practice self-care. It made me look at long buried and very challenging feelings. I won't go so far as to say it was revolutionary, but it helped unlock lots of 'wonky' thinking that I had, including that most notably called 'imposter syndrome' (syndrome – again).

Three other things happened in succession over the following two years. The first was that in my desire to be outward facing and network for school, to be covered later on in the book, I came across an organisation, and I met the founder of it, Al, for an impromptu coffee in Liverpool that turned into a whole day. We traded stories, and he reinforced the idea in my head that I absolutely should do a TEDx talk, as I had been asked to do by the most lovely 'Adam', and about which I was obsessing and very distressed. He reflected back much of what the therapist had told me – I confess here and now that I never did complete the full therapy sessions, by the way . . . I had heard enough about myself and couldn't face myself anymore at that time! Later on, Al came to school and worked with my entire staff, many of whom claimed it was their most profound Continuous Professional Development (CPD) training experience ever. Many of them cried, and most of them wrote to me to thank me for my honesty and my forward-thinking attitude in asking someone like that to come in and work with them, and for sharing with them all 'why'. This was, of course, timed to perfection as within weeks we were in another lockdown situation in our country, and mental health issues were on the rise in a dramatic way – plus several staff had lost parents and were struggling with grief.

And then I was struggling with grief. It was my turn. A significant adult from my childhood, Griff, died at an early age of the most awful cancer; my young beautiful and talented cousin, Heather, died at a very young age of the most horrendous cancer; and my broken heart was bleeding out for the loss of someone I loved very much along with the death of these two people. I had to employ every strategy I had in my arsenal. I was hurt, angry, confused, and I was in disbelief at the injustice and the lack of logic and sense in it all. The waste of lives. I was raging at an unjust world and the futility of life for a wee while until I regained control of myself and was able to process it. I saw Rev Jackie for a coffee one day and wept unashamedly in her presence, so angry and full of pain.

Coaching and growth

At this time I was invited, by a woman I had never met, Christina (I talked about her in a previous chapter), to join a walking group for networking purposes, around West Kirby Marine Lake. My posts on social media hadn't changed – I am always posting thoughts, poetry, words, reflections and anecdotes about life lived, observations and so on – and something in my posts resonated with her. So, encouraged by her, literally given courage by her request that I seal the deal with the universe by committing to meet her, I duly turned up at 0700 on a dark Sunday morning in January in the freezing North West of England and set off on a windy and wet seaside walk. Our friendship, sealed that day without either of us realising it, was transformational. She is a wonderful woman, and through our conversations and subsequent meetings, our duo increasing to become a trio, we have a strong unit of support that means we can help one another through not just the professional hurdles we three face, but the growing pains of parenting teenagers and young adults!

Christina has coached my son, in the same way that Anne Marie (of the previous chapter) has supported my daughter with decision making and healthy boundaries in relationships, and I see this is a strength, that my children can approach adults outside of my family and seek guidance and alternative frames of reference for themselves. I see it as a strength of my parenting that I could model doing this, whilst not becoming reliant upon it to function effectively, and removing any stigma from this as a strategy.

Christina then did a coaching session with the whole staff, again for their mental health, and once again, the staff saw the benefits of having a coach to support your frame of reference and your thought process to ensure that you are not derailed by life experiences. That day the Senior Leadership Team did not attend the session, but more than 50 other staff did. SLT were in the throes of closing school on the back of immediate action required by government the previous night in light of the third lockdown in our country due to Covid-19. However, one of the staff lost her mum the same week and wrote to both Christina and I to tell us that her work and her way of talking to staff was so beneficial that it had lifted her and enabled her to work through what needed to be done for her mum.

Counselling and growth

I have brought in an anonymous counselling service for staff called 'Employee Assistance' for many years, and I never know if staff use it or not. I often suggest that they do if I am supporting them with grief, divorce, ill-health or separation, but I am never sure of its efficacy. It is not for me to assure myself, only that as a leader I acknowledge that investing in myself on a number of levels is essential, and therefore providing ways for staff to invest in themselves on a number of levels will also be essential – whether they access those resources, and to what extent, is up to them as sentient adults.

Peer coaching and growth

I have been coached as part of a group as an early career stage Headteacher and found it hugely beneficial, not least as it facilitated me doing the job, but also as it provided the foundations for my doctoral research. This spurred me on to both teach coaching at MA level in several universities, which I found rewarding, and also practice coaching in my role as Headteacher. I am a @CollectiveEd Fellow at the Centre for Mentoring, Coaching & Professional Learning at Leeds Beckett University and strongly support the work of @DrRLofthouse and her team.

I have had talking therapy and found it beneficial in knowing myself to a deeper level, which (as stated previously) I think is vital in being a self-regulated human and good leader. I have offered the same to my staff who have all engaged with it to a greater or lesser degree, but all of whom know now that there is no stigma associated with doing so if they need to in the future. I have had some coaching sessions and offered them to my whole staff as they are positively influential to our personal and professional development. I exercise and have offered our staff the chance to exercise in a different way during lockdowns in our country, in order to facilitate the impact of exercise on them. Investing in me, and signposting 'investment in self' to others over whom I have influence, is a big driver in how I lead, and lead with love.

So what?

Although leadership coaching or therapy are just two 'meta-methods' as a perspective on how to unlearn negative habits, along with how to institute good habits, there are many other ways of finding time and opportunity to invest in yourself, facilitating tenacity, and therefore enabling you to be more successful at achieving your dreams and goals and those of your team. The internet has a wealth of tried and tested methods, and you only need to tweet out the question to get back hundreds of responses.

If you invest in yourself, then you can invest in others; it is the old 'oxygen mask' analogy – for those of you too young to have come across it, the idea goes that if you are on a plane in trouble and are told to put on the oxygen mask, you do not put the mask of your child or elderly parent first – you put your own on first so that you are able to help not just your child put theirs on, but also anyone else who needs help.

What has all of this to do with leading with love, with you?

The point of this chapter is:

- As a leader, you need to ensure that you invest in yourself and model this because you want your team to have faith in themselves whilst building internal resilience (which means that you can . . .)

- Absorb a lot of pressure in a healthy way and have a range of strong outlets as a leader (because . . .)

- You can't be all things to all people all of the time (because . . .)

- Without an escape valve in the form of thinking and reflection time through exercise or creativity, an external voice or critical friend telling you how and when to regain perspective, you can lose it (also . . .)

- Your team seeing you explore issues and develop self-awareness and understanding means that they can do the same with you, thereby elevating and sustaining high levels of morale (to make the best team you can).

Further reading/listening

If you like a podcast and 'self-investment' is something you want to know more about in terms of leadership:

1. Inspirational Living Podcast offers motivational broadcasts for the mind, body, and spirit. https://tinyurl.com/Success-and-Happiness
2. TED is behind 'WorkLife' with Adam Grant. https://tinyurl.com/Work-and-Life-in-Balance

3. There Are Other Ways: Conversations About Living Life a little Differently, presented by Fiona Barrows. https://tinyurl.com/Live-Differently
4. TED Conferences. https://tinyurl.com/Stress-impact-on-our-bodies_

If you like a book and want to get the best potential out of your team in a number of levels:

1. Moody, Claire (2020). *Coaching Mindset: How to Use Personal Coaching Skills to Reach Your Goals.* Independently Published. ISBN: 979-8629891130.
2. Stanier, Michael Bungay (2016). *The Coaching Habit: Say Less, Ask More & Change the Way You Lead Forever.* Box Of Crayons. ISBN: 978-0978440749.
3. Brown, Jeff (2017). *Love It Forward.* Enrealment Press. ISBN: 978-0980885934.

Choices can reflect your hopes, not your fears

No choice where we start but . . .

I think that the concept of 'choice' could be highly contested, mainly because it automatically implies that as individuals, we all have the same freedoms, agency, knowledge, cultural and social capital to exercise any kind of choice. The reality is, of course, that we are born and have no choice about where, to whom and what innate skills we are born with. '*Obviously*', you will all be saying, but this is not necessarily obvious to policy makers, those who create from the ether a social structure that dictates what is seen as successful, judged as a positive contribution and the methods of measuring this success for all to see. Those policy makers may perhaps be unaware of the adverse additionality (or, to coin a technical phrase, the 'co-morbidity') for people who may have limited qualifications, possibly limited support networks, who may work, yet struggle to provide for their families due to simple facts like the cost of living increasing, prolonged austerity measures and latterly the Covid responses, such as enforced closure of businesses.

We may have first hand experience of not eating, in order for our children to be able to eat. We may have personal experience of the raw hopelessness of thinking about tomorrow, or next week or 'the future' when it is uncertain, or the worry of providing a basic roof over the heads of our family when there are no cash reserves, but in the main, policy makers are divorced from the visceral ephemera that affect the lives of 'Joe Public'. I think perhaps this is where our personal and professional leadership comes in, and where we really can make a profound difference to someone else.

If you have ever worked in an area of deprivation, or with those whom life has deprived in some way, in a nursery, a school, hospital or GP surgery, the prison service, homeless charities, food banks, ecclesiastical establishments, the Youth Offending Service, large organisations such as any arm of the British Armed Forces and so on, then you will have at least witnessed the disintegration of social infrastructure that leaves people largely without genuine choices in life. As someone who has cooked food once a month for a local charity that fed the homeless, I know that they simply eat what is made by those offering their 'charity'. They were not selecting from a menu; they had no autonomy.

 DOI: 10.4324/9781003281313-12

The rhetoric that we are fed in the UK, without getting too political here, and that has been spun for the past 40 years in fact, is that *everyone* has a choice, and if people choose to engage with free education, then they can lift themselves from the level where choices are limited to the reality where the sky is the limit. Although the irony here is not lost on me (sure, didn't this happen to me?), remember my lovely young soldier from Germany? There is a very clear dissonance between the theory and the reality because education is not a simple transaction. It cannot be patched up with Pupil Premium Funding for the disadvantaged, and more so than ever in the last 100 years the impact of a global pandemic has instantly stripped back the façade behind which poverty and inequality have been lurking and brought it to the foreground. We all see it, and not just because Marcus Rashford made 'hunger' public.

It would appear to me to be a moral imperative to ensure that, where possible, we equip as many people that we interact with on a daily basis with the skills, knowledge and understanding of the world outside our organisation to be able to one day make informed choices. We are duty bound to help them to build the path before them, step by small step if necessary, even if it may not look like 'The Yellow Brick Road' but more of a healthy personal construction site where progress is being made. Imagine one of those practical 'leadership' type activities where you balance on a can of beans and have to put the plank out before you can traverse the piranha infested waters scenario. What does this look like? What barriers will we need to overcome? What has this to do with leading with love?

Choosing to limit oneself

Firstly, we can help people overcome the barriers of 'self-limiting'. When my son (who as I have shared already) was coasting through secondary school in a disinterested and disenfranchised way, largely because he had decided from an early age that he was joining the Army at 16 so he didn't need to work in school, I tried to explain to him the value of 'choice'. Even with his choices based on his hopes and dreams, things went awry.

I tried to verbalise and illustrate the potential negative repercussions of not gaining the GCSEs that our education system sees as the Golden Tickets to the next stage in life, to limited avail. He didn't work for his mocks, and when he had the rude awakening that was the dawning realisation that if he failed maths and English, then this would not bode well for the Army (not himself, just the chosen pathway to a future career), he decided to get stuck in. Too little too late, sadly, and Covid-19 prevented him from demonstrating this newfound enthusiasm for learning because teachers rightly had to make rapid and pragmatic assessments, under difficult conditions, based on mocks and prior attainment. He failed English. He then spent a considerable amount of time unhappy at the Army Foundation College, Harrogate despite the excellent set up that it is, because I told him gently that he could not leave, no matter how miserable he was, until he had successfully passed and gained the GCSE English pass equivalent that was needed.

He had limited his own choices and options by being narrow minded (and a little dogmatic – the privilege of the young and also the older and less growth-minded among us). He had not created a contingency plan. With no 'Plan B', he had to learn the hard way the benefit of creating a situation for himself where choice was a real possibility. I could have forced him to put in time for schoolwork and GCSE preparation, prevented him from watching TV or socialising and made him work, but that is not my parenting style – rightly or wrongly. I felt like a bit of a failure as a parent for a time, but actually I realised that for some people, it is the experience of making the mistake and the feeling of being hamstrung that creates the very best learning, and the most appropriate and invaluable thing for me to do was to coach this young person, my young person, through rectifying his mistakes, learning the lessons and creating choice.

There are so many people in this position, though – not just parents but any-one working with young people, whether that is the cadet force, youth clubs of any description, sports teams and so on. Each of those people can make a difference, and I would argue that if they are not actively seeking ways to make a difference, then they perhaps need to re-evaluate their own importance and their role. As our soci-ety has disintegrated from the nuclear families of old, it is the very people in those privileged roles who have access to young people who can make the most significant differences. They are not 'just' a youth worker, or 'just' a coach – to some children they are everything they aspire to be: they are shamans and gurus, they are heroes.

Thankfully my son's is a good news story – he applied for and was successful in being allocated a place on a highly competitive 'pre-apprenticeship' course at the Engineering College, and the rest is history. Not everyone has a strong, capa-ble, supportive adult in their corner at home helping them to navigate potentially life-changing decisions and supporting them when they make the wrong turn. If you can be that adult for someone, even if they are not *your* young person, then you should be. The repercussions of living this way of life is that your influence will have an impact on your own close circle and wider.

Whilst labouring for someone, between the Army College and his Engineering College (another thing I made him do was secure paid work before he left – adults do not usually have the luxury of leaving a paid job for nothing . . .), my son came across an electrical apprentice. He lived with his nan, his mum's boyfriend didn't like him, he hadn't seen his dad and he was recovering from cancer. He made a costly mistake one day when unsupervised, and mortified, my son told me about it because he felt so strongly about this young man. He actually said to me, 'Mum, what happens to those who don't have anyone fighting for them?'

I posted a tweet in relation to this, and other socially problematic things that I had come across that week, most notably the situation in Afghanistan, and was speechless when several people that I did not know, other than through social media, messaged me to offer financial support for the boy to pay the bill he had incurred. Between us we paid it, and a little more for a wire detector! It was a defining moment when I wrote to him a message that said

> Not everyone in the world is there to exploit you. There are grownups who don't know you but who want to help you succeed. Remember this random act of kindness in the future when you own your own business and can make a difference to someone else – pay it forward.

My son said, 'I knew you would pay that bill for him, mum'. He was right. We don't need to be in formal leadership roles to do things that are, in effect, the lived reality of leadership through love. We can, just like our words, have a huge impact on others with small things that we do. I know lots of people acting in randomly kind ways such as this without even knowing that they are leading through example, and without spending hundreds of pounds – leadership is, in this context, showing others the best way to behave.

Making the 'right' choice

Choices, decisions, options, resolutions, possibilities – your head can spin at times from both the lack of options and choices you have and the huge range.

How many of us have been in positions where we did not know which decision to make and our head was so clouded with anxiety or fear, ignorance or poor education about something that we have struggled to make a decision and just marked time? Not making a decision can be as catastrophic as making one, so it is easy to see why so many people falter, prevaricate or procrastinate where decisions need to be made – particularly when the outcomes are perceived as 'high stakes'.

Every day, as leaders and in fact as humans, we are faced with making both large and small decisions. In a world of connectivity and unlimited choice, constrained only by financial and human resource limitations, decision making can be fraught with anxiety as we navigate the 'right' decisions for the right reasons and whilst we work out what is 'right'. From the married man who tells a woman he is interested and that he is 'married but not married' and 'what if' their connection was 'life changing?' knowing that he is lying and simply wants to exploit the woman; to choosing to take on a six-year course that will result in a qualification that could change the direction of generations of your family; from choosing to sell your Bitcoin options today rather than tomorrow and losing thousands to choosing to book a holiday and spend your savings on making memories rather than a new boiler – everyone is struggling with working out what is 'right' to them, and this is the same in our work places as well as our personal lives.

Who are we pleasing?

A second consideration with regard to decision making is for whom we are *really* making the decision. So much of that is based on our own frames of reference, created when we were small, and often reinforced by successive decisions that we make in the same way and for the same reasons – confirming our bias, strengthening our views and honing the internal rationale that we create for our 'life navigation' tools.

This can be both positive and negative. For example, if we are adults and base our decisions only on what our mum or our dad would want us to do, or expect us to do, or have told us to do, based solely on her or his values, then it is highly possible that we are basing our decisions on outdated and potentially inaccurate perspectives on life as our mum and dad's schema was created in a time in history that has subsequently evolved. In the same way that if we judge our mum or dad for their decisions, made decades before, using our frame of reference as it has been developed today, we would be doing so from a perspective where we are able to use hindsight, and improvements in awareness, research and knowledge, which would be just as unfair. Although the views and support of our mum and dad may be well respected, to live life *only* through or because of them could be a huge mistake as we are surrounded with up-to-date information and can educate ourselves further. It is certainly worth thinking about.

One of the saddest things I have heard, talking about decision making for the satisfaction of others, is a family friend who was not given permission by her parents as a twenty something to marry the love of her life (sadly, based only on the man having a different religion!). She is in her 70s now, has never had a boyfriend before or since and has lived, by her own confession, a truly lonely life. Her parents were happily married, had two children, worked and lived their lives as they chose but prevented their daughter from doing the same. It was a different time, we tell ourselves, but still, a life unfulfilled makes me feel sad. One would hope that things like this are really consigned to the past, but we don't have to search too hard in order to find examples of bigoted behaviour throughout our society even today.

Imagine if the same logic applied in your role as a leader. Someone who looks up to you, who relies on your guidance and support, asked you about a career course, and you chose to refuse them doing the course based on your views on the value of it to your school, or to you not understanding the intrinsic or tangible value it could have to them. Imagine if you chose to refuse the request of a staff member to attend a funeral because you did not see the value in the perceived relationship between your member of staff and the deceased. Imagine if you chose not to help someone, where it would be easy to do so but demanded your time, and they unnecessarily failed at something as a result. These things do happen; even in a 'caring' profession such as education, they happen. It is a question of whether you want to be that person or something else entirely.

What are our choices driven by?

A third consideration is around what actually drives us. Whilst some more instinctive decisions can also have fear associated with them, it is rationalised fear, and instinctive choices feel like the easiest ones because they are the most aligned with our values, demanding minimal logic or analysis – they just *feel* right. We have all made these and know the joy they bring and the freedom from anxiety because they come from our authentic selves. Each of us has made decisions we regret, usually because they are not aligned with our core values, and often because they were made based on other people's expectations, ego, or in the heat of the moment. Earlier chapters have discussed the importance of knowing yourself and what motivates and triggers you, which will assist in identifying where your core decision-making processes are situated. This is naturally the first step towards informed decision making that serves both you as the leader and also the organisation and its stakeholders. Your legacy as a human being and as a leader, as someone that people look to for how to behave, is a vital consideration when making a public decision that other people will evaluate.

I resigned with immediate effect from a lecturing post based solely on a disagreement between me and the course leader because I was essentially being asked to mark papers that had clearly failed as 'passes' for political reasons. I struggled with the binary aspect of this decision as I felt I was letting down students in resigning, but I could not stay and continue to work for someone whose values were so clearly different from mine. It was a painful but professional end to a long-term relationship, but I was nevertheless hurt by it. I did not want my legacy, my professional identity, tied up in a situation that I fundamentally disagreed with and therefore made the decision based on my core values – despite the loss of secondary income and the guilt I carried at letting down students mid-year.

This can be the same in relationships, both personal and professional. It is better to end them in as healthy a way as possible rather than allow them to deteriorate and putrefy. If you have made clear your values, then the ending of something may be painful but will come as no surprise because the other party will be aware of the boundaries and expectations you have.

Fear as a driver

Most decisions have four key drivers, with fear being the one that is hardwired into our subconscious in order, physiologically, to keep us safe. Fear exists in each of us, to a greater or lesser degree, and needs careful regulation, often via self-talk and other strategies (discussed in the next chapter) in order not to sabotage us. Ultimately though, when making decisions, as humans we base our rationale on either fear or love. You get to choose which you will let override you.

Fear (of the unknown, success or other people's judgement) may encourage us to accept something we don't really want to and stay in jobs we don't really like, and even prevent us taking steps to leave disempowering personal and professional relationships – even when there are amazing and life-affirming options open for us to seize.

Making decisions from a position of fear of the future, or fears carried over from the past, prevents us from enjoying the present, and this diminishes our potential and abilities in the here and now, and also an unknown future full of possibility – as a school leader that can hinder vision, as a person, fulfilment. Often decisions made in this stage of anxiety are filled with regret and self-perpetuate the negative associations that we started with, leaving us disappointed and emotionally crippled the next time a similar decision presents itself. This is why knowing yourself and investing in yourself are so important to your successes as a leader and as a human being – you risk self-sabotage if you don't, and in sabotaging self, you can sabotage the organisation.

I once knew of someone whose partner threatened them with public humiliation of being called a 'paedophile' as a method of control – which worked (the person was in no way a paedophile, but the fear of 'mud sticking' was enough to control that person for years!). This person had their life ruined, and naturally the lives of all who loved them, because their choices were influenced by fear of their ex-partner. I also knew of someone whose partner refused to let them see their children unless they capitulated and did as required as a form of control (this is wrong on so many levels, not least the harm done to children in the middle of these tornadoes of narcissism). I knew of a Headteacher who threatened people with the sack if they did not conform and staff who were pressurised to work on the holidays and do some unsavoury things through fear of repercussions from this person. The list is endless, and I know for certain that every person reading this is either nodding and thinking to themselves that they too have a list of similar stories or perhaps have even done things like this themselves in the past.

Creating fear in others as a way of controlling their decision making may work in the very short term, but this is unsustainable as a human being or as a leader. It does not create the kind of productive and mutually beneficial culture and atmosphere where people grow and develop capability or personality. It actually stunts growth. People learn to live within the confines of this way of behaving rather than look to the sky or the horizon for ways to challenge themselves, and before you know it, glass ceilings become concrete ones, permanently detrimental to mental health.

Decision making from a place of fear can ensure that an individual continues to live a life where true potential is diminished. From a leadership perspective, this can be disastrous for the staff you work with, the organisation as a whole and outcomes for your community. If you are sitting there reflecting on times when you may have been afraid, where you have regrets, then talk to someone about it – find the learning in it for you and that you can share with those you lead. If you are reflecting on a time in your life when you created that fear in others, then coach yourself through accepting that painful truth and own it. Make sure that you do not do it again by evaluating exactly what made you do it. What was the point? What did you gain and lose? Allow yourself to feel the medley of emotions that come with realising that at times you have been less than the person you aspire to being, maybe less than the person you are now, and take steps to prevent it happening again.

Love as a driver

Making decisions from a place of love, self-awareness and understanding can facilitate an environment of fulfilment, abundance and joy, even in a work setting, and gives agency to others to do the same. This is based largely on your own modelling as a leader and showing others how it is done. You need to verbalise your processes, in the same way that when teaching children how to write a non-chronological report, for example, you would initially do so through modelling what happens cognitively and what comes out of your mouth and onto paper. Doing the same with decisions means your peers will pick up the nuances of the process. They will be able to stop themselves at key decision points and take stock of their behaviour and thinking, asking others to check them if, like me, they have a healthy team who have been coached in how to do this.

If you know yourself and the rest of your team, and when you are under pressure you take collective responsibility for decision making, then although the final accountability and last word will be yours as the leader, the process is co-created effectively.

Although it is very useful to take advice from other leaders, our parents, external consultants, or leaders in diverse fields – especially those who have proven success – making decisions purely based on the opinion of someone else and their track record can prove to be disadvantageous because each of us is unique. Each situation has been arrived at through a complex interface of a range of actors, and the outcomes may need to be crafted differently depending on the context. Making decisions based on other people's expectations can also create issues with relationship integrity if things do not unfold as anticipated – blame and resentment are very real risks for when things go wrong, just as much as hero worship when things go right, and of course we as humans are always looking to confirm our own bias.

Decisions making as leaders – choosing how to respond

As a leader, I always take the views of others seriously and explain that I am happy to be corrected or my views to be modified, but I know that the final decision has to be mine. Knowing myself and my team well means that I know the domains in which I may suffer flawed decision-making capacity, and it is at these points that I expect others to provide information to assist and guide me, assimilating this information and reminding myself though self-talk that the outcomes will be mine to deal with. Where choice exists, so does the expectation that the consequences of those choices will also exist, and someone must be prepared to accept those. The leader.

There are so many bi-directional variables which can affect any outcome in a school, no matter how predictable it may appear, that applying logic or scientific paradigms onto decision making can sometimes be fruitless. Logical decisions, although sometimes essential, because they are purely cognitive and have no heart involved, can often leave me feeling flat, unenthusiastic, and a little disengaged. Again, it is crucial to share this feeling with your team so that at such times, your flagging morale can be buoyed by the collective team spirit.

Leadership of a school is fraught with complex and competing priorities that are not disappearing, in many ways they are multiplying, and this can mean therefore that many of us in this role feel disengaged from the purpose we set out with. It is at those moments that we must make the most important and effective choices that we have at our disposal. We can choose how to respond. This is something that transcends poverty, intelligence, social capital and acumen, role in society, gender, and ethnicity etc. How we choose to react or respond to something is really our only autonomous choice in life, and this is possible to exercise every day in our workplace.

I won't lie, it has taken me considerable time and energy to firstly work this out. I began to understand it as a response to events in my personal life where I was confused and bewildered about how I was treated or how I witnessed others being treated. I was hurt and betrayed and could easily have lashed out and in return betrayed others. I could have revealed secrets told, confidences I carried, yet I chose not to. I took the only course of action I felt appropriate to my core values and remained stoic. I chose not to engage in unhealthy and unpleasant activity – despite the behaviour of others – and remained true to my own values. This choice eventually liberated me from any anger, any resentment that I may have carried towards the individuals themselves, but most importantly, in the longer term view of my life, it taught me a valuable lesson in the power of our choices and where lies our real ability to choose.

In my workplace this is crucial. I have, over the years, been let down by others, in just the same way that I fear I may have let others down with an idle word, or a misunderstanding from time to time. When I am feeling aggrieved in the workplace, I bring to the forefront of my mind the certain knowledge that I am in control only of how I choose to react to being let down. I teach my own children this. I model it to the staff I serve and articulate it to the children I work with in school. They do not need to lash out verbally or physically; they need to pause, breathe and consider the potential consequences of doing so. Then they need to simply tell themselves that they are making a conscious decision to respond in a certain way and repeat this in their head and to their peers, thus making a verbal contract, a commitment, with themselves and those closest to them that they will act with integrity and in tune with their world view and values. They will sleep better, suffer less anxiety and in the end feel better that way. This takes time and practice, but don't most things? It won't come easy as our immediate reactions may need tempering, but it is worth putting the time in to learn this strategy or else face a working life, and a personal life, full of unnecessary sleepless nights – you will have enough of those worrying about other things, so try to minimise the ones you will have that are caused by not taking control of your choices.

Values lead decision making

The key to making the right choices and decisions for me is that they always serve my highest moral expectations and the collective good of all stakeholders. The best decisions come from being connected to my values *and* intuition, coming from a place of love, not fear, and taking cognisance of the fact that occasionally I need others to point out that I am off kilter to keep me on the straight and narrow.

What has all of this to do with leading with love, with you?

The point of this chapter is:

- Leadership is full of decisions, from the macro to the micro level, some of which need to be made quickly and others which can be discussed and pondered, but all can be made from a place of love (which means that you can . . .)

- Always make decisions that you do not regret, particularly with training (because . . .)

- You can resist pressure to conform to stereotype and resist fear dominating you (because . . .)

- Fear of the unknown, or the future, can take over alignment to your values and detract from your main effort as a leader (also . . .)

- Your team being involved in decision making can coach them through the process you go through, thus supporting them to avoid making emotion- or ego-led and regrettable decisions, but rather those based on the greater good and the shared value system of the organisation (to make the best team you can).

Further reading/listening

If you like a podcast and 'hope' is something you want to know more about in terms of leadership:

1. Ideal Day Podcast. https://tinyurl.com/Overcome-your-Fear
2. Lewis Howes: How to Overcome Fear of Failure. https://tinyurl.com/Summit-of-Great

If you like a book and want to get the best potential out of your team in a number of levels:

1. Stone, Stella D. (2016). *Overcome Your Fears and Live Your Dream Life*. XLIBRIS. ISBN: 978-1524525293.

2. Estacio, Emee Vida (2018). *Fear Is Not My Enemy: The PAME Code to Retrain Your Brain from Fear to Courage and an Amazing Life!* MLP. ISBN: 978-1790953448.
3. Tomsett, John (2018). *This Much I Know About Love Over Fear, Creating a Culture for Truly Great Teaching.* Crown House Publishing. ISBN: 978-1845909826.

Talk to yourself as you would a loved one

Let's talk mental health!

If we know, talk about, and accept the importance of mental health in our colleagues, if we believe that the biggest influence on teacher retention is burn out and stress, then we need to be actively on the lookout as leaders for all manner of mental health issues, both the chronic ones and the acute.

There are people in our care for whom mental health is a daily battle, something they have lived with for years, that often has underlying issues that they need help with. There are others in our care who suffer from immediate issues, perhaps a change in their circumstances or their environment, and this has a negative impact on them. If there are people suffering with both, then as a leader you may well need help from occupational and HR sources to support them effectively. More and more in our society, with increasing issues that we all face, there are people who suffer, and I cannot imagine that this will change any time soon, so it needs to be something that is in the forefront of our leadership thinking.

I believe that in creating an environment where we are all aware of these things, and where there is no shame and only support, then this can only be a good thing. This may have nothing of relevance to you, and you may have switched off, thinking it is all too 'touchy feely', but I can only talk about what I believe and how I work as a leader. I do not have a road map for any other way, and the health and wellbeing of my team matters to me. I think, how can I create a culture of mentally healthy children if we as adults who work with them cannot model that self-regulation, co-regulation or moral challenge and support for one another?

Good mental health rarely happens by luck, chance or osmosis these days; it is usually due to environmental factors as much as innate traits, and the environment is exactly where we can exert influence as a leader. What I will model (the values and standards I live by first and foremost), followed by ensuring that others are supported (through them, how the wider community is supported) really matters to me. Whether I like to acknowledge the 'influencer' part of my role, or not, as a leader it is inherent. How we talk to ourselves is as important as how we talk to others, and we cannot have positive and healthy conversations about and with

DOI: 10.4324/9781003281313-13

ourselves unless we work within a healthy organisation and exist in a healthy social group.

Where to even start with mental health? As ever, with yourself!

The best leaders realise through working on themselves, whilst developing their emotional intelligence and awareness of others, that they do not need to prove themselves to anyone. (Man, I wish I could do this better and be up there amongst *the greats*!) They operate on a simple philosophy of 'be the best version of you that you can be' and model this. I aspire to this on an almost daily basis, by the way, and although I know that I am only partially there all of the time, I am striving to be there *most* of the time. I am sure that, had I more knowledge and in-depth understanding of psychology, I would be able to work out the reasons why I am always trying to prove myself to myself, test my limits, find my boundaries so that I could cease and desist forthwith – I don't, so I keep finding ways to try do so. I suppose in the grand scheme of things, this isn't the worst character flaw I could have, but I am working on moderating it so that rather than launch from one challenge to the next, I do actually pause for breath between them – it is in those pauses, I think, I hope, that the increased wisdom comes.

I do not yet know what motivates me to push myself and seek challenge other than to see where life takes me and to explore the edges of my enjoyment and abilities. I am not competing with anyone else, only myself and the inner voice that wonders if I am 'enough'. Where the end of those abilities is I have yet to find out, but I can now say with certainty that I have learned so much about myself in the process of seeking my boundary lines – my 'left and right of arc' as they say in the military. When I say that I have 'learned', it is because I do things to test myself, just to see the outcome, not for the end product (which can sometimes feel like an anti-climax), and often I am asked why I am signing up for something or why I am not satisfied with what I have already achieved. I have no answers.

What can help with mental health? As ever, your team!

It is often said that I am 'driven'. I don't do things because I need the kudos or cachet of the achievement itself. For example, I can run a marathon with little or no training, but not in under 3 hours, or even 4. So I know that my body is capable of pushing forward for 26 miles, both in mild and also very hot weather. I did not set out to run either marathon in a specific time, didn't do it to compete with others, only to try to complete them physically in one piece, whilst also trying to raise money for good causes. It wasn't about self-aggrandising or self-promotion; it was about self-challenge. I could have worked harder, run faster, been better, but . . .

From those experiences I learned that there are people in my life who wanted to come and support me to do things like that, simply because I am loved and good to be around. I learned that I can exercise mind over (very reluctant) matter, and this (as you know if you have read previous chapters) has come in very handy at times. I also enjoyed the experience, the train journey down, the snacks my friends provided, the company and the 'bants'. I loved wandering around London the night before and being immersed in the buzz of anticipation, the swelling in the numbers of people and the chat with others in restaurants as we talked 'running' (I can evidently run, but do not class myself a 'runner'). I loved being hugged by my most gorgeous friend, and one of my biggest and best advocates, Bruce, at the end of the first marathon and my beautiful friend Clare, finding me some flip flops to ease my painful feet after the second one. I loved the train journeys back both times as the collective euphoria and sense of achievement and wonder surrounded me like the orange glow of the 'Readibrek' advert (those of you in a certain age bracket from the UK may know what I am talking about!). After that, the next day I was in school, and it was all but forgotten, the next challenge already forming in my subconscious. The memories linger, like kisses on your soul really; the feeling of deep safety in the strong arms of my friend will never leave me, and the night-time sharing of secrets with Clare cemented our friendship bond, something that is unshakable. Your support crew, your team, make anything possible.

What else can help with mental health? As ever, your wiring!

Sometimes what you learn about leadership while doing things that are technically completely unrelated to leading is stuff that you need to tease out through reflection.

I have already talked about resilience so I won't bore you again, but for those who are reading this chapter in isolation, I will quickly say that in running the second marathon, pretty quickly after having breast surgery and with no training at all, just relying on latent fitness built over years, I struggled in the heat. At times in the post–20-mile haze of agony I felt I was in, I wanted to give up. I had an internal argument (yep – an actual argument in my own head) about what I should do, one voice telling me there was no shame in giving up and to go to the medics and tell them I had nothing left, and the other telling me there was no way on earth I was giving up and just to keep my legs going until the next purple balloons or the next lamp post or the next Macmillan stand in the near distance. Small goals. You already know that the voice of determination won. I use that voice, and the feeling it evoked from the time, even the playlist I had on in my headphones, when I am seriously 'running on empty' in school, and even when I have been seriously empty emotionally following a painful break up. I give myself the metaphorical small goals and get to them – the end of the day, the next mealtime, the weekend.

When I think I can't keep going and I literally have nothing in the tank, usually at the end of the term or school year, or a particularly stressful school event that has lost me sleep, then I dig deep to the point where I have a reference. For me, it was that day in London with the big toenail hanging off my right foot inside my running shoe, the heat in the high 20s (°C) and the purposefully overtight sports bra holding my reconstructed chest in a vice-like grip, when I thought I couldn't run on (and I did), that pushes me to keep going. So, there are benefits to my wiring, but there are definitely drawbacks! It took a year for my beautiful feet (my best feature) to recover!

What else can help with mental health? As ever, influential others!

I listened to the American Special Forces veteran and Ultra Marathon Record Holder, David Goggins' autobiography recently on one of my 'tabs' (weighted walks) to school and was struck by some of his similar thinking about this kind of thing. It made me realise that I was actually doing myself a disservice by not sitting and allowing myself some time to simply sit with the feelings, the genuine emotions of satisfaction and joy that a task, a trial or a challenge had been completed, with all of the inherent learning extracted and the cognitive links made, before moving on to the next one.

Since hearing him talk about pushing himself, I was forced to accept that I am not the only person 'driven' in this sense. I am weird, but perhaps not alone! I have a feeling that there will be some of you who reach out having read this chapter and let me know that I am definitely not alone, and that you too do this crazy thing that I do, and then I will feel part of a huge gang of people who set themselves personal and professional challenges and then resolutely refuse to give up no matter what until they have completed what they set out to . . . Does this resonate?

My loved ones, particularly my mum and my youngest sister, tell me often and plenty that I have nothing to prove. I do not need to prove to anyone that I am worthy, or good enough, clever enough, fit enough, strong enough mentally, caring enough, loving enough – nothing. Lots of people tell me to be kind to myself and to listen to my body, to rest and to stop pushing (mainly they just say I am nuts, which is a fair point if you are outside and looking in!). I have not listened to them, instead smiling at them, seeing their lips move and hearing white noise that does not seem to register the positives in my brain. It is as if I could not accept the praise of my loved ones, mainly because it is not them that I have been seeking approval and acceptance from. I have come to the conclusion that I had to realise for myself that I was enough. I had to accept that before I could finally grow.

Realisation

Now that I have realised it, that I *am* enough and have done enough, I can refocus my energies – not change, not stop doing the things that I love, but do more of them and less of the ones where I am on a permanent loop to be out of my comfort zone physically and academically. I can now talk to myself like my loved ones do. I can tell myself that I am indeed kind and that I have been loving and have loved fiercely and without constraint or condition. I can accept that I have intellect. I can tell myself that three MAs is enough, and I do not need to test my aptitude any more having done a doctorate and so on, and the best thing of all? I believe myself when I say it. It is an odd sensation, and to begin with, when you start to tell yourself that you've done okay, as the burgeoning realisation starts to manifest, you feel very strange indeed. You are so used to ignoring other people's positive affirmations and thinking people are 'just saying it' that you struggle a bit with your own voice giving you the affirmations – it has taken me 47 years. But owning this, using your voice and really listening to yourself, is such a valuable leadership ability for many reasons.

What is the point of this ramble? What on earth does pushing yourself to excellence for no apparent reason have to do with anything 'leadership'?

As a leader, I need to be aware that people do not always know their limitations because they have not tested them. They talk themselves out of taking steps towards their own success (see the previous chapters) because of a sense of paralysis around decision making, imposter syndrome, fear of failure, lack of support and resources and so on. They also may not know themselves or see their skills in the way that someone invested in them to do so, like their leader, can. They may be under the influence of a negative relationship or working through the legacy of a previous negative professional experience and therefore unable to see their gifts and skills. I view it as my job to make sure that I coach them through this and ensure that I do all in my power to ensure that they realise their potential as human beings and professionals, especially those who work directly with children, or who have children they are raising.

If I create an environment and a culture where this is the norm, and they are able to grow, then they will perpetuate this not just for themselves eventually – and let's be honest, it took me decades – but in a much easier way for their colleagues and the children with whom they work. They will become, through their own evolution, the role models needed in the school environment and moreover perhaps in their own lives with their families and others they come across. I think that if more people were invested in working on themselves for their personal growth and success, rather than looking outwardly to blame others for limiting them from achieving, then the world we live in would be a much better place. This may seem a lofty ideal, but even if you only influence one person in this way, it is one person more in the world who is going out advocating personal reflection and endeavour, success being something intrinsic rather than measured and measurable by external things, being prepared to fail at something in order to work out your limits – if, indeed, you have any.

I know someone who has been failed by the promotion system in the military, their annual reports, OJARs, are all extremely good and enough to effect promotion, but because of the niche jobs the person has done, their reports have had no impact, and they have made limited progress through the ranks. As a result of this, their self-esteem has taken a nosedive, and they talk about themselves in the most derogatory way, which is painful to hear. They are a good person, do anything for anyone, they are self-sacrificing and altruistic but because of the narrow system they are in and the impact of the very worthy but 'different' roles they have undertaken, they have not been rewarded, and this has taken its toll on them. Thankfully the education system is not the same, nor is the route to promotion. It is difficult to compare, but in my army leadership role I need to take cognisance of the report writing that I will do; it is imperative and career limiting if I do not.

As a leader, I need to be aware that people are not always kind to themselves; they don't need to be extreme and actually 'harm' or 'sabotage' themselves, but sometimes they are not kind – there is a subtle difference here. If they don't have a team of people around them being kind to them, and not everyone does, then we have a collective duty to make sure we address this. If I wasn't necessarily kind to myself, and I have done considerable work in understanding myself and my impetus for doing things, then the likelihood is that others will be as clueless to the damage they are either doing or perpetuating to their own self-esteem and self-image as I perhaps was.

This isn't as obtuse or rare as it may at first sound. The most marked example of this I have had recently is when one of my colleagues, the most beautiful soul, kindness personified, a person with an endless supply of patience and love for others, confessed to disliking themselves in a way that was painful for me to witness. They sent messages to people where they talked disparagingly about themselves, and this was a huge red flag. I wanted to help this person but was not necessarily knowledgeable enough to do so. What I was, however, was someone who had cultivated an environment where the conversation with this person was possible, and where they felt comfortable, if emotional, in letting out their personal battles with their body and their relationship with food. They went home and discussed it with their partner and made a start on what I am sure will be a successful journey towards being able to have the sorts of conversations with themselves that I can now have – even if it takes them years. Part of that journey will be bringing their public and private persona together, and part of it will be learning to talk to themselves as they do others – to champion themselves and see their worth as we all do. I am proud to have the kind of workplace where this was shared and support offered freely.

Why being authentic helps

I think that the best leaders realise that it is too much emotional effort to be different for different people – good leaders are authentically themselves, and often 'their people', those with congruent values, will find them. We all gravitate towards those who are likeminded or have our minds changed over time when we are with inspirational people – it is human nature I am sure, and what makes Twitter and other media platforms sometimes an echo chamber (some conspiracy theorists would argue that it is what sets the algorithms for us seeing certain posts, but we can all choose to override that!). As discussed in the previous chapter, good leaders seek coaches, seek counsellors, seek those who will facilitate them becoming better, knowing themselves profoundly and as a result becoming comfortable in their skin. The next logical step to that is to start to talk to themselves (in their own head, not actually out loud, although . . .) in a compassionate, understanding and kind way.

You sometimes come across those facilitators purely randomly, and they don't always just agree with you (we are not talking 'yes-people' here), they will listen to, really 'hear' you and challenge you if you need it. They need to see the real you, however, to help you grow and accept that to try to be someone else as a leader or a person is just not constructive.

Some of the best people who have challenged me, and continue to, are people I have connected with during lockdown, but also those most dear to me. One of the loveliest people I know, known literally around the world as Yozzer, has been in my life for almost a decade. I love him. More than anyone other than my blood relatives, I love him to the core. I literally love him to bits. He has hurt my feelings, opened my eyes, made me see the wood for the trees, forced me to reflect on the broken and unpleasant parts of me and been a catalyst for change in my thinking that I will be forever grateful for. We met at the gym, doing circuits, and our friendship grew from there. He wasn't a paid coach or a guru of any sort, and at times, by his own admission, he was as broken, if not more so, than I was, but nevertheless he shone a light for me at my darkest times and loved me when I needed to be loved. His life has moved on and we are rarely in contact now, but I will carry his love with me. How many of us can say that we have been the kind of friend, through thick and thin, who remained stoic through being pushed away and still gave the kind of tough love that needed to be given? How many of us can say as leaders we have been the same? It is not too late and is within the reach of each of us to be like this.

Scott, Kyrstie, Joanne, Lee, Deborah, Rachel, Ricky, Matt, Anthony, Paul, Kari, Ben and Dave are all utterly beautiful souls who I have connected with on Twitter and who have listened to me and coached me through some personal challenges in the most recent year or so, letting me see that I was not alone and making me actually braver as a human being than I was before. The impact of their conversation has been not just in school, where I feel buoyed up by their advocacy, but also in my personal life where I see that I am much stronger than I was giving myself credit for!

Because of them, I am now beginning to talk about myself in a public way that is much more positive, modelling how it can be done, and for people who see me on Twitter or LinkedIn and think I am invincible, inspirational, strong etc. (YES! This really does get said!), I think that it is important for them to know that whilst this may be the appearance, actually I am just like everyone else, just like them, overcoming the same issues, anxieties and fears, with a huge team of people around me – I think if you have read this book so far, then this is obvious. We each can be a part of the team of someone else, near and far. We can change the way we see and talk to/about ourselves – it really is possible.

Self-judgement

Good leaders spend less time worrying about the judgements of others than on how they judge themselves. Again, they work within a belief system of 'if someone judges you – let them. If they judge you harshly or unfairly, don't let it detract from you being the authentic "you" that they don't see'. In a world where social media, the press and public opinion can be so polarised, damaging and damning, it is important to gain some perspective on this very, very quickly. There is always going to be someone who does not like you, who may absolutely refuse to like you, even if you are the loveliest person and best leader around – FACT. Sometimes this will be precisely as a result of the fact that you are the loveliest person and best leader around because something in that triggers them and they can't cope, so they will reject you out of hand and try to destroy you; other times it is because of a visceral clash in values or the way you operate.

You have no choice other than to let it go, or it will eat you up. The only way to combat this is to ensure that firstly you make every decision based on integrity, and run those ideas and decisions past your trusted team as a filter where possible; secondly to live your value set; and thirdly to have developed a way to talk to yourself as you would another person in the same position whom you like, love or respect. Then you may be temporarily hurt, saddened and upset when you are judged unfairly, after all you are human, but when you analyse this, you will know that you have done all you can in the best way that you know how to, and you will be able to let it go.

At times I have struggled badly with this, and there are times (especially when extremely tired or triggered myself) when I have no choice other than to sit with the feelings and let them wash over me. I do, however, have the immeasurable benefit of Sue, Sharon, Clare and Alice as the non-teaching element of the team, with Lottie, Laura, Lou, Emily and Arzoo as the teaching element who remind me that it is our *whole* SLT who make the decisions after discussing and going through our quality control, checks and balances – this can also involve the governors. We would all agree, and they will have challenged and perfected the final decision before it is shared, so anger from parents and complaints at decisions I make is largely futile. That's not to say I don't make errors – I always apologise for these and say when I have been mistaken – but my team will say 'what would you say to us if it was one of us telling you this, now?'

Anger and personal slights against me, my team defend and talk me through, as I do when there are complaints levied at them. When I am struggling with parenting or relationships, they talk to me. and I talk to them. What happens is that the dialogue merges, and in the end, you talk to yourself as those loved and trusted people would because you learn to love, trust and respect yourself. If you are anything like me, then it is exhausting and takes ages; you will have to unlearn years of ingrained and learned behaviour – so don't expect a quick fix! I am still a work in progress. Equally, the opposite is true. If you are surrounded by toxicity, or not surrounded at all, then you have only the negative voices echoing in your head and are unlikely to ever be able to find the compassionate voice you need to give you licence to thrive.

You are enough

Even though I know that I am not *quite* there yet, maybe I never will be, maybe none of us ever are and that is the whole point . . . I do know that in order to maintain emotional and mental equilibrium, I must keep being myself, the best version of myself that I know how to be, part of which is linked to self-awareness, being physically connected and being dedicated to lifelong learning discussed in previous chapters.

I think it is really important to separate the 'being the best you can be' concept from 'being better than everyone else' rhetoric that the marketplace, Ofsted judgement culture and the 'every man for himself' attitude in our society can perpetuate. I think the best leaders know these things; they know that they just need to focus on growing as a person, on cultivating this on a wider scale, so that they demonstrate that when they know better, they do better. It isn't about stepping on others to prove you are better or being relieved that it is the school down the road that has the poor Ofsted judgement and not you. It is about focusing on being the best leader you can be, with all that this entails, so that if the worst happens to your school (as a result of the destruction of social infrastructure, the constantly shifting sands of Ofsted and government expectation or a global crisis such as the Covid-19 pandemic), you are equipped to deal with it pragmatically and not allow it to destroy you. The best leaders know that this is hard emotional work that takes mental exercise in the same way that physical strength takes physical exercise. Nobody said leadership was easy – nobody said life was easy either, but the potential for personal growth is limitless!

The best leaders also know the value of real self-talk. If you would not say to a loved one that they are not good enough, could never do it and so on, then that kind of damaging talk has no place inside your own head. The best leaders, therefore, never tell themselves they can't – they know that the minute anyone tells themselves this, then they will be right. Even I have never told myself I can't. I don't know if I can, but I don't tell myself I can't. I verbalise the anxieties and the doubts, I allow them airtime, and then I let my determination silence them. If I do not accomplish something, it is never for the want of me giving it 100%. Therefore, with the right self-talk, allowing yourself to be encouraged by your inner monologue rather than discouraged, the best leaders do not let age, gender, marital status, ethnicity, dependents, sexuality or anything else *ever* impede their decisions about their lives, and they are creative when appointing people, making sure that none of those factors affect anyone with whom they work either. One of the greatest privileges of the leadership role in a school is seeing others overcome the self-imposed barriers that their own negative voices create. It is akin to the lightbulb moment that we have when a child grasps a tricky concept and we think – YES!!!! It happened in my recent commissioning course also, seeing those from diverse backgrounds all thrown together and learning under pressure; it was evident that we all overcame barriers, and this was because we worked as a team.

Your legacy, your impact on others, matters

You will likely get only one life – you need to know at the end that you have lived it, and part of that is being concerned with creating your legacy, not your CV. You are more than the list of things you have achieved and accomplished. You need to tell yourself that. Each accomplishment is a result of a coalescence of events and opportunities at a specific point in time that you have been able to take – it is not a definition of you. What will define you is the learning you take from those accomplishments, how that learning shapes how you talk to yourself and others, how it moulds how you behave towards yourself and others and how that impacts on your circle and beyond.

One day I hope to be a very old lady, living a simple life by the sea, walking on the sand each day and falling asleep with the sound of the waves on the beach. I want to know that I have squeezed every drop out of life, taken as many opportunities as I can, and lived to tell the tales, 'spin the dits', of not just the experiences but most importantly what I learned from them. I want to know that I have loved and nurtured myself as I have loved and nurtured others, and as a result, I have strived to touch the lives of every person I have come across and left them the better for it. Even in knowing that this is not possible, endeavouring to do it is enough, I think.

What has all of this to do with leading with love, with you?

Self-talk then, that powerful internal monologue, how you *actually* talk to yourself, is vital in relation to happiness, productivity and performance, and as such has been studied in sports for the last 40 years. Less prolific in education or leadership spaces, but the same principles apply, I think. I believe that self-talk has equally important applications for self-efficacy in both leadership and educational domains no matter the stage in your career. In fact, in pupil/student or professional worlds – developing your ability to use language to revolutionise your own life is just as important as doing so for others.

You will be familiar with the summary by now, but the point is:

■ Life is full of opportunities to challenge yourself so that you can positively impact the work and influence of yourself and others, both created and spontaneous (which means that you can . . .)

- Train yourself to talk to yourself as if you are a cherished loved one, rather than someone inadequate (because . . .)

- You need to be your own best advocate (because . . .)

- Good self-talk definitely impacts on how efficacious you are (also . . .)

- If people hear you talking yourself down, then they follow your lead, and this is a self-fulfilling prophesy; if you tell yourself you can then you can, if others follow then you have a staff of highly motivated and committed individuals (to make the best team you can).

Further reading/listening

If you like a podcast and 'integrity' is something you want to know more about in terms of leadership:

1. The High Performance Podcast: Chris Hoy: Keep Raising the Bar. https://tinyurl.com/Chris-Hoy-High-Performance
2. Bruce Van Horn's 'Life Is a Marathon' Podcasts. https://tinyurl.com/Life-is-a-Marathon

If you like a book and want to get the best potential out of your team in a number of levels:

1. Knight, Sam (2018). *Self-Talk Your Way to Success*. Independently Published. ISBN: 978-1731543257.
2. King, Vex (2018). *Good Vibes, Good Life: How Self-Love Is the Key to Unlocking Your Greatness*. Hay House UK. ISBN: 978-1788171823.
3. Goggins, David (2018). *Can't Hurt Me: Master Your Mind and Defy the Odds*. Lioncrest Publishing. ISBN: 9781544512273.

13 Your body may be present, but your soul isn't

Connectivity and alignment

We spend an awful lot of time in our workplace, an awful lot of time. If we are not connected to our organisation, through the strands of relationships, values, purpose and legacy, then it can be a source of depression, demoralisation and anxiety because we are there only in body. Whilst this is the same for many personal relationships and home lives, it can be our work relationships and work lives that cause us the most pressing anxieties as we rely on this to provide for us and our families.

Choosing a career that aligns with your values and lights a fire in your soul is so important to the essence of living a fulfilled and happy life – and yet so many people are either unable to achieve this or unwilling to search for it. That isn't to say that at times, even when you are completely happy and motivated, your job (particularly as a leader in any field) can seem simply untenable for a range of complex reasons. Safe to say that the majority of us realise that we don't exist in utopia and realistically, would we want to? Life would be pretty 'vanilla' if we had 24/7 perfection, and what would we learn from that?

The previous chapter dealt with talking yourself through situations, and this one is about the practical side of 'doing' something to move your body out of those difficulties, finding the motivation to reconnect your physical and your emotional so body and soul are in the same time zone. I am a firm believer that unless you are physically and emotionally in good shape (don't freak out here, I don't mean Olympian fitness standards when I say physically in good shape!), then how on earth can you be personally or professionally productive and the best version of yourself? If your work is affecting your ability to connect on any level, with yourself and others, you need to find some ways to remedy this, especially as a leader. You need to do this for yourself and also for others. Before you glaze over, allow me to elaborate . . .

 DOI: 10.4324/9781003281313-14

Sometimes we need more than the abstract or esoteric

Many of you may know that I am quite happy in my own company. You may have heard me talk about my small dream of a quiet cottage by the sea, on an island (preferably of the west coast of Scotland), with a log fire, lots of books, a bottle of whisky or gin, and a comfy sofa with lots of cushions and a big blanket. This dream has at times been all that has kept me going throughout periods of personal and professional 'madness', most notably in the two years of managing the impact of COVID-19 on a school and its community and managing a challenging personal relationship and its eventual breakdown. Focusing on that goal has become a visual mantra at times; I am able to see an image in my mind of my dream. You will all have something you aspire to that keeps you moving forwards, keeps you placing one foot in front of the other, but I have also needed more immediate, concrete and tangible solutions – something which, again, may resonate.

You will all, no matter where in the world you are when reading this, recall some of the things that I am talking about, but between schools closing/not closing; what felt like last minute updates on 'Key Worker' lists (that included everyone and their dog really, because in our interconnected society, who isn't 'key' to keeping the cogs of capitalism going?); having to take a moral stance on who can work from home and have conversations with angry (and understandably strung out) parents; my own two teenagers being under what they called 'house arrest' (tough love is, after-all, tough . . .) and both of them having their GCSEs affected; and simultaneously keeping a whole staff buoyant who were naturally anxious about exposure to the most aggressive and deadly virus humanity that has been encountered in our modern times (all with no other adult at home to share this with) – I needed to up my mental and physical game to stay healthy (all of this with the gym being closed). I won't have been on my own, many of you will recognise yourselves in this, I am only scratching the surface of what we all endured.

The world felt a sense of isolation, we all felt distanced, detached, cast adrift from our fellow humans during that time – connected in our disconnection. Relationships in their infancy foundered as people were forced to remain at home, as it happened not just for three weeks, which was what we were initially told, but for months. Relationships on the verge of being rekindled were snuffed out as international travel was banned for over a year, changing the courses of lives forever. Businesses closed and people lost their livelihoods, homes and security, and this placed huge stress on established relationships and families, some of whom went hungry and were unable to get help. Couples who had been unhappy for a while but used the distraction of outside activities to perpetuate momentum suddenly found themselves thrust together in an enforced, highly pressurised and (as it happened) very hot situation. Milestones for every age bracket were lost forever, births, marriages, deaths. Social lives and self-care stopped as restaurants, pubs, cinemas, gyms, hair dressers, beauticians all closed indefinitely, and as everyone questioned 'what is the point to anything?' people no longer had the ability, or necessity, to create a socially acceptable mask. Parents, siblings, friends and relatives died, alone and without having seen their loved ones for months. The world was turned on its axis, and suddenly the work of educators, the NHS, refuse collectors, cleaners, retail workers, lorry drivers and so on became more important than politicians', as we all recognised those who keep us fed, cared for and healthy as the true heroes. People grieved all kinds of losses, some of us still do, and at the time they did not have the socially well-trodden paths of collective support that they would have had in order to help them in dealing with their grief. It was a time of introspection, and a time of collective national and international fear and severed connections.

For some, it was business almost as usual. Like many in education, I continued to work. I didn't usually go to the pub or out for meals, so the social side of things didn't change my daily routine greatly. Although I missed the camaraderie of the gym, I caught Covid early on and was so unwell for more than seven weeks that I couldn't have done much exercise anyway, so daily walks in the sun, when I was able to enjoy them, were perfect. Initially, I worried for the future of my children, who were both in GCSE years, and then I talked myself and them through the worst case scenarios, and although it wasn't ideal, we realised that the whole world was going through this, and any employer in the future with an ounce of sense would understand – the main thing was that they were safe and healthy. Although the three of us languished at times, each in our respective worlds, like islands in an archipelago that was our home, as we navigated the interminable days and weeks, we each grew in ways that we recognised and celebrated.

Sometimes we walked together. My daughter, who had been struggling for some time under the influence of some pretty negative friendships, was suddenly liberated and, with the weight lifted from her, began to thrive. She attended the online learning sessions that her creative and dedicated teachers held and was quite happy. My son reflected on his future and the mistakes he had made with his mocks, we discussed saving and house purchases, finances and mortgages. He was 'scammed' out of his MacBook, and although it cost me £1000 (yep, a whole thousand), he learned a valuable lesson that has served him well since. Around work I considered life, love and the universe, as I am wont to do, walked miles each day, initially alone but eventually with Yozzini, noticing the changing world around us on our beautiful peninsula, spending simple times with someone I love very much.

I was quietly content in my solitude the rest of the time. They say no man is an island, but I felt like one. I suppose for me, like for many people, it could have been easy, in the heat, post-illness, with a world 'locked down', to become quite apathetic. I wondered how many people, even without the added issue of a pandemic, who are post-surgery, post-illness, going through a change in life, could struggle with a sense of futility and listlessness. I know of a couple personally who will just say to me that they are so weighed down that they 'just can't' – can't put on their trainers and walk the dog, can't get up and make a meal, can't shower and wash their hair and so on. Their body just won't listen; they are there in body but not mind and soul. They don't feel connected.

What we can learn from the concrete and tangible

At the time, I was thinking to myself, what can I take from my reactions to these things? After all, my take on life and leadership is that it is about growth and reflection in order to enhance the present lived experience and inform or streamline future decision making. I have said already that I cannot separate out the personal from the professional development I undergo and how each informs the other – this was no different.

What I did at the time was to play a simple game in my head, © 'Desert Island Discs', and I came up with my Top 10 essentials for being an island, in my own life and my own home – and surviving it. I reflected on times when I had been in the throes of lethargy and had been unable to revert to my usual exercise and reading self-motivation package. Those times had indeed been 'post-surgery' and when I was very much struggling with mobility and isolation, or when I was going through a really painful relationship breakup and just didn't have the capacity to move my body in any kind of meaningful way, or focus to read. The concept of actual movement as a way to connect the dots for me, of a sense of the 'physical', was quite meaningful, and it started with the concrete act of making a list – don't most things in my life?

Making a menu!

The Top 10 list really worked for me, like a menu from which to select things that I could cope with, even just one a day or one a week to begin with, writing it down on a calendar or a planner, and if pulling them together here may inspire some of you to find your own top 10 'go-to' strategies for coping with the demands of leadership, or crisis management, or change, or physical incapacity, then great. Feel free to substitute anything on my list for something you find helps you connect the sometime disparate parts of yourself; alternatively, you could always just steal mine, they are not subject to 'copywrite' (unlike Desert Island Discs!!!) to reconnect your brain, body and soul, to reconnect your whole self with your joy of your job and your personal life.

At the top of my list, turn to music. Genuinely. Those of you who know me, know that I love music, and I love singing. All. Of. The. Time. I don't care how badly I sing, I love it and there are some songs that just lift my heart and take me right out of any sad situation I am in; some even give me a sense of euphoria. Perhaps this is associative and subliminally I am thinking of the emotion I felt at the time I heard that tune first, or what I was doing, who knows, but there is a reason for the saying 'Where Words Fail, Music Speaks' (good old Hans Christian Anderson, he obviously had a way with words!). My mum is the most hilarious person with music and has these epic 'dance' moves that she will throw out as soon as a tune comes on, and it is so comical that the joy she creates just by watching her 'freestyle' is infectious (it is matched in its opposition only by the irritation her humming causes as she freestyles that also!). We all have those tunes, no matter whether they are rock anthems or rave classics – dig them out!

To that end, my suggestion is to create playlists – this is pretty easy to do on most phones, and in fact if you have Spotify or Applemusic, they will even do it for you if you are strapped for time. My advice on this is, when you are in a very good frame of mind, create the uplifting playlist. If you do it then, you will be prepared for when it is needed. Get something in there that has you tempted to dance in your office with tears streaming down your face, or makes your chest vibrate with the bass, or makes you want to sing as if nobody is listening. I once blasted Adele's 'Someone Like You' at the top of my voice (luckily with her accompanying me) when I was breaking my heart, and it totally worked. I cried, I sang out loud, and the act of doing something connected my component parts, and afterwards I got up. It really helped.

So, which tunes can I not live without? If you want some pure bangers and need inspiration, here goes, for a wee list – although not a definitive one by any means – and remember, you need to pick music to match your mood for this top tip to work . . . dancing around the house, mellow by a fire, having a cry, face timing your mates . . . variety is key here, and listening to new music to see if you like it is essential, too (remember what I think about comfort zones – Radio 1 isn't just for the under 20s)!

Ben Howard – his first two albums in their entirety (there isn't one bad song!), any and all of his acoustic stuff on YouTube is also simply epic. Genuinely, the memories I have of his music can and will paint pictures behind my eyelids forever. He is amazing, and so was my trip to Amsterdam to see him play, as were the hours up and down the motorway to The Sea Mills Hotel, numerous trips to Cartmel with him in the background, so many once-in-a-lifetime experiences with a once-in-a-lifetime human. Ben Howard makes me cry and smile simultaneously. Kings of Leon – their entire library. Truly uplifting music, their track 'The Last Mile Home' was on my playlist for the second London Marathon that I ran (no joke), and as for 'Comeback Story' – I mean, I challenge anyone not to sing out loud to those songs (although when I went to see them live in Liverpool, the fan in front who was 'air guitaring' was a little irritating!). Mumford and Sons – their entire library, too. No explanation needed! I went to see them live with my mum, mate Sandy and daughter. Mind-blowingly fabulous and again, more than a little memorable – even if some of their tracks also make me cry. Ed Sheeran – saw him in both Birmingham and Glasgow on the same tour, and I will never forget either event. Similar vein here I know, but bear with me. These guys all have powerful lyrics and brilliant tunes to commend them, as do Sam Garrett, The Proclaimers, The Saw Doctors, Catfish and the Bottlemen, and Nothing But Thieves. Finally, no decent Desert Island playlist would be complete without a bit of Eminem, George Ezra, 50 Cent, Aitch, Aloe Black, Callum Scott, Calvin Harris, The Red Hot Chili Peppers, Bob Marley, The Beatles, Abba, Mary J Blige, Gaz Coombes, Gerry Cinnamon, Lewis Capaldi, Billie Eilish, James Bay, Sam Fender and Nirvana! I could go on, but I won't. If you haven't heard of all of those people, then open your mind to something new today and check them out (I am not on commission by the way!).

Number two on my list was always going to be books. Seriously. BOOKS! Get into reading. I love reading anything: the classics you may not have read since school, from Jane Austen to the complete works of Shakespeare, the plays of Oscar Wilde to the poetry of Wordsworth. Let the words created by others envelope you in their beauty and allow you to escape into their worlds. Contemporary literature is astonishing: there are biographies of amazing people like Michelle Obama, books on leadership and sport like *Legacy*. Two of the best I have read in the last decade are *Any Human Heart* and *Normal People*, both made into their own TV mini-series. Mind bogglingly good. Read anything! Before you tell yourself you have no time, you can access talking books now, as discussed in earlier chapters, so there really is no excuse not to. Books are life!

They can reconnect you in so many ways, they create hooks to our subconscious and our conscious, inspire us to behave differently and respond more effectively just through auto suggestion – I think of reading like I would someone letting me out of a junction with a smile on a very busy road. Tell me anyone for whom that doesn't make their day?

I am still passionate about a book shop. There are few greater pleasures than a walk through the aisles, touching the covers, looking at the colours, the fonts, the titles, the smell. Glancing at the blurbs and wondering if this is the next great read. The physical act of doing these things is cathartic in itself, strangely comforting and calming. Book shops for me, like libraries, are cathedrals of hope, full of challenge, ideas, love and joy. The best book shop I've ever been to is a choice between Shaun Bythell's in Wigtown, and Fred Holdsworth's in Ambleside – for different reasons. If you cannot get to a bookshop, there are loads of great suggestions for good reads both on the internet in general or by following wonderful curators of reading lists on Twitter. Seriously, get into books.

In the top three, of course, is some exercise! Ok, so this may prove easy, or it may not. I have accumulated a lot of gym equipment over the years; some of it you may have seen on my social media feeds, which makes exercise at home much easier perhaps. Some of you may think, 'this is beyond me', the exercise or the kit collecting, *but* you'd be wrong! One of the legacies of lockdown is that people have learned how to access exercise, for so many reasons, from home, on their phones! My first port of call as a lead into exercise would not necessarily be the nationally well-known faces for workouts, but something like Apple Fitness or the 7 Minute Workout app for your phone – both of which are *so easy* for all levels. We all have seven minutes a day for ourselves, and neither app requires any equipment at all if you don't want it to – body weight is more than enough.

I love Asana Rebel for yoga, having never considered yoga 'exercise' in my whole life until last year, and if I could now say one type of 'exercise' that connects mind, body and soul, it would be this. The breathing, purposeful movement and conscious knowledge of your specific muscles is just wonderful for connecting all elements of your body.

Alternatively, you could just throw on some music and dance like mad around your house; even if wheelchair bound, or physically incapacitated, you can dance. Moving your body and raising your heart rate, especially to music, is so therapeutic and such good medicine for the soul. Try it and see, don't take my word for it.

I have already talked about food and nourishing your body. There is nothing better than the little treats you love at a time when you are feeling disenfranchised. As you know, for me, feeding my body nutritious food, home-cooked, and trying new recipes is a family favourite. We do a version of 'Come Dine With Me' in my house, we cook and judge . . . it can be scathing (when I got 2 out of 10 for my courgetti) but also hilarious. My daughter makes a fab banana and chocolate chip bread, and although it took me an hour to clean the kitchen, this was also part of the fun. My son makes a pretty good cooked breakfast if truth be known, but whatever it is, you are not just going through the motions, you are connecting several senses to your physical act of cooking. Smell, taste, if you are with others then it can be uplifting to share the chopping and preparing just as much as the clearing up. Without even being aware, you are synchronising your body and thoughts, whilst also creating something to fuel yourself. Just an idea, and this doesn't mean I am suggesting giving yourself the green light for eating whole pots of red pepper hummus (I can sometimes do this in moments of disconnect!).

I am not accustomed to sitting around and watching TV. I think it is obvious to everyone that my strategy in life for avoiding self-reflection about my inadequacies, social anxiety and general weirdness is to keep myself as busy as possible, so sitting down for an hour or two is not really something I do. BUT, when I was unwell, and after breast surgery, I prepared myself with my all-time favourite movies and box sets to just embrace 'slobbing out'. If you need inspiration and to widen your movie repertoire, mine are (in no order at all): *The English Patient*, *Local Hero*, *Out of Africa*, *Band of Brothers*, *Lord of the Rings*, *Pacific* and *Harry Potter* box sets, *Avatar*, *Star Wars* box sets, all of the Marvel movies! I am sure that I do not need to say more. You can combine this with food and do it after exercise and lo and behold – there is a pretty legendary day right there that will really boost you and ground you back to being connected to what you love!

I love my garden. I love to tidy it up and make it look lovely. It requires time and physical effort, and I can do it whilst listening to music or a book (see what I did there?). You can do it in stages to break the day up, or give it some real care and spend a whole weekend there. We all need to get outside for a little while, and being industrious will aid in a sense of satisfaction and productivity, as well as giving us an essential dose of Vitamin D. Visually it can be appealing too, but not everyone has a garden. What then? You could walk on a beach carrying a bag and collecting flotsam, jetsam and rubbish. You could offer to do the garden of a friend or a neighbour and feel connected to your community as well as your body. You could create boxes on your veranda or plant potted houseplants in your flat;

the greenery will not just purify your air, but make you see colour and texture that changes in the light.

I have to confess, I am better at outdoor plants that require little to no care from humans. Green-fingered I am definitely not – any plant surviving in my garden needs to be literally a survivor, so this one may be easier said than done!

Something that I find so satisfying and grounding is when I tidy my wardrobes (fridges and cupboards too – don't leave out the worst storage spaces)! It may sound awful, but I have several wardrobes, and I occasionally do sort them out – boring, mundane, routine tasks that get you moving and noticing what you wear, or could wear, reminding you that you have choices and options, and that keeping good things for 'best' isn't really necessary – reminding yourself that you can wear what you like and celebrate every day if you so choose can be so re-invigorating! The last time I did this (embarrassingly), I challenged myself not to wear the same outfit for the whole school term . . . and succeeded. To be fair, I rarely chuck things out, don't really buy fashionable clothes, and look after stuff, plus I rarely fluctuate in dress size (I have been 12 stone there or thereabouts for decades!).

This is a great opportunity to colour code your shelves and hanging spaces ☺ or simply sift out things that could go to a women's refuge, a charity shop, a community organisation that clothe the vulnerable for nothing etc.; wedding dresses can go to charities that make funeral attire for stillborn babies, bras can go to charities in so called third world countries that protect women from rape; you may be a book hoarder like me, and you can declutter your bookshelves by posting on Twitter that you are happy to send random books to people if they send you their address, you can play @Ready Steady Cook with the random items you locate in your kitchen cupboards – it's potentially a time to get inventive, or obsessive!

Mindfulness has maybe become synonymous with yoga and meditation, which it doesn't really have to be. For me, being mindful is as simple as walking to school and feeling the sun warm my face and enjoying the sensation for a moment, just as much as it is doing the same activity and feeling the rain hitting my cheeks. It can be when you light those special candles, do an online art class, colour in, do a jigsaw, sing, learn to sit still – this I am working on – and just 'be'. Being mindful can be assisted by apps on your phone, but for me, I keep this one simple.

I am never without my phone because I use it as my camera – you can take close ups in the garden, or random sky shots, or daft selfies all day long. The funny thing about this is that it will help chronicle your day, days, weeks, changing self, whatever! I did this after breast surgery actually, 'one day', I said to myself, 'when this is over, it will be consigned to a dusty memory, like childbirth, too painful to revisit and impossible for the mind to embrace. So these images will prove a funny way of recalling these disconnected days and weeks'. And the images of that time really are a reminder of what we can overcome as humans and how we can pull ourselves from the brink of despair. I suppose that there is potential, combined with the content of the next paragraph, to make for a best seller and something that lives on in posterity – think a modern-day *Samuel Pepys' Diary* (except who would want to read the Chronicle of Vic's Boobs?)!

There is something so satisfying about the feel of a nice pen and writing in a beautiful book. Obviously e-diaries will count, but imagine if you made a scrap book diary with your photos and thoughts written in your hand with a beautiful pen; your children and grandchildren and their children will read in amazement about our day and age, for example, when a mere bug caught us all out and brought our modern and fast-paced world to its knees in just a few short weeks, in the same way that we look back on significant events of the last few hundred years. If nothing else, then when you are old, you can remind yourself of the ephemera of your life and reflect on all you have seen and done, all you have known and been a part of. Your reflections on this, and the observations we have made on humanity via social media, will entertain, baffle and disgust us all for years to come – unlike times gone by, the internet stores things forever. The good, bad and ugly are pre-served for eternity now effortlessly; our world has shifted, and hopefully we will value different things in the aftermath of such an event as a pandemic. Now is the time to write the history of the future, but to connect and ground us, we can also look to the past to make sense of ourselves now.

What has all of this to do with leading with love, and with you?

How we treat ourselves, our communities and our planet affects our connectedness and how we are therefore able to react to crisis situations. As a leader, the more connected and grounded you are in yourself, the more easily calm and informed decision making will occur. You will find your own ways of connecting all aspects of yourself, your components, and once you discover your most effective methods, you can fine tune them – think of assembling an F1 car. It is made of the highest quality parts, put together by excellent technicians and driven by experts in their field. Yet, its high performance and impressive speed isn't perfected in a day, it also takes a number of technicians to work on different aspects of it over time. It also takes subtle changes to manage changes in weather states! Nor will you be able to perform at a high level immediately, even if you are equipped with all of the right knowledge and skills and have all of the environmental tools and structures. As you go along you will need to adjust yourself accordingly to ensure you are get-ting the very best from all of yourself. Embrace this. Just understand it as another element of leadership and life, and be aware of when you need to recalibrate.

The point of this chapter is:

- Life is full of complexities that can become barriers to us being our best and most connected selves (which means that you can . . .)

- Remember to focus on looking for the ways in which you can reconnect yourself to your 'why' or the love of your job (because . . .)

■ Sometimes action is the way you need to react, rather than thinking or reflection (because . . .)

■ We all need a tool kit at our fingertips that facilitates us activating a positive mindset; sometimes this involves our bodies, or our minds or both (also . . .)

■ Leading by example matters – physical and emotional health are so closely affiliated and need to be attuned so that others in your sphere of influence can see it, can visualise what it can look like, to replicate it in their lives (to make the best team you can).

Further reading/listening

If you like a podcast and 'mindfulness' is something you want to know more about in terms of leadership:

1. The Mindful Podcast. https://tinyurl.com/Mindful-Podcast
2. Soul Music from BBC Radio 4: Each Episode Explores One Song and What It Means to Different People Around the World. https://tinyurl.com/Soul-Sounds

If you like a book and want to get the best potential out of your team in a number of levels:

1. Dweck, Dr Carol (2017). *Mindset: Changing the Way You think to Fulfil Your Potential*. Robinson. ISBN: 978-2133487514.
2. Hill, Chase and Scott Sharp (2019). *How to Stop Overthinking: The 7-Step Plan to Control and Eliminate Negative Thoughts, Declutter Your Mind and Start Thinking Positively in 5 Minutes or Less*. Independently Published. ISBN: 978-1098853372.
3. Mate, Gabor (2019). *When the Body Says No: The Cost of Hidden Stress*. Vermillion. ISBN: 978-1785042225.

People, not systems, change the way that people work

Life is to be lived not survived

It feels to me that life is not a passive activity, although for some people this may well be how it is lived. For me, life is filled with transactions, compromises and shared understandings that are constantly being revisited in light of new information or learning, almost daily. I know that it has been like this with my home life, my work life and indeed my personal life since I was very young. I suspect this is one of the reasons I am so focused on personal growth and professional development. There are many examples of when I have understood conceptually a scheme or a structure but not actually found it easy to put into practice to begin with or understood how to review and make changes to it.

When I embarked on being a parent for example, little did I know that you are totally unprepared for it no matter how systematic 'feed, change, sleep' can sound. I am not sure that I was a natural . . . I did read a book on it (well, glanced at the book) and kind of pieced together the 'How to' manual of motherhood from observation of others. I was an epic 'aunt', I like to think I still am, but at that time I had only my rehearsal role as aunty to go off, a kind of pseudo-parenting role with all the fun and none of the responsibility.

Despite my lofty (control freak) assertions and expectations that my children would be perfectly well behaved and do as they were told, carve a linear pathway from birth to adulthood (with absolutely no issues) simply through the force of character of their mother, I had to eat humble pie. I knew the mechanics (no smutty jokes please) obviously; didn't pay any attention at all to the birth information, after all women had been birthing babies for millennia; and basic principles such as babies need milk, warmth and love were well-known facts, even to me – *but* the skill of raising a child, of knowing why they are crying and what each cry might be telling us, was mortifyingly esoteric and required the hive mind of those who had parented before me to give me the skills and knowledge that I needed.

 DOI: 10.4324/9781003281313-15

I entered blindly what I like to call a 'steep learning curve' for about three years of what felt like permanent pregnancy, maternity clothes, nappy changing, sleepless nights and breast feeding from which I thought I would never emerge. The other surprises came when the nappy stage was over, or the primary school stage was over, or the secondary school stage was over, and I realised that this learning curve is never over, and each time you make a transition, it is like an assault on your senses and cognition. Time passes, though, and you emerge from the grafting part of parenting with a few life lessons tucked under your sleeve, and lots of memories.

Evolution of leadership

So what? There is no difference for me as a leader. This evolution of me as a parent has been almost identical to me as a leader and as a functioning adult – and just as painful and messy! Try not to panic at this point, the nation's youth really are safe in my hands but . . .

We all know the principles of leadership. There are a million manuals on how to do it, from the theory behind it, to the pedagogy of how leaders develop, to how to square away challenges such as Human Resources issues, tricky conversations or burn out. There are books. We can access courses and qualifications in leadership, where our academic understanding of the conceptual can be tested out and critiqued; we can expand on the repertoire of tools available to use in myriad circumstances in our organisations. We can apply for and successfully attain leadership positions, either based on excellent interview technique or past experience, but each new organisation is unique and presents its own trials and contests that must be engaged with, and we never know what they are until they arrive in the unsuspecting inbox or on the innocent desk on a Monday morning or Friday night.

I think, then, that the art of any systemic change is not what you have read necessarily (the irony is not lost on me here, given that you are reading about my stance on leadership!), not on your CV or academic experience, not even on what you have done before in similar situations, but on *how* you do things, the foundations. I think it is the *how* that is the transferable skill and the one that can facilitate and enable sustainable change – no matter where you find yourself or in what kind of setting.

This is quite an unnerving thought for a new leader who has yet to form a picture of their individual style of leadership in their own minds. I know it is because I have been there. When losing sleep over what to say or how to say it, when deciding what the rationale could or should be for something, or when deciding how to ensure that you are being fair, reading a book, looking at a policy or someone else telling you what they do and how they do it may not necessarily be too helpful. If you are considering leadership and not yet embarked on it, but just in general really, I would highly recommend what I have suggested in Chapter 1 – know yourself first. If you know yourself and you are content with who you are, then you can begin the work of eliciting what it is that drives you and the kind of legacy that you want to leave in your wake. These things should then give you the final piece of the puzzle about how you want to do things, the kind of team you want to build and how that team will build the necessary skills to create systems that work and do so effectively.

Is it as binary as chicken or egg?

I wondered, before I became a school leader, what comes first when establishing an effective and productive culture – the people or the systems? I am now of the opinion that it is neither and yet both. The people you choose to work with you are also the co-creators and curators of the effective systems you create, and any system is only as good as those contributing to it regularly. When I let that sit in my conscious for a while and try to challenge that thought, I find it difficult to. I am sure that there are exceptions, I just can't think of them.

I think of school. We have many systems, for example, the system of assessing and tracking pupils. If I apply my logic to that system, does it work? If teachers assess children's progress in differing ways and input individual information into the tracking system, then it could become ineffective and unfit for purpose, which is to track progress and make comparable what is largely not easy to compare – both qualitatively and quantitatively. If the same teachers are consistent, both in the way they apply assessments, therefore actually 'assess', the way they cross-moderate assessments, the open way that they will work out nuances in understanding and decision making across teams, and finally the way that they input and analyse the data, then the system theoretically becomes much more effective and produces something more like useful information for leaders to have a broad brush understanding of progress. Therefore, it is the people co-creating and sustaining the system that are the key, not the system itself.

Implementing a system of tracking progress was one of the first courses of action that I took when I arrived in my current school – a school of almost 600 children – where there was no electronic tracking and more than 25 teaching staff. The operating systems available at the time were researched by the Deputy Head – in our school that is how we operate. We do the research before we spend the money and ensure that the product we are buying is fit for us; on this occasion it involved me resisting external pressure to get something in quickly, and also resisting my own urges to use what I was used to.

There are so many educational options and products out there, and everyone who is accustomed to their own standard operating procedures will wax lyrical about the ones that they use, so I always bring it back to what could work in our context, given our size, configuration, staffing, training needs etc. I also try to ensure that the activity of research and implementation is beneficial to both the individual and the organisation, creating a congruence that also facilitates staff professional development.

I had suggested to my Deputy that she should do the National Professional Qualification for Headteachers (NPQH), and quickly the assessment systems in school became the focus for her project. This was hugely beneficial to both her and our school, another way that we work. We bought a super new system when it was in its infancy; this has proven to be one of the best decisions for our school and has continued to evolve with us and our changing needs over time. What has also been key to the success of this programme, however, is the fact that we consistently apply the way that we work with one another as staff alongside the way that we work with the system. The people in our school enable the success of the system, and the way that the people work together is related to the culture and the shared expectations we have.

If I apply my logic to the performance management system in school, which is about managing people and appraising their impact on the organisation, I wonder if it is the macro-level system that makes this work, or the way it is enacted? I think I have been 'performance managed' so terribly in the past that it cannot be the macro-level, or else everyone would have an equally good experience of it, so it must be the individual school, and therefore the people. I should perhaps point out here that I see Performance Management as a different process from managing capability and competence – this is a different topic altogether and definitely for another day.

In our school, I eschew the performance management time frames of the government as they are farcical and have little connectivity to the natural cycle of annual school improvement. I have worked with successive (and progressive) governing bodies in both schools where I have been Headteacher in order to have my performance assessed in July – at the end of the academic year and in line with evaluations of the school development plan.

From there, because we as leaders know our schools inside and out at all times of the year (not just when Ofsted are due!), my targets are set for the following year based on what we want to work on and the strategic direction we are taking the school. With my targets set, I then create suggested targets for my staff, which I send them in advance in order to give them time to consider, adapt and amend if they wish to. I ask individuals to review their own progress against their current targets, and we meet in September to both review the previous year and also finalise the new targets for the academic year ahead.

I have usually collected and collated extra supporting information throughout the previous year, sharing this in the September meeting in full and ad hoc as they arrive to me, revelling collaboratively in the achievements of each one of the staff, be that letters from parents, emails from members of the public who see staff out on educational trips, thank you cards from other schools about the help they have given to colleagues etc. I also look at what they want to share and celebrate with me. It really is a huge highlight of the year. It is also productive; we discuss the future of each person, the direction their career is taking and could take, courses they could do, how we can support with funding or time for courses etc. It feels collaborative, supportive and celebratory. It isn't the system of performance management, but the people in our school who enact it, that makes it so effective.

Coaching at every level for systemic change

I met up with a group of educational buddies recently, and we were discussing this very point – but in the context of how I work on sustainability when change is the only certainty. Naturally, I talked about systems that we have in place to make sure that we future proof the organisation. Let me give you an example.

I explained in more detail what I said earlier; to reiterate: we have performance reviews annually, as most organisations do (some done better than others, as we know, before you roll your eyes at the page!), and ours are early September. These are informed by my performance review, done in July, and that in turn is informed by the evaluation of the needs of the school – assessed annually in the summer. The reviews that I conduct with staff are also mid-term appraised in February, and this gives us a chance to discuss barriers to achievement of the objectives of each staff member, and also celebrate the work done towards achieving them to date – in addition to all of the other value-added activity the person will no doubt have been busy doing.

For me they are a chance to connect on a 1:1 basis with people, to discuss much more than performance but vision – their career, their growth and what they are passionate about. Without fail during these meetings someone will surprise me with an idea or a quietly burning ambition, and I am usually quite sparked up and determined to see their idea to fruition by supporting their enthusiasm and making magic happen.

One of those people I have met with is a young aspiring leader with a very strong personality and a forceful way of delivering information. She came to her performance review, without me asking, with the most amazing portfolio of work that she had done. It was simply incredible. But she showed me it and was rattling through the information contained within it, promptly closing it over before I had time to absorb any of the information, saying that she was proud of her work. For me, it felt somewhat like a verbal assault, simply as a result of her delivery – which was a total shame because the content was magnificent. So I stopped her and asked her to pause whilst I looked at and enjoyed her work, the work that she had taken the time to create and bring to me and was proud of.

I read it and felt extremely proud for her and told her so, and then I had a tricky conversation with her that highlighted why she sometimes did not receive the kind of outcomes she hoped for, and that she wanted, from her colleagues. I gave her some strategies to slow down her thinking, to expand on her methods of eliciting the views of her team to make sure they felt valued and heard; I then suggested ideas of how she could synthesise her final plans as a result of the process – blending the thoughts of her team into something even better than her original seed of an idea whilst also moving forward apace with all members invested. I talked to her about applying what she would do with children – pause and allow them to think for example – and how she should employ those same strategies in her professional conduct with colleagues and be prepared to evaluate her success in this aspect of her leadership development through having a chat with me the following month. We discussed this as an element of leadership capacity and as a way of understanding her impact as an aspiring leader. Since then, she has commenced an apprenticeship in leadership in school and has had all of this reinforced by the academic.

It was fascinating. She wrote to me the following week thanking me for the conversation and telling me that she was so grateful for the opportunity to explore the ideas discussed, and also she had put the same strategies into her personal life already to huge success!

The group of educators listened to this exemplification, but one dissented – I am all for challenge and diversity of thought, so I was keen to hear their views. I believe that occasionally it is my job to work quickly, authoritatively and decisively. This more so in the military work I may do, but equally in the education settings where I work. Time sensitive and critical situations require quick thinking and commitment to my vision and plan. The vast majority of the time, however, I believe in coaching and constructive conversation. I want to show people divergent thinking and how not to be threatened by it, but to embrace it and all of the opportunities it can present as you evaluate solutions that had previously not even been thought of! I recognise that this method takes a little longer than just telling people what to do or transactional leadership, but in terms of capacity and sustainability – this is the way I prefer to work.

The dissenter challenged me directly and suggested that an innovator, a leader with strong ideas and creative passion, should be allowed to express themselves however they choose, and if others feel uncomfortable with the delivery, then essentially it was their issue to resolve – which I agree with to an extent. Equally, I believe that if you can avoid anyone having to waste time clearing up misunderstandings and making reparations to those they have offended inadvertently, then it is worth exploring that avenue from time to time to see if they prefer it as a strategy or to know when it may be wise to deploy it. We agreed to disagree and remain friends – it takes all sorts, and their way is their way, just as yours will be yours.

In examining other school systems, to try to test my theory, we have both formal and less formal systems of pupil inclusivity in their own growth. We buy a cohesive character education programme called Commando Joes to support our 'Social, Moral, Spiritual, and Cultural' (SMSC) development, but I like 'joined up thinking', also known as cohesive planning, and also proactivity – and try to model this at all times across school. When I talk to children in assembly, particularly those at the top end of our school, I talk to them about their legacy. I do not think it is too young for them to think of being role models, not just in our school to younger pupils but in the way we celebrate now, through Twitter and so on; it means they can be role models across the world if they desire. I ask them how they can start small in our school and to think about how they can build on that.

In the past that has involved children coming to ask me if they can raise money for charity, create and lead assemblies of their own (no mean feat in front of 400 other children!), create a school newspaper, an ethos group etc. Children are passionate about a lot of things, and these days more than ever they have voices that should be heard. The government ask them to do more in terms of academics at much younger stages in life than they would ever have in the past, it makes sense then that they would be able to assimilate information and articulate their views far earlier than perhaps they would have in the past. They should perhaps be afforded rights in school commensurate with the understanding and acceptance of their responsibilities in a future global society, therefore. If we are expecting them to engage with challenging concepts in primary school, such as democracy, violence against females and hate crimes, and if we want them to be constantly preparing for the next stage in their lives rather than enjoying the present, then it is perhaps important that the government learn to listen to what is being said (in a range of verbal and non-verbal ways) by our young people, and as such maybe we need to listen to them. This for another book, perhaps.

Equally, I think about the military and essential systems that keep the cogs turning. There are people trying to make informed and beneficial changes to the systems, keen to embrace the progressive cultural developments in our society and see them fully incorporated in what could be considered a traditionally male-dominated environment. So many committed individuals, keen to progress the development of military personnel within the huge multi-disciplinary machine, are what will change the systems and the narrative of the people coming through today. It is the cognitive dissonance between what the visionaries have known and what they see as the future that permits them to think creatively and make ripples of change.

I was so very privileged to be asked to talk at an event at the Army Foundation College (Harrogate) to more than 300 junior soldiers and staff about my experiences as a 'woman in defence', I identify as female by the way, so wasn't offended by the title. I was asked there by the forward-thinking CO, Lt Col Simon, and was able to share some of my life experiences as well as the military journey I have been on and how the two things have worked in my favour, not too dissimilar to this book. I felt a profound sense of being part of a systemic change narrative at grass roots level when I said to a mixed audience, but to a majority of impressionable, female junior soldiers,

> I want to tell you that you will be surrounded by strong female role models now, some of whom you will hear from today, because in 40 years things have moved on and in the military more so than ever (even if there is further work to be done). I want to remind you that when you can see it, you can be it – so look around you to the women in uniform that you can emulate and who you can learn from.
>
> I say this because one day, 20 or 30 years from now, you may be stood in front of a group of young soldiers and you will be talking to them of your

experiences and how they have shaped you as a human being, your career as a professional solider and potentially beyond. You will be considering where you began, here at the Army Foundation College, and each of the key events that led you to that moment in time in the future.

These will be the people who change the systems of the future.

I have no idea if it will make any difference to any of those who heard the talk, but what mattered was the intent of the person who had the vision and brought together the speakers. It is always people who effect change, and change is inevitable. We can each be, at times and within the constraints of our role, orchestrators of change or actors within it, and how we choose to react to it can create either magic or catastrophe. As Ken Robinson illustrated, shift does happen, reform is constant.

The 'what' can change, the 'how' maybe not so much

In such a big school now, I have the luxury of a large and diverse senior leadership team. What I do now is different to what I did before in my last school, which was a third the size, but how I do it is similar, again, to how I am in my military and academic roles, and my personal life.

Firstly, I look for the spark of passions in people that can be encouraged into flames. I look for skills that are emerging and need coaching or training to become matured and embedded; I look for talent – it's really that simple.

I don't worry about prickly bits, or personality 'edges' too much, especially not in those with little or no experience. Usually those edges are sanded off by the daily grind of life experience, and any kind of gentle polish can usually be added later through self-reflection and absorbing other ways of doing things.

All teachers who come to work in a school are equally qualified; when you arrive at a school and inherit a team, they may have been through a meat grinder, or they may have been blessed and lived in halcyon times – they will behave differently for you than they did your predecessor, simply because you are not your predecessor, and you change the dynamic! When I am appointing new teachers, I just look for those who look to engage with the human side of themselves, and I then have faith that good humans can usually become good leaders, and then the systems we implement will sort themselves out.

Secondly, I have a goal in mind – a big map, that I point to with my small hand. I share that end goal with the team, and I explain the part each of us will play. I suggest opportunities and constraints that I have observed and ask them to consider those I may have overlooked or am ignorant about through newness or lack of specialist knowledge. From there, we devise a system, and usually this involves going outside of our organisation and asking others what they use and if we can compare our practice – taking care to be cognisant of contextual nuance before making our final decision.

Thirdly, having devised the system as a collective. We create time to implement it and then build time in to consolidate the use of and evaluation of the system, monitoring the curriculum, moderating writing, tracking, whatever it is, it goes through the same process and the outcomes are always the same. The majority of the staff implement the system as per the agreed parameters; a minority are unable to without support from the team, not the senior leaders necessarily, but their colleagues, in order to be able to implement the system in the same way as those who they work alongside for parity. We review it, as part of the revisiting of initiatives that also form a systemic part of how we work, and then we iron out misconceptions, errors in original thinking, or problems that have arisen that we did not foresee, and we make the system better. Relentless attention to detail, lack of complacency and determination to do the best we can with what we have is what underpins our work.

The system, whichever one we are looking at, now working effectively, gives us the product we need, serving the purpose of the original brief and supporting an essential aspect of organisational life, which is the fourth piece of the cycle. If it no longer supports something essential, and even with modification it is unable to, then it is not retained as a system. Staff know this. We all embrace the collective ethos and work towards the common goals and outcomes, and part of that is being honest about the efficacy of a particular product or strategy that we have created and seeing it for what it may have become – defunct and not fit for purpose. We never discard anything that has value, intrinsic or explicit, to children, their families or our staff, only that which does not add value, or save us valuable time.

How can we judge if we are getting it right?

I never expected to have to test my theory on people versus systems, yet I have done so on four separate occasions so far, in two different schools. In the school where I completed my first headship, I had a bilateral mastectomy which required me to take some time off to recover. In the years preceding that surgery, which was the longest period of absence I had taken since starting any kind of work at 16, we had indeed worked on systems in school – those that supported distributed leadership, those that facilitated parental engagement and also expectations of parental and pupil behaviour, those that enabled the rigorous monitoring of educational standards and so on. My two Assistant Headteachers (AHTs) at the time (Cath and Kev), both extremely capable, dynamic, fast-thinking and skilled individuals, were rightly apprehensive about me being off for 12–14 weeks, and I was, too. As a control freak, and someone not accustomed to sitting around, I was pretty anxious about it to say the least.

None of us needed to have been! They were absolutely brilliant, on every level, in every respect, supported by a very able and committed Governing Body. One of the AHTs even quipped that they had made a few decisions because they knew that I would have made those decisions as we worked so closely together and our values were aligned. Some time later, when I needed additional surgery, the remaining AHT took it all in their stride and was totally unflappable (one had left for a promoted post). Knowing that I could leave school in capable hands and knowing that our systems were such that they had empowered staff who professed to never want to be Headteachers was incredible. That AHT covered my secondment to the school where I work now and actually became substantive Headteacher on the basis of their merits and the way they had demonstrated their skill set in the time when they acted as Head in my absence. That is succession at its finest.

Similarly, in my current school, in order to be able to attend Royal Military Academy Sandhurst (RMAS) recently, in order to complete the commissioning process as an officer in the British Army Reserves, I needed to take three weeks out of school, and my Deputy Head Teacher, Sharon, who has been at the school for many years and is not only extremely competent but also well-liked and respected, covered my special leave of absence.

She had completed her NPQH, worked alongside me for three years, and made all decisions together with me, so she was well versed in the multiple layers of complexity we work with across so many different facets of our large school. She was brilliant in my absence and was able to put many aspects of her theoretical training into practice during those three weeks of real responsibility and accountability – at a time when we were expecting Ofsted!

Some would call my absence at such a time foolhardy, or plain old professional suicide – if Ofsted had arrived to our school, which was in its second Requires Improvement (RI) judgement cycle, while I was not there, and they had given us a bad report, then the blame could have been laid firmly at my feet. Yes, this was a risk, but a calculated one (remember calculated risk in the previously chapter?). I assessed the situation and was satisfied that the systems in our school were so effective, the people working in our school used to operating in a high stress and yet emotionally healthy and supportive setting, with shared vision gluing them together, that Ofsted would see that, witness the authenticity and even if I was not there, the systems and the people running them would still work. Risky, and some would argue arrogant, but I choose to believe that this demonstrates the faith that I have in the people I work with, and their professional excellence, as it did my Governors' belief in my leadership.

Why people are key change drivers

If we focus on the people whom we work alongside, those we serve as leaders, and consider their traits, drivers, skills, and fears in a holistic way, we can truly engage them in organisational transformation. It is possible. I believe that it is more important to do this, in terms of reflective school improvement, than anything else. To arrive at this point though, you need the processes, discussed in previous chapters, firmly embedded in your organisational systems and standard operating procedures. Some of those processes begin and are nurtured in their infancy in very early stages of career development when leaders don't even realise they are gaining the skills they will need – when leaving secondary education, for example, or engaging in a degree, or specific training, as I have discussed earlier. This means that we have a duty of care at any point in supporting future educational professionals to acquire the foundations of the skills they will need for the long term.

This methodology, essentially based on collaboration and coaching, having honest and supportive conversations, is not necessarily conducive to short-term results, which can be a battle in the school improvement discourse, but harnessing individual aspirations alongside generating 'shared values' and whole school vision will remove any barriers to collective participation in creating positive systems that create beneficial outcomes for *all* stakeholders.

Imagine if organisations linked to the government, with a vested interest in school improvement, could change the rhetoric around what it is to be a 'good' school? If they could begin a seed change on the understanding of what it takes for leaders in disadvantaged areas, or those taking on schools in difficulty, to be able to turn around the fortunes of those establishments and retain their own mental health and that of the people working with them – for the long term?

Imagine if the larger 'meta-systems' that our small cogs fit into were able to be changed by one voice, or a small group of voices collectively calling for this change and actively working towards it? I think there are organisations out there to support educators in effecting change, and I believe that it will be people, those who are a part of the system, that will change it in the end – not external actors and accountability instruments. For change to be embedded and lived, it needs to come from within.

Most school transformations focus on increasing accountability metrics, which (at best) offer short-term solutions, and often come with the by-products of high levels of burn out through staff working in unsustainable ways. This has been cited as the cause of shortages in education for decades; there are less people willing to work in the factory of education as the accountability infrastructure becomes increasingly suffocating. In fact, through leading with love and compassion, as detailed throughout this book, both individual and also 'hive' mindset can be changed for the longer term, but this takes a degree of bravery from leaders at all levels. It takes us giving agency to all members of our staff body so they are empowered.

We will rehearse this narrative often in school. I will often remind staff who are asking me questions that they may have forgotten the answer to that 'the answer always starts with "In our school"'. We have to acquiesce to the expectations of the government of the day in terms of curriculum content, assessments, inspections and so on; *how* we do so is our own affair. We can waste valuable time lamenting the injustices of such a futile system, or accept it and choose to focus on the everyday genius that we are generating.

Staff will come to realise eventually, if the same reassuring story is repeated, that satisfying external agencies may bring the short-term results, may keep the inspectorate at bay for a while, but in co-creating and then sharing the narrative and doing so through the systems of your school, and explicitly understanding all aspects of it, they will be engaged, find a new level of mental energy and have the capacity to create enduring intrinsic results. It is then, when staff feel able, that they themselves can be instruments of change.

Unless, as a leader, you are able to identify both your own mindset and that of others (those that are limiting and also enabling your vision to be realised), your improvement initiatives, both in system and people spaces, may simply be a waste of human and physical resources. You can only work on altering states of mind and systems through consistent behaviour and commonly understood values-based actions. This involves having difficult conversations to both establish and reinforce expectations, and this naturally involves respectful honesty.

What has all of this to do with leading with love, with you?

You will be familiar with the summary by now, but the point is:

- As a leader you have to think about capacity and sustainability (which means that you can . . .)

- Ensure that your legacy continues after you leave. You must take your time to get to know your school and staff (because . . .)

- In knowing yourself, and them, you can work effectively together to make long-term systemic changes (because . . .)

- It takes time to build positive relationships; the resulting relational exchanges are what influences organisational systemic change the most (also . . .)

- In working with the people first, and empowering them, not only do your systems take care of themselves, but the people you work with are happy to run those systems effectively, thus sustaining high levels of 'buy in' and morale (to make the best team you can).

Further reading/listening

If you like a podcast and 'people centred' is something you want to know more about in terms of leadership:

1. Brenee Brown: Unlocking Us. https://tinyurl.com/Unlocking-Us
2. The Tony Robbins Podcast. https://tinyurl.com/Tony-Robbins-Pod
3. Sir Ken Robinson: Changing Education Paradigms. https://tinyurl.com/Robinson-TED

If you like a book and want to get the best potential out of your team in a number of levels:

1. Hanley, Kate (2018). *How to Be a Better Person: 400+ Simple Ways to Make a Difference in Yourself – And the World.* Adams Media. ISBN: 978-1507205266.
2. Moore, Rob (2019). *Start Now: Get Perfect Later.* John Murray Learning. ISBN: 978-1473685451.
3. Rees, Tom and Oliver Caviglioli (2018). *Wholesome Leadership: The Heart, Head, Hands & Health of School Leaders.* John Catt Educational Ltd. ISBN: 978-1911382706.
4. Hilton, James (2020). *Riding the Waves: Finding Joy and Fulfilment in School Leadership. Bloomsbury Education.* ISBN: 978-1472967992.
5. Morrish, Andrew (2016). *The Art of Standing Out: School Transformation, to Greatness and Beyond.* John Catt Educational Ltd. ISBN: 978-1909717831.
6. Waters, Steve (2021). *Cultures of Staff Wellbeing and Mental Health in Schools: Reflecting on Positive Case Studies.* Oxford University Press. ISBN: 978-0335248896.

If you want to go fast, go alone; if you want to go far, go together

Even introverts can be outward facing

I am the same with everyone that I know, and even those I do not know. I can laugh and joke, chat to and banter with people at train stations, men in red shorts in bars, couples that I meet on the beach – everyone and anyone gets my time and my attention. In work I interact with student teachers, colonels, generals, cleaners, captains, soldiers, chefs, parents and children and am always keen to know how they are and be a listening ear if they need one. As a neighbour I go out of my way to offer help and support in times of illness or incapacity, or even if I can just do a good deed like drop off freshly laid eggs from the chickens, or Sunday lunch. I have evolved into the person I am now. I know that I am someone who is kind and caring, compassionate and authentic. I like myself – finally. I travel alone and feel like an adventurer rather than a 'saddo' with no mates. I am as happy to have dinner alone as with a friend, so here is the thing: even though I am the same with everyone, even though I am genuinely outgoing and friendly, and people think I am a party animal, I actually have another side to me. The introvert. Yup. True story.

I am quite content on my own. I am. I find a lot of energy restoration takes place when I am simply 'contemplating', either walking or running, on the beach or in the hills and, failing that, on the roads and through the woods where I live. I love the safety and harmony of my house and the peace it creates in all who come here – not one person who has ever set foot inside my house disagrees – it is a sanctuary (well, a sanctuary of pushbikes, books, dog paraphernalia, sports kit and other ephemera). I do not fear living alone and quite enjoy my own company, and I find that I am at ease in solitude. Many of the sports I enjoy are, or could be, solo endeavours, and I do enjoy reading, which, unless it is with children or random Royal Marines, is usually a solo activity, too. I can do most things on my own – gardening, planning for home improvements, measurements, basic DIY, decorating, lifting and shifting. I generally ask for help and support on very rare

DOI: 10.4324/9781003281313-16

occasions, usually only when I am physically incapable of doing it myself, and on an existential plane, this could be both a good and a bad thing.

I wonder to what degree that this was always in me; perhaps the generation who are no longer here could tell me if I was always predisposed to do things on my own, I am not sure. I do know that when I was married, in view of my ex-husband's job, I was often on my own for prolonged periods, and I was able to function because I had strategies for coping, so I must have learned how to do so at some point in the past. This, if anything, gives the starkest indicator to me that if I am alone, then I can work very quickly and accomplish a lot. In the absence of my husband, when I was married, and the absence of a partner since, I have been able to complete a significant amount of study, work in a relentless way in school, and take on additional roles in university and the Army Reserves. If I had a partner, then the time devoted to these endeavours would likely have been shared with, if not devoted to, them.

In recent years I have made the difficult but conscious decision to begin to allow other people into my life, to spend time with me and be absorbed into my personal space – something that I have guarded so carefully for the longest of times. Some of you reading this will already know what I am like, a tough cookie, or an ice maiden on the surface – when in reality nothing could be further from the truth, as you will also know if I have let you into my home and you have therefore met my children and could make judgements about me based on how I live. I am not an ice queen. I am just guarded about the spaces where I feel safest: my home and my heart. This has led to some quite painful experiences, trust me, and an awful lot of learning about myself and how I like to operate in the space in which I feel most comfortable – in so doing, I have also been able to identify the outside limits of that zone and the reasons for not liking to stray out there.

Work out where to find the edge of comfort

None of this has been easy, and none of it has come without a significant amount of heart ache and angst. I am contacted on Twitter from time to time by people who see posts I share, usually random interesting quotes or pieces of poetry, and they will tell me that there was a message in that post for them, that it resonated. I know that although I am alone, I am also not – there are many of us, all ages and ethnicities, genders and backgrounds, coming to terms with our emotional constipation, and yet none of this is usually expressed or spoken of publicly, especially by the successful. I don't class my personal growth as a mental health issue, but there is always the possibility that someone surviving life's threshing floor is developing one, or surviving whilst also carrying one.

Locking myself away personally may have facilitated a huge gain in qualifications, but other than that, it hasn't really helped me develop my ability to interact. It may have protected my heart from being hurt, but it hasn't stopped me from feeling sad. Stark lesson.

As I have already said, once I have identified lessons from my personal life, I am usually applying a similar lens onto my professional life to see if the same traits have hindered me or enhanced my practice, thus giving me insights into how and where I am most comfortable, and what work I must do on myself to exist more around the edges of that zone, in order to effect personal *and* professional growth. I like to be rounded and tackle myself in a holistic way.

If I had behaved through the years in my work as I have done my private life, then I can 100% guarantee that I would not be as successful now as I feel that I am, and other people tell me that I am. In any way. That is because I have chosen to lock myself away and study, protect myself from the possibility of being hurt, and not engage with many people who may have wanted to share my life – I know, leave the most shocking revelation to the almost penultimate chapter of the book! I have created so many barriers to people 'getting in' that not even Prince Charming, looking like Channing Tatum with James Bond's jet pack, could breach the walls!

Good news, though! I think.

Permit the epiphany!

Firstly, this has all changed. During the pandemic I had an epiphany. This may seem more than a random thing to say, after all, the Covid-19 measures simply served to legitimise my self-imposed preferred 'self-isolated' state, surely? Something strange happened, however, that was essentially the catalyst for several things, including this book and many podcasts that I have done, and that was that people connected more on social media – they had to, and many of them chose to connect with me.

In so doing, I was suddenly being asked for my opinion on a range of topics, and as you may have noticed, I usually just say it how it is, and often say the first thing that comes into my head (this has at times rendered me no better than a social hand grenade because I have an incorrigible sense of humour, also ask *way* too many questions and can overshare somewhat!). Anyway, people seemed to like what I was saying, surprisingly because I say the same things over and again, and seemed to like my connectivity and compassion with others. Therefore, from the safety of my home, I grew and grew as a person upon seeing reflected back to me the idea that there were other people out there who were similar.

I found my social anxiety at being with others and feeling ugly, or boring, or unattractive, or not good enough (controlled only by my strength of will at times and by not wanting to let others down if I had agreed to go out) begin to diminish. Who knows why, but the trigger was definitely around that time – perhaps more reflection may bring me the answers. I do know that on the back of this my very good friend Adam (also known as 'Tiny' – in view of his 6'9″ stature – typical British sarcasm and humour) also insisted that we go out and celebrate some of the brilliant things that had happened to me, that I had simply let pass me by, because he was so pleased for and proud of me. Thus, I went on my first night out in Liverpool.

There will be some readers actually scandalised by this revelation. I, at my age, having not been on a night out in Liverpool when I have lived 20 minutes from the place for the last 13 years. Imagine.

Find the small steps and bravely take them – even if you are holding the hand of someone else

Adam managed to work around my usual modus operandi and called me two days beforehand, telling me it was my Warning Order. He said that he would be collecting me at a certain time, that I had two days to select my outfit (I am notorious for not doing this until the last minute and then utterly freaking out), and he knew I would be trying to think of excuses not to go out so I shouldn't even try to give him any because he was taking none of it. He told me where we were going and talked me through the whole thing in so far as he could.

I realise that it makes me sound pathetic, and I do actually know that I am, but it worked. I was beside myself with stress about the outfit, but my beautiful daughter helped me pick it, my lovely mate collected me, the lack of crowds and imposed table service at the bars we went to meant I was absolutely fine and, get this, it was past 1 AM before I suddenly felt the need to leave and go home. The only time I was even a little bit anxious was when we left the bar and suddenly there were a lot of people, both revellers and police, on the streets. Tiny just told me to walk behind him, which I did, and we were in a cab and on our way home faster than you could say 'Taxi!' I had an amazing time and another light bulb moment.

I may have been the answer to Adam's prayers when he was struggling to deal with his personal issues, and been an amazing friend to him, signposting him towards our local rugby club to create a 'surrogate' family for him of more sensible people for him to hang out with (lots of single young men his age, for example!) as he tells me. I may have been the enabler that my sister Sarah thinks I am, and brought him and the place where he would find friends for life together, but only because he listened to me. He grew confidence over time as we met and had very civilised old lady coffees over the months, and I coached him through one transition after another. Because he listened to me, and found confidence in himself, he stepped outside his comfort zone and went to the rugby – without me to hand hold and introduce him. He introduced himself, not really too tricky as everyone's eyes were drawn to his diminutive 6'9" stature and nobody saw a role for him on the second team at all . . . ! (If you know rugby, you know that he will have been immediately roped in as one of the scrum 'engines'). Despite never having played rugby in his life, he has become an established member of the club and a well-loved member of the gang.

Equally, he may have been just the nudge that I needed when I was ready to receive it. I have never looked back, and although the feelings of anxiety remain,

I have been agreeing to more social events and planning ahead, and actually enjoying myself in a way that I never thought I could, with other people.

I know that I have been a source of disappointment to my children, and many a friend and partner over the years, with my lack of desire to go out to go shopping in the city (or at all!), to go to crowded places, and the fuss I have made of what to wear and how I look – I am pretty mortified about it now to be honest, but no more. Tiny broke the duck for me, for which I am eternally grateful, as is my daughter who finally, at 17, has a shopping buddy (*occasionally*, let's not get carried away!).

Secondly, I am much more able to see this trait and its damaging effects in others. I have a friend who (for reasons best known to himself) shuts himself off from any kind of love, affection and happiness. He exists alone nearly all of the time except when in work. He chooses to holiday alone. He chooses to spend Christmas and birthdays alone. He will experience such piercing moments of elation and contentment, which cause him to feel utterly wracked with guilt, that he cannot cope. He thinks himself unworthy and undeserving of such joy because he has fallen short of the constructed and largely false expectations of others – including himself.

As I have grown and been involved in the messy process of 'growth', I have hoped that he would see it in me, as one of his biggest advocates and someone who loves him unconditionally, and start to give himself agency and licence to grow himself. This has not been the case. He listens to what I say but does not hear. He perpetuates a rotation of sadness and sorrow; rather than try to break the destructive and self-sabotaging cycle, he refuses, and therefore remains tortured. Who am I to say anything about these choices, other than – it really does not need to be this way? What I know is that others must have been as frustrated with me over the years as I have been and am with him. When we know what another person has to give, the wonder that is a particular human being and the presence that they have, we want them to share it, and we want to be a part of it with them. But, we all have to be ready to receive the concept of change at a time when we are prepared and have the courage to engage with the blinking hard work of it.

Maybe we are simply better alone?

Sometimes we are better on our own. We can work quickly, come up with good ideas, or rejuvenate our energies, feed our minds, or just switch off. This is a truism, and despite any personal or professional development I have experienced, it remains the case that I need time alone to recoup energy.

But sometimes our friends, in work or at home, see in us what we miss ourselves. They see our gifts, our skills sets, where we can excel, how we can improve. They know what we need to do in order to effect growth and push on, even with something so seemingly insignificant as a night out, or a shopping trip, and if we resist forever, we are doing ourselves a disservice that may permanently affect us and our relationships with others. We absolutely need those invested in us to tell us these things, but we equally need to be open to receiving the messages. We need to surround ourselves with people whom we trust to tell us unpleasantries about ourselves, those brutal truths none of us want to hear, and then take the support they offer to make the necessary changes. It is exactly the same in the personal as it is the professional domain.

And maybe we are not better off alone . . .

One of the most beautiful souls I have met, Anne Marie (I have spoken of her before), had the difficult job of being my Chair of Governors in the early days of my first headship. She knew me in my rough diamond mode, when I was really rough and learning my trade. For her, it must have been like trying to work with a thunderstorm, and I must remember to give her a hug and apologise when I next see her, because she certainly had to give me brutal truths on a professional level as she does a personal one.

I am passionate and driven, you may have picked this up, and have a busy mind and a physically active persona. As a new Head I had yet to master these things to any degree and felt, perhaps as I did when having children, that through sheer force of character and passion I would be able to get things done properly and serve the children we worked with in the best possible way. I was able to restrain myself from dragging staff with me if I had a new way of working, in part largely thanks to Cath and Kev who were my exceptional assistant heads and managed to remind me of the details when I came up with the grand plans. We complemented one another so that the blunt instrument of me was refined by their situational awareness and knowledge of the ground in general. But what I had yet to master at that time was my 'frustrations', shall we say, with politics and injustice.

This led me to a decision that I took to send an email, which was the same as poking a huge and angry wasps nest with a large stick and standing there with maple syrup all over me.

Anne Marie not only advised me that my heart, which was my biggest strength, was also my greatest weakness (correct), but also supported me through the shocking few months that followed where I inevitably lived through my reprimand (relieved however that I had also taken one for the team and the email saw fruition for our school). Her guidance and support and her suggestions for my professional development were instrumental in me making sure that I never made or make the same mistake twice and that I flourished. Proof, as if it were necessary, that we need a team. The old adage *no man is an island* is so true; no woman is either, not if they want to be the best versions of themselves.

The work of educational leaders is and has always been a complex, nebulous business. I can imagine if you are reading this now (and you are one) that you are throwing your hands up and shrugging, 'tell us something we don't know' – if you are not in education then let me state the obvious: educational leadership involves so much more than the public understand. Society moves apace, and we are expected to serve not just the school and its community, but also the external political narrative, and create the workers of the future that the government of the day have decided the future needs based on funding models of the last century – thus informing the diet of education that we offer the children in our care and the support on offer to them from outside agencies.

The role of a school leader now is more than teaching (if it involves teaching at all) as there is so much bureaucracy, although there are some poor souls who must do the job of leading and teaching simultaneously, and for them I have nothing other than respect – more on this in the next chapter. Educational leadership is about establishing relationships, through creating a culture, based on not just the systems of administration and operational integrity but also real time complex decision-making based on long-term strategy affected by national political agendas. Let that sit in your mind for minute. Not only a mouthful to think, to write and to say out loud, but imagine trying to create it without a magic wand and with no money . . .

Right?

This, by the way, in a context of daily management of multiple personalities, emotional transactions, Health and Safety/building maintenance, multiple 'moving parts' and conflicting stakeholder views and priorities, whilst also responding to constantly developing personal circumstances in staff, parents and pupils, against a backdrop of political tug of war because we all know that 'education' is contested by one government after the other with what the opposition believe.

It is not possible to do this role alone and survive for long. You need to turn to those in your team in the first instance. This involves all of the things I have talked about in the previous chapters and all of those in a nuanced and individual way that suits you, the school and the context in which you are working. But one thing is for certain: you must turn to them. You cannot work quickly or alone in a school and expect results.

You must work out between you what you are not doing that you could or should be doing to enhance your workplace – you may be shocked at what I am about to say but here it is anyway – in terms of things like leaving on time or (heaven forbid) early, in terms of eating lunch, or not checking work emails after a certain point. Then working out the nuts and bolts of the job, the curriculum you want to teach and why, how you will teach it and why, what training you need and why, what purposes will it serve and who will it benefit, how you can minimise time wasted by staff and maximise time put in by staff for optimal results for children. Working out affordability and budget management, sustainability and distribution of resources for maximal gain. You need to assess how to share information, what information to share, whether you can store or share information and how you manage staff time to do so. There are a million decisions and even more outcomes of those decisions that you must realise before making them – on a daily basis. If everyone in your team, be that large or small, is working on the same goals, looking out for one another, trusting one another and supporting one another to be better, then you will go far. I can only say this from my own experience. This has worked for me now for almost 10 years in two very different and complex schools in diference circumstances in what reductionist rhetoric would label 'deprived areas'.

Building a team to drive you forward

People go far when they work in a team, and this involves trust and belief. When this hasn't been the case it is obvious, as obvious as when it is the case.

But what of those leaders who still lead in an autocratic way? Who still want to control everything and micro-manage (don't be shocked they still exist even now)? I don't know. I am not one and do not work for one, so it is difficult for me to discuss this. I have worked for people like this; the workplace has been toxic, created ill-health and ill-feeling amongst colleagues, destroyed careers and lives. If you think you may be one of these people, my advice would be to get a coach and talk through why in the first instance and try to rectify the issues you may find in your own practice in the second instance – and good luck developing your growing self-awareness.

Team building is such a complex business though, isn't it? We may arrive in a school to a team that has been formed, in whatever way, by a predecessor. They will have had their own way of doing things and sometimes that way is not congruent with your way. The first job is to politely and professionally begin to change the way things are done without being disrespectful to the person who has gone before, and this can be like an odd kind of dance where you must give and take a little as the new relationship foundations are being formed.

The best way that I have found of doing this is to simply give the rationale for the changes that are made, keeping the personal out of it. Ask for ideas to solve a problem that has been identified, and involve the team in working on the solution in a manner conducive to how it will be from then on under your leadership. Try not to criticise but instead model how it is you want things done and why.

This can take time, and being a diva or a bit like a bull in a China shop may well not be the best approach. Sometimes I have had to give myself a serious amount of self-talk in order to go a little slower, to enable others to keep up, or to enable them to create the ideas that will drive our relationship forward, and thus forge the strategic direction of the organisation. If people you work with see that there is a positive outcome to what you want to achieve, and the way you want to achieve it, or even smaller positive 'stepping stones', then they are more likely to buy in. If they see that you are just going ahead on your own, more of a tactical bound ahead, shouting 'follow me!' rather than encouraging people from beside or behind you, then they will begin to fall behind and lose momentum. Worse still, they will feel inadequate as they see you charge ahead and compare themselves as not as quick, intelligent and agile, and you will lose respect.

My natural predisposition in things, or so I learned many moons ago, is *impatience*, mainly because my brain works quickly all the time, and *perfection*. I want things to be right, to be done correctly, to be done quickly. This is easy in tasks that do not involve other people, of course, if you are alone. It takes considerable training yourself out of this mindset to work well with others. If you want to go fast then, yes, do things alone. In a team environment, this speed and professional aggression will be your undoing though, because by steaming ahead of your team, you will have no back up, no support. This is where listening to key members of your team and fostering that open dialogue, those lines of communication that keep you as a leader grounded, is so vital.

To go forward as a force, then you must work as a team and be prepared to listen to members of the team who would caution you against speed vice detail and potential hazards or risks. Genuinely, the greatest example of this outside of the education world in which I spend the vast part of my existence is something in the Army call 'Advance to Contact' – which, although I have never done it in real conflict, can be done in 'pairs fire and manoeuvre'. This is where two pairs of soldiers will move forward providing covering fire for one another, each pair communicating together and with the other pair all the way. It is slower than perhaps the fastest of the four running on ahead and opening fire on the enemy, but it means that all four are much safer, and four people are all firing in a concentrated effort, rather than the single one who is ahead but with no back up. I have probably scandalised my military friends with such an oversimplified description of this, but essentially, four all working together is better than one superspeedy person forging ahead.

If we accept that team building (that building a team that *works well* to be more specific) is an important method of improving the overall way that the organisation functions, then building an effective team must also be linked to the creation of not just the physical but the psychological climate in which the team operates. This is really too crucial to leave to chance, and therefore many aspiring leaders, or those taking on a challenging environment or starting from scratch, turn to literature – look for the 'how to'.

There is, of course, much extant literature on building teams across many disciplines, in education, and in educational leadership, and that research is situated within a range of conceptual, methodological and applied domains – each of which has the potential to advance theory within the leadership field with more research that is current and focuses on the new and emerging challenges that we face that were not evident 10, 20, even 5 years ago. The problem is, however, lack of any firm conclusions about what constitutes effective team building, and the possibility of a good team being influenced or affected by several uncontrolled aspects of an organisation have left many practitioners feeling overwhelmed at the choices available to them in terms of which is the best fit model for their own setting.

If you were to ask any school leader, in any phase of education and any kind of setting, they will have undoubtedly read a book about leadership in the hopes that it will give them the handrail to being able to successfully do what others have done before them. It is like searching for the Holy Grail because there are too many moving parts in education to find a one-size-fits-all solution, and some of those 'moving parts' are actually inherent in you (whether you realise them or not).

I personally came to the research aspect of leadership long after I had been practicing it, and thus, again, much of my knowledge is practice (mistake) based, so please remember the caveat – this is my take on it all, and based on my experiences (both good and bad).

Be clear on expectations

For me, key components of team building start with emphasising the necessity of the role you are asking someone to fill, clarification of the expectations and demands of that role, effective goal setting, cyclical periods of 1:1 time to 'progress check' and give authentic positive feedback, effective interpersonal relations that create a conduit for information from both leader and follower, and ensuring effective lines of communication the larger the team grows. Essentially, choosing the right person, for the right role, explaining this to them and supporting them to do it – good recruitment and performance management!

Sounds like a piece of cake, I am sure. Understanding this apparently simple metric, however, involves any leader expanding their mindset to understand that the scope of team-building strategies extends far deeper than simple group cohesion activities planned for In Service Training (INSET) days, or weekly staff meetings with cake and tea (although these are MOST welcome additions to the week). It is the relentless and daily attention to detail, constant modelling of expectations and behaviours, the positive and supportive relationships you build, the love you share by letting others see that you are as imperfect and human as they are and trying all the time that matters in a team.

I think that team building has the greatest potential for improving employee perceptions, workplace attitudes and most importantly the behaviour of individuals within the organisation – all of this inevitably leads to organisational effectiveness (or ineffectiveness). Each member of the team has their own specific role to play, but each member of the team has a collaborative role to play in the decision making and shaping of the direction of travel. If you are recruiting, then naturally this is huge and has lasting repercussions.

If you want your organisation to go far, empower individuals, give them the opportunity (if you can) to work within your organisation as a member of a team, but make sure their roles are clear and they are rewarded or congratulated appropriately. That is as sophisticated as it gets.

I focus, in my three-form entry school, on teacher teams led by subject matter experts, and I enhance the ability and credibility of those leaders to ensure that they are a lever for change. I expect them to challenge me and one another, to support one another in terms of outcomes and consistency and to achieve the organisational main effort – whatever that is in a given year or for a specific project. I want challenge and someone I trust to tell me about my blind spots, my areas of weakness, how I can best develop myself, and in doing so I work with people who ask me for the same in return.

If I were autonomous, if I were closed off and unresponsive to the perceptive and sage advice of my school friends, as I have mortifyingly been in relation to my family and friends in my personal life at times, then I would never have been able to create the amazing teams of people that I have and am lucky enough to work with. Only by trusting others, having professional respect for them and permitting them professional agency have I been able to harness their energy, and we have pushed the school improvement narrative hard and fast to great collective success.

There are so many obstacles to effective team building, including, but definitely not limited to, budget constraints and endless national cuts, or reforms which inevitably mean new formulae for this that and the other; unions and militancy, teacher knowledge and training – something currently being contested nationally; teacher fatigue and dedication; communication and team function – something that can change overnight in some situations; capacity and sustainability that you really do not want to be another barrier – nobody needs a dictatorial and micromanaging leader who doesn't listen or grow and likes to work within their pre-established comfort zone.

Exceptional leaders build an internal network of diverse and committed people. They build a team and where appropriate are actively involved as members of other people's teams, which we will talk about in the next chapter. At times I have got this totally wrong, by the way; or I have got it totally right for the time it was needed, but some people I have employed have not grown with the organisation, and as the organisation has matured and evolved, it has become apparent that they no longer align with the values. I have learned not to take this personally, but it has been a steep learning curve. This is where the personal and professional lessons overlap again for me.

Sometimes we have to 'let people go' in both a practical and emotional sense. As leaders we are often not immune to human relationships (as much as it may appear that we are!), and we can build paternal/maternal bonds with colleagues that are very strong. The nurturing that comes from being a leader can sometimes cloud the decision-making process when someone evidently has slowed in terms of their enthusiasm for school or for us. This can be a short-term fix, fatigue or a personal issue that is negatively impacting on engagement or performance, and sometimes a longer term and more profound issue. The only way to maintain the health of the team as a whole is to manage this, as unpleasant as it sounds, with effective and honest conversation, and sometimes difficult and painful action.

Is there any difference in our personal lives? I think not.

Exceptional leaders are kind and generous with their time but move on if they are not valued – accepting that some things are time limited and that is okay. They know when the right time is to move on – it can almost be like Nanny McPhee, because the business of leadership is about creating a legacy of sustainability. Creating capacity in others to do the job you are doing, making yourself in effect 'redundant', is part of succession planning and is healthy. Each of us knows when this time has come, and we survey the team and just know, as parents also do, I am learning. When it is time to let go, because your job has been done and done well, you will know. The beauty then is that you know your legacy will be in what your team propagate after you have gone. Three times in recent months I have been told in completely random ways that ex colleagues of mine have said to others, and it has travelled back to me, that they know that they would never be where they are now had it not been for me and my leadership. If that doesn't take the wind out of you and leave you blubbering, then I don't know what will!

Professional jealousy – the undoing of any effective team

One final observation about creating and leading a team, moving far with that team because they are a team, is that it is important as a leader never to be jealous of others. If people in the team support shared organisational and therefore personal values, then good leaders raise them up! If those people are different, good leaders will celebrate what it is about them that complements the leaders' strengths and mitigates for their weaknesses. This involves the leader actually knowing what their strengths and weaknesses are, as discussed in very early chapters, 'owning' them, and not being afraid to share them, as self-reflections, with their team – model this, and it gives agency to team members, allowing them to reflect on themselves without censure. It is in this that the leader has the most power almost, not over others, but in giving others power of knowledge of themselves.

What has all of this to do with leading with love, with you?

The main point of this chapter is:

- You can't lead in isolation without followers, who naturally become your team as you build relationships on trust (which means that you can . . .)

- Co-create the team to make up for any skill and knowledge deficits, and also plan for sustainability (because . . .)

- You will not be there forever and sustainability matters (because . . .)

- Opportunities are always coming, and growth is essential (also . . .)

- In training others to do the job you do, it means that the next generation of leaders is prepared, but still working alongside you until you are no longer needed (to make the best team you can).

Further reading/listening

If you like a podcast and 'teamwork' is something you want to know more about in terms of leadership:

1. 'Leading and Learning' with David Spell. https://tinyurl.com/Leading-and-Learning
2. Team Anywhere. https://tinyurl.com/Team-Anywhere

If you like a book and want to get the best potential out of your team in a number of levels:

1. Widdowson, Lucy & Paul J Barbour (2021). *Building Top-Performing Teams: A Practical Guide to Team Coaching to Improve Collaboration and Drive Organizational Success.* Kogan Page. ISBN: 978-1789666762.
2. Rogers, Michael G. (2017). *You Are the Team: 6 Simple Ways Teammates Can Go from Good to Great.* CreateSpace Independent Publishing Platform. ISBN: 978-1546770855.

16 Collaboration is multiplication

Neoliberalism and accountability – what they mean for unique schools and children

In the last four decades, school-to-school collaboration in the English school system has deteriorated, compromised and contorted by myriad policy initiatives which have formed part of, and underpinned, the inherent competition ideology of the marketplace environment co-constructed in the Western world by Margaret Thatcher and Ronald Reagan. For a more detailed sociological and conceptual understanding of this, you would need to do some research into neoliberalism, globalisation and so on, but I promised at the beginning that this book would have fewer big words and more real ones, so I won't bore you too much with the reasoning behind it all; suffice it to say, schools compete with one another.

The competitive cycle begins and ends with two main things: firstly, Ofsted and secondly, the published (and highly contentious) data that relies on pupils completing exams.

Simply put, the system says that pupils all arrive at school – a free endeavour for everyone in this country who wishes to take advantage of it – and they have the same opportunities as the next child, and if they choose to access those opportunities, then they can perform well in tests. If they perform well in tests, at 4, 6, 8, 11, 16, 18 and so on, then they can collect little nuggets of something that enables us to buy a 'Social Capital Passport', which enables us to travel to a world where we can find all we all need to make money to buy bigger and better houses and cars, live in better and more affluent areas, enjoy physical safety, healthy pensions, leisure time and health (both now and long into the future) etc. Those little nuggets also give us little units of self-esteem, like calories for our souls, and are called qualifications.

Conversely, the system is designed so that if you do not perform well, then it is your fault. The education system is there, and if you choose not to engage with it, then you punish yourself and do not get qualifications, and therefore, you do not have the opportunity to travel upwards with your social capital ticket and must live in poverty unless your family are wealthy in their own right.

DOI: 10.4324/9781003281313-17

The only small issue that I have observed with this model, which relies on children being like empty vessels awaiting filling as they travel on the conveyor belt of state education, is that I've yet to meet two children who are exactly the same. I realise that (on the same premise as above) this is perhaps my fault for not looking hard enough for the homogenised children of our time, but genuinely, I have noticed that children are all different!

Children who arrive at school do so in the context of the homes they live in, and here is what is so interesting: children spend approximately only 950 hours a year in school, leaving 7,810 hours at home. There will be mathematicians amongst you reading that and doing some mental calculations, simplifying that ratio, but I think even for a very non-number mind who is reading this, it is obvious that children spend at home approximately eight times the hours they spend in school.

Let's imagine, then, that children are not identical and do not arrive in school at exactly the same and ready to absorb learning in the same way. Bear with me as we build some completely fictitious images of three children, fictitious so far as they are not based on actual individual children that I could name, but many that I have come across over a 25-year career, and even then only choosing three belies the multitude of combinations that you could find of the following characters.

Let us pause and consider the child who has no parents – there could be any number of reasons why – the child who may be in a care home, separated from their nine siblings, who may be fostered, possibly not their first care home or first foster carer, who may have suffered at the hands of their parents, or as a result of their parents' issues, to such an extent that they are emotionally traumatised and need significant support from psychologists, therapists and carers.

Let's imagine that child arriving at school, perhaps not their first school, or even their second, an environment that is alien to them, frightening, with any number of barriers – language perhaps, culture, or even just that the child has never learned to trust any adult and has significant attachment issues. The range of complex needs of any child is so wide, is so difficult to reduce to a bite size 'quick fix', hence schools must try to work with several professionals, who may or may not have the capacity and manpower to offer and sustain provision of support for this child, but nevertheless they do their best. Staff work into their break and lunch times, they work at night catching up because perhaps during the working day the child has had multiple crises and been completely dysregulated so has needed a team of adults to keep them, and other children, safe.

Their learning will have been disrupted, as will that of the other children; other children may well be afraid, and that child may be shunned because of their erratic and unpredictable behaviour, but staff persist in trying to work with all of the children on tolerance and understanding and British Values, and maths, and literacy and a rich and challenging curriculum. That tricky day is repeated, perhaps each time the child has contact with a parent in their home, or at the prison, perhaps as they move foster carers or are adopted, that day becomes multiple days. The inclusive school works hard with staff, children and other parents; governors discuss the situation, and as Head you are fielding complaints and still fighting for the needs of the child to be met.

Before we get to the bottom line, let us also consider the child from the very affluent family, the family who all live in a lovely village in a detached house, no mortgage, stay-at-home mum and one sibling. The family on the surface have it all: two cars, money to burn, fabulous lifestyle, but the adults do not love one another, and the depressed atmosphere in the home begins to have an adverse impact on the child, who begins to act out. In an attempt to maintain appearances, the parents lavish the child with the material.

To the outside world, what can be the matter? The child acts out in school, has violent outbursts, is unable to express unhappiness in any other way, but it is unclear why. The child's behaviour dominates the family, adding to the dysfunctional dynamic already present, a tool for the mother to blame the father, the parents' relationship deteriorating and creating ever-decreasing amounts of stability in the home. The father leaves, and the mother prevents access, increasing further the destabilisation and the child's confusion, anger and hurt.

The child has violent and destructive outbursts in the home and the father returns, under duress, to try to repair the damage. To no avail. The child, more confused than ever, continues to behave in a way that makes it difficult for the adults around him to help. Still, outside of the home, everyone thinks all is well; they are an upper middle class, respectable, family conforming to all social expectations and norms. The adult relationship, however, is broken, and the negativity permeates all activity within the family, including Christmases, holidays, birthdays spent apart, a method of the mother punishing the father, periods where he is banned from seeing the child, exacerbating the anguish. The father meets someone else, and the child comes to understand this information in a very upsetting way, their behaviour deteriorating now to the point they are no longer attending school, and at some point, the father ends his relationship to try to fix the child, again to no avail. The father is depressed and unhappy. The mother is unhappy and angry. They take out their dissatisfaction with life on one another and possibly self-medicate with alcohol, the yoyo effect of their erratic relationship only serving to undermine the child's understanding of relationships, as well as who to trust and how to make sense of the world.

To the outside world, nothing is known or seen, only the child's behaviour. The child can tell nobody as he has not learned communication from his parents through anything other than anger and sullen silences.

A final scenario, the child from a very wealthy home where both parents are professionals, but not home too often; perhaps they are doctors, lawyers, academics or in finance. The child attends breakfast and after school clubs, a range of sports clubs, is very high achieving as they have a tutor for every subject, holidays abroad in all of the school breaks, and a disposable income paid into the bank account they have access to.

Nobody would assume that a child like this could have needs that could affect their education – they have it all, surely? Yet the child craves attention, periodically they will get it, in a range of ways, but at other times they get bored. They may explore risk-taking behaviours, a normal developmental milestone, but with the unsupervised hours they have and the money they can spend, they turn to drugs, they develop issues such as eating disorders and may end up pregnant as they find some kind of love that was missing in their family lives invested in a child of their own. Equally, they may break a leg when skiing and be unable to attend school for a considerable time. Or suffer a dreadful illness such as leukaemia and therefore be unable to attend school for some time.

'More than a score'

Three children – we all recognise them, or elements of them. We have taught and supported them, spoken to parents and carers, professionals and specialists about them. Now imagine they are all in the same class, or in any one class there are multiples of them, 2/3 or more.

At some point in the year, tests take place and the children do not perform well, may not even sit the tests, may be excluded, refusing to come to school, hospitalised with eating disorders, self-harming etc., and in any case, the other children in the class may have had multiple sessions of learning disrupted by them and their behaviour so they may sit the tests but may not actually perform to their best ability either. The school are worried about all three, for different reasons, but because they are inclusive and care, they worry for each child. They know the potential outcomes for the school, and there is nothing they can do, so they must instead satisfy themselves that they have fought for all three, and their siblings if it is appropriate, and supported their family members and signposted them for help and support.

The results of the tests are published, and the school is judged on the basis of the results, primarily; they hit the headlines because there are league tables, like in football or rugby. A school with low test scores evidently is rubbish; they are clearly not doing a good job! What kind of school would only allow 50% of their children to pass a test when they are 4, or 7 or 11? What kind of school does not force parents to drag school refusers to school under threat of fining? What kind of schools are our children in unless they are all getting the highest possible scores, and actually, what kind of parents are allowing this shambles to perpetuate? In fact, what kind of government?

Well, the kind of successive governments that preside over a metric that limits each year the number of children allowed to 'pass' exams, particularly as children get older for GCSE/A Level examinations; if nothing else the pandemic illustrated all that is wrong with this system really. The playing field is never level if the statisticians are going to create the bell curve every year. Someone inevitably will have to fall below, some above, the majority in the middle. Schools, however, are judged on this. Not systems.

The fact is, none of us know the lived experience of any of the fictitious children I have described, or their peers. None of us know how prepared they are to learn, how calm their minds are when they arrive each day, or how full their bellies. We know that one displays the symptoms of dysfunctional attachment, but at this point we are overlooking the fact that any one of the children may also have ADHD, ASD, ADD, ODD, dyslexia, dyscalculia . . . the list is endless. They may have rare genetic disorders, they may have siblings or parents who have died, the list goes on. What we know is, regardless of any individual barriers to learning that any single child in our schools has (as a result of something beyond the scope of the school), the school is judged on it as if all children enter it, and the exams they will sit, the same.

Those of us committed to creating the best possible environment for children to grow and thrive, which involves caring for their physical needs (feeding and clothing them) and their emotional needs (supporting their mental health and cognitive development), which in turn will affect the child being able to access education in their way and make sense of it at a time when they are able, eschew things like Ofsted.

We accept that they must come, like winter rain, freezing cold, being taxed and death. We see the car crash of it all in slow motion and believe ourselves strong enough to withstand the impact, hoping that our communities will know the work we do on their behalf, feeling that we can transcend Ofsted and league tables, believing that most parents (rather than relying on the ridiculousness of using the outcomes of children in standardised tests to make decisions about a school) will rely on the feeling they get when they walk around and seeing the joy etched on the faces of their children as they leave each day. We plough on regardless of the limitations of the neoliberal system, the negativity pushed in the press though league tables, empty rhetoric. We push on because we want inclusivity and equality for all children.

How pseudo-inclusion creates explicit exclusion

Finally, imagine that we are the opposite to an inclusive school. Imagine our school is only focused on Ofsted Outstanding, for which we will possibly need all (or most of) the following: no exclusions, 100% attendance, a zero-tolerance policy to virtually everything, oversubscription in every year group, enough money and space to build additional classrooms when needed, enough money to ensure every child has digital equipment and that they can use it at home at the drop of a hat (or a pandemic), enough money to ensure that all trips and visits are paid for and do not affect the high-achieving pupils, enough money to pay for all training for staff and also all morale boosting including hotels and pamper packages, supportive parents, 100% parental support on the feedback app, no complaints, no changes in staff or governors, governors who are in school weekly and have few commitments in their day jobs etc.

Imagine that the parents of a child with issues of any description applies to our school and comes for a walk around. We observe the challenging behaviour or the challenges, and (filled with dread) we tell the parents that our school may not be able to meet the needs of the child, and they would be better at the school down the road. This is something we have done for years, to excellent effect, our reputation gleaming.

Meanwhile, the head at the school down the road, who clearly doesn't care about standards like we do, welcomes anyone and everyone and, wait for it, is a school REQUIRING IMPROVEMENT! The parent may be socially mobile and equipped with the wherewithal to challenge the head's attitude and insist that their child attend. Imagine that immediately on attending the school (through a zero-tolerance policy) the child becomes distressed and is excluded. The frightened and distressed parent may then be encouraged in the direction of travel that the head suggested previously, as in, the other school down the road, and the issue (the actual child) will be swiftly removed from roll and despatched to said school down the road, possibly the day after October census (that's the day that all subsequent funding for the school year is decided and the decision is made on number of children on roll that day!).

Imagine the dystopian world we would have created. Flipping heck! Isn't it lucky that none of the above are *ever* seen in our schools, children are perfect and leaders never off roll children to preserve their data . . . oh wait, this is exactly the dystopian world we all exist in, a direct consequence of a broken and twisted system!

In recent years, as government policymakers have experimented with reforms and directives based on the concept of a self-improving system in which schools will support themselves and each other to raise standards of teaching and learning, there has been increasing scope to work in a formalised collaborative way, not least through Multi Academy Trust organisations.

This dismantling of the 'local authority' system of old is purely to centralise control to Westminster under the guise of it being about autonomy between schools in formal partnership. Local Authorities (LAs) were often socialist strong holds, and the wresting of power from them has served only to increase the power of national government – one only need recall the threat of the government to take the local authority in London to legal action if they closed schools early just before Christmas in 2020 due to Covid-19. This was an actual life or death situation, yet the national government took control, in the end being embarrassed because it was entirely the correct decision by the school and the LA and internationally validated as such only days later with a second wave of the pandemic hitting the country and another national lockdown being enacted.

If multi academy trusts (MATs) are the only way to go, then this is where we will all end up, and we will have to navigate that new landscape. Meanwhile, the capitalist model of giving choice to parents and allowing anyone to set up MATs, or schools (free schools), or allowing anyone to be a principle or a CO of a school or MAT, means that those establishments have to be run as businesses.

There is no option for a local authority to support a school in crisis financially; they must sort themselves out or close. The end. Unless the government choose to write off the debt. This means that national government have all the power, but each school or MAT has all the responsibility and none of the support of a local entity with a vested interest in the local community and its prospects. It has all happened without anyone actually understanding the implications because the political spin doctors have been at work and once again explained that it is about under-performing schools.

Pause for a moment and consider where the majority of these schools might be – given the criteria we have already highlighted for success.

Dystopia and the resistance antidote

The professional and cognitive dissonance caused by the issues located within the profoundly competitive English educational arena, which sees schools contend for pupils, fight for funding and resources in order to survive, and employ inhumane unscrupulous tactics in order to preserve their reputations, means that it is debatable, the extent to which authentic collaboration between schools can exist in any capacity, let alone whether it can meaningfully facilitate educational improvement for all.

And yet, the most meaningful relationships that I have built as a leader are where I have willingly entered into cost-neutral or free collaborative arrangements that have had many mutually beneficial outcomes. Obviously, the concept of collaborative practice and what that means can be debated, but as stated in previous chapters, if you have an altruistic view of leadership, then you will behave in certain ways and communicate in ways that resonate with your values. That communication, done in the way that the vast majority of us now do, via social media, acts as a beacon. That beacon draws like-minded individuals, other leaders, to you, leaders who will be able to amplify your shared vision, thus positively impacting on not just your school or setting, but a wider context. If you are a small school, then you will need to use this as a lifeline – nobody can be subject leaders, Heads, teachers and all things to all men and also stay sane and also run a successful school.

Never more so was this evident than in the last three years, particularly in view of the pandemic and how our working practices changed. As we reached out more on a virtual level, connections grew and grew. @WomenEd, a brilliant platform that enables women to reach out to other professional women who share the same philosophy, is a super group to belong to, and most recently I have become part of the Army Servicewomen's Network @Army_ASN, which provides a platform to develop and expand the professional and personal interests of women in the army, enabling them to reach their full potential – a cause close to my heart.

Through my #AVicCarrCalls calls, and reaching out on Twitter in the past year, I have also ended up becoming an active and vocal part of a few educational movements, two of note are More Than a Score @MoreThanScore and also The Education Roundtables @EdRoundtables. These platforms have afforded me to collaborate and multiply the voice of many professionals, resulting in me being nominated as a Fellow of the Chartered College in recognition of the support I offer others, I think, but also because colleagues look to people like me, with a voice, to speak for and on behalf of them.

This may sound arrogant on the surface, and I hope that having read the past 15 chapters you know that I am not, but I can appreciate why it may sound that way. However, as I think I have said throughout, if whether by design or inadvertently you become a person who can influence, then you should do it for the greater good. When the profession that I have steadfastly dedicated my professional life to for a quarter of a century is at threat of being decimated by the press, or the government, then I will speak for us all and suffer the consequences (remember the story from the previous chapter about the 'hand grenade email'?).

This attitude led to me also being asked onto a national Sunday politics show, to speak on behalf of the National Association of Headteachers (NAHT), to welcome Sky News to school to do a documentary about the realities we face and so on. I am asked to be a voice, and I step up that role willingly, hopefully sharing what I know of the struggles faced by colleagues in Pupil Referral Units (PRUs), special schools, nurseries, further and higher education, primary, secondary, academy, free and state-maintained schools. I try to be inclusive, and if I get it wrong, I tell myself that my intent was altruistic and came from a place of love for my fellow educators.

I have been asked to speak at International Women's Day events about overcoming adversity; to University students about SEND and assessment, leadership and carer development; to Newly Qualified and Early Career Stage Teachers about time management, mental health and stress; to leaders navigating tricky conversations; and to master's students about academic rigour. I do so on a small scale, for free unless school is offered something, to try to foster a shared love of our profession. A profession slowly dying because the system makes it so disparate and lonely, that many people shout out into the ether that they are isolated or feel overwhelmed with the job as they are struggling in their schools.

So what?

It really is possible to navigate this curious hybrid of competition and collaboration because, in spite, and perhaps as a direct result, of the marketised environment in which schools in England operate, there exists an appetite among school leaders with similar mindsets to work with, learn from and support their fellow leaders.

The Education Roundtables tribe are an incredible bunch. It was easy to collaborate with them; we all share similar mindsets, but are totally different; we are all keen to share, be open and support one another and the wider profession; and the majority of us want nothing in return.

When I collated our Ofsted inspection information, I offered it to anyone keen to read it and ended up nearly burning my lap top out by sending more than 3000 emails in a single weekend, not to mention my own eyeballs for looking at a screen for three days solid. The result of this was that firstly Paul Garvey offered to host the information on his website, and people could then download it themselves, and The Key asked if they could share it – meaning the reach for this was huge. There was no financial gain whatsoever for our school, just the knowledge that we were living our values and supporting our colleagues. The same with our school dog information – @GorgeousGus has been such a source of love and comfort in school, and of course he is a very publicly recognisable black Lab, and this sparked interest in many people about how they too could facilitate having a school dog. I have shared our information now with more than 2000 people. That is a lot of school doggery and love!

Reaching out to networks on Twitter, Instagram, LinkedIn and so on enables people to connect and collaborate, and through networks and organisations, it is possible to meet inspirational people, generate opportunity, and may even link coaches and mentors. There is often a preoccupation with 'followers' and how many you have; I would say don't focus on that! Focus instead on what you send out, develop your own voice, share and comment rather than just like and re-tweet. You will soon have a tribe of like-minded souls ready to collaborate with you. Then watch the magic happen effortlessly!

Gravitating towards me with my mindset was Kyrstie, @KyrstieStubbs, who does the most amazing work for equality and diversity and who is an absolute inspiration to me; @CensoredHead, who must remain anonymous but will be immortalised as my first ever #AVicCarrCalls; Ed Finch, @MrEFinch, the most lovely human ever; @Alienwife99, who again, must remain anonymous; Sarah Watkins, @mini_lebowski, who is just a creative legend for Early Years and Foundation Stage (EYFS) pupils and an all-round beauty. I literally could carry on and use the entire word count of the book on my Twitter heroes, but I won't!

There are, of course, 'network' theories, which are underpinned by the concept of moral purpose which can facilitate a cognitive understanding of the rationale for collaboration between humans, and naturally this lends itself to collaboration between schools. These theories, based on research, discuss the conceptual, the optimal conditions in which collaboration is likely to succeed and the reasons also why it might fail. But if you want the simplest answer? It is the underlying desire to transcend the competitive and lead with love, passion and authentically help one another that enables this vision of true collaboration to be realised.

I am not naive enough to think that if we were all in neighbouring schools and competing for pupils (which equal money, don't forget), then we would all work together so supportively. We could never know the impact of this unless those conditions were met, but something tells me that the characters of the individuals in the @EdRoundtables would work just as well if we were neighbours.

Voluntary collaboration, in which school leaders choose to support each other built on a foundation of shared values, which then facilitate the identification of a common interest, can create sustainability between schools, and I really do think that this movement is the start of that.

Twitter, linking and collaborating, has also provided me the opportunity to do lots of pro bono development work with schools, in finance, curriculum design, managing difficult situations, appraisal and performance management (if this is you, you will see from the book that everything I say in those sessions is really what happens!). Latterly, it has also enabled me to encourage members of my team, those with confidence and those who want to develop it, to share best practice as we understand it, offer support to other colleagues, and raise their own professional profile in a positive and rewarding way.

The beauty of making links beyond your school is that you can reach outwards if you have limited capacity and ask for model or template policies and protocols that could save you hours of valuable time. You can ask for help with looking at applications or help with brainstorming ideas for dealing with any situation you could come across, and perhaps the most important one, ask for a listening ear if you just need someone to talk to.

If I could encourage you to take anything from this book, it would be to know yourself and to make links inside and outside of your school with like-minded and positive people with diverse backgrounds and skillsets. In the last chapter I spoke of teams and the absolutely crucial aspect of having a healthy team to surround yourself with – not everyone is that lucky. What if you are in a very small school, geographically isolated, or you are struggling to connect internally? The only way of surviving beyond that is to reach outside. You can do this virtually through social media, as we have discussed, or in person at events such as the recent @NAHT conference. I would urge any person in education to ensure that they become part of a union, to protect themselves in the case of needing legal representation at any time. In the same way that driving is not permitted unless the driver is insured, working in education should not be permitted on the same grounds. Union meetings can provide people with equally healthy collaborative support, and this is usually wide ranging and permits networking with a whole plethora of different people.

If we accept that connectivity is power, is a 'force multiplier', we must ask ourselves what puts people off being connected? Ok, maybe, one reason could be the temptation for interminable hours spent scrolling – many of us do spend hours every day tethered to our devices at the expense of other activities. Social networking platforms are designed to make us feel more connected, yet an over-reliance on technology can result in stress, addiction and anxiety at times as people search for validation through 'likes' or 'follows' and so on, but with some focus it is possible to find excellent free resources, endless inspiration for classroom activities, and with a # the topics of the day are brought to you.

Who knows, years from now we might evaluate the emergence of social media through a lens of humanity maturing, and we may well have grown out of the need for it. Those who do not like to connect in this way often refuse on the basis that they want to take charge of how, when and where they connect with people. For them, socialising and networking may be focused on physically touching, talking and being in the same space. This has certainly evolved for @EdRoundtables and especially so as the effects of the pandemic begin to recede. I think that if you view the use of social media networking as a start, which allows you to build into real life and safe exploration of connections, then you will be less put off.

Because part of the problem with social networking platforms is that they are not just used by us for us – the interactions are channelled through the platform to create 'data', which is ultimately fed back to a range of brokers to use for marketing – they also promote a particular way of being connected to and supportive of those around us, and this engineered way of working, with the associated adverts and algorithms is the most off putting aspect of it all for me. I am hopeful that with ever more sophisticated technology, this will be rectified in the future; however, if we can freely use social media as just another method for making those all-important connections and allowing us to cast our net far and wide and reap the rewards, why would we not do so?

What has all of this to do with leading with love, with you?

The point of this chapter is:

■ As a leader, you are committed to your own development and that of team members within your school (which means that you can . . .)

■ Share your skills with members of the educational collective outside your school (because . . .)

■ Working with and for others is the socially and morally right thing to do (because . . .)

■ Not everyone has the same internal support network you have, or access to training and resources (also . . .)

■ In sharing their skills with others, not only do many other people benefit, but your team will feel ever more empowered, and their self-esteem will increase, complementing your main leadership effort (to make the best team you can).

Further reading/listening

If you like a podcast and 'collaboration' is something you want to know more about in terms of leadership:

1. The Better Networking Podcast. https://tinyurl.com/Better-Networks
2. Newgen Networking Podcast. https://tinyurl.com/Network-pod

If you like a book and want to get the best potential out of your team in a number of levels:

1. Pollard, Matthew *et al.* (2021). *The Introvert's Edge to Networking: Work the Room. Leverage Social Media. Develop Powerful Connections.* HarperCollins Leadership. ISBN: 978-1400216680.
2. Smith, David (2020). *Emotional Intelligence: Improve Your Social Skills & Relationships, Achieve Self Awareness & Self-Management, Boost Your EQ and Control Your Emotions.* Independently Published. ISBN: 979-8667050247.

From playground to parade ground

Leading with heart

Love

From the playground of my youth (which was far smaller when I returned in my 40s than it felt when I was five), to the parade ground of Royal Military Academy Sandhurst, from which I recently marched up the steps into Old College into a commission in the British Army – and all that has happened in the years between – I know that I have been loved, and I have loved fiercely, and when I am long gone all that will remain is the essence of that love in the memories and behaviours of those whose lives I have touched, and who follow in my wake.

Threaded throughout the book, in my own haphazard and random way, the book which has attempted to stitch patches together to form a quasi-cohesive narrative of my take on leadership, is hopefully the essence of leading with love and compassion. In our modern world, so often devoid of basic humanity, where millions starve whilst billionaires take to space; where children drown as we close invisible borders; where those voted to protect us lie and exploit our resources; where fabricated lives are lived in and through social media and reality TV; where capitalism and money are king – doing *anything* with love matters, but leading with love matters more so than ever.

It may not be 26.2 chapters, but it may feel like a marathon read if you have reached this point – so well done, or 'BZ', as they say in the Navy! The finish line is in sight, and having been chief 'dit-spinner' (story teller) for the last 17 chapters, you will be glad to know that I am almost done.

I have been thinking that it would be amazing to find some of the people that I have referred to in the book and do a follow-up interview or podcast with them to tell them about the impact they have had on my life and see if they realised it, but I have never hosted a podcast, and I am not sure I would be any good at it. . . . This could be an idea for the future perhaps, although slightly suggestive of a 12-step addiction management model, wherein one of the steps you have is to find people

DOI: 10.4324/9781003281313-18

whom you have hurt in the past to make reparations, only this could be conversely to show gratitude. Incidentally, although not in an addiction management process, I could, and perhaps should, find those whom I have hurt and make reparations, but that is also a story for another day! Unless I just do a genuine and public message to them all now.

An apology

Please know this, there have been times in my life when, for reasons that I did not know or understand at the time, I have said and done things for which I am both ashamed and sincerely sorry. Some of you, like Mrs King my Physics teacher, I have bumped into over the years and been able to apologise to in person, for being the class clown (her recollection of me differed to mine, which was odd!). There are others for whom I will never have the opportunity. Growing into a version of myself that I like has not been easy and has taken a long time; I have had my heart broken and have probably hurt one or two people in the process of becoming 'me' – and thankfully there have been people like Bruce who have loved me even at my least likeable. If you have come across me in the past when I have been in the throes of metamorphosis, and any of my words or deeds have hurt you, then I am truly sorry.

There are so many more stories I could tell, but if you sit reading any longer, you're likely to grow roots, so it's time to wrap it up – I will keep the rest for my proposed 'dit-off' with Spence (yes, Captain B, I have not forgotten the challenge!). And I am sure that there will come many more opportunities for chapters to be formed – I recently applied to be part of an all-female team that would row the Atlantic . . . and having known people who have done so, I feel fairly sure there would be a story to tell upon completion if I was successful. Even though this may not come to fruition (this time), imagine the sense of honour I feel to have been shortlisted?

Loves

I guess if we are talking about love, which I have been for the past 17 chapters (in case that golden thread has escaped you), then we need to talk about 'loves'. Why? Because how we treat ourselves and others is innate and the bedrock of how we lead. However, I am smiling in a slightly wicked way because I can imagine several people suddenly feeling very panicky right about now . . . no need, I would never 'kiss and tell', and this isn't the kind of book where an exposé would be acceptable! I have loved many people and places in my life, too many to mention here, and all have mattered, all have contributed to the 'me' that you all know now.

My last love recently exited my life, for reasons beyond my understanding, but all that brought me through its highs and lows was learning. My first love was my best mate, a boy called Richard. We lived opposite one another, him with his mum, Irene, next door to Mrs Clarke who had a piano in her 'parlour' and who was a great advocate for children being children – lucky really because we got up to all kinds of mischief and shenanigans. He sat on my doorstep with me as a tiny child, one of the few photos of my childhood that escaped the carnage of my dad slitting his wrists all over our memories in one of his suicide attempts. Me in a crocheted bonnet and frilly nickers, him in the knitted shorts ensemble so popular in the '70s. We climbed up the drainpipe and onto the roof of my dad's pigeon coop together, and promptly fell off – together (him needing stitches and me getting a beating); we played endlessly on the bomb site that was known as 'The Bondi' at the end of our street, with the broken glass, discarded fridges, and other genuinely life-threatening paraphernalia that these days would give parents high blood pressure, yet everyone was totally unconcerned about 40 years ago; we ate 'sugar butties' together (literally two slices of buttered bread with sugar sprinkled on them!) and generally loved one another in the innocent way that children do.

Sadly, after my siblings and I were forced to leave our home in a hurry, bundled out into my grandad's car, him wielding a shot gun and threatening to shoot my dad dead, I never saw Richard again. But he was my first best friend (the OG as my daughter would say) and my first partner in crime. He taught me that friendship transcends gender, just as well because my most recent partners in crime (and nonetheless important in their own way) are all men also: Bruce, Yoz, Johnny, Richard, Michael – I could literally write a book a piece about each of them and their impact on my life – but we are wrapping this up, remember! Richard also taught me that girls can climb, run and ride a bike just as well as boys – and who would argue that these were not excellent life lessons?

Since 'The Bondi' days, there have been many people who have taken pieces of my heart with them; some have left me with pieces of theirs as patches. My interests in life have led me to having many male friends, but this has never been an issue. Friends, boyfriends, mates. Names like snowflakes, drifting and spinning gently through my head as I reflect on a life well lived, drifting before settling upon and wrapping around my soul, creating a wonderful blanket of peace that stretches through the annals of my life. I have been so blessed.

Loss

Of those who have been with me the longest, you all know about Johnny, and Richard. There are people right now that I do not think I could live without and who are tattooed on my soul along with my wonderful work colleagues who have found their way deep into my affections; and people whom I thought I could not live without yet whom I have survived losing, despite the desperate, manic, suffocating, crushing pain of it, so I do know that it is possible. The indelible mark of their absence has been left, teaching me that those who feel the same about me will also survive when I am no longer around – for whatever reason. I believe this in a professional and a personal sense. I left my previous school, where I commenced my headship journey, cut my teeth and learned about leadership on the frontline; where I felt such visceral connection to staff and had a six-year history – yet everyone managed without me, and this is part of the natural cycle of any organisation. I felt heart-warmed that the work that went into cultivating the culture there meant that people I left behind were empowered to become leaders and recognised as such in their own right.

Loving

Love. Love is a funny old concept, I think, elements of which I have yet to finesse the art of – if truth be told. Evidently, as a single person (eye roll!), I have been at times tricky to love, although it pains me to admit it; and at times I have found loving people a very tricky endeavour because it involved giving my whole self, and this is not a thing I felt brave enough to do. I have given my whole self and been humiliatingly rejected and survived that. When I see children or colleagues hurting, and they are like wounded animals, metaphorically snarling and snapping at those who care for them, I am often quietly reminded of what it feels like to be enduring such pain, and it drives me, through love, to reach out and help them even more. There are several people who have suffered as a result of my limited ability (at times) to love, to my shame, but I was incapable during my 'growth years'. I have persisted in trying to work on the aspects of my wonky self that needed it because giving up on love is not an option – especially when it is the fundamental force in humanity.

I feel that in the writing of this book, and the putting down on paper just a fraction of the flotsam and jetsam that bobs around my head, that has shaped me as the person and leader that I have become, I am more ready than I have ever been to embrace a future where I no longer have to thrash myself to achieve, I no longer have to wrestle with the demons of self-criticism, and no longer feel inferior to my own version of me. I have, as I said to one of the young teachers aspiring to leadership in my school recently, found out that I am okay, and they will too, in time. Right now, I might be at my most easy to love, and I feel that I may even be ready to love again. We shall see! I have certainly made this public pact with the universe, and this makes me more accountable in many respects to find happiness and contentment where I have felt dissatisfied with myself. We each owe it to ourselves to be most loving and compassionate to ourselves, and in so doing, we will be better placed to create the kind of environment for others to do so.

Acceptance

This 'calming down', the quiet acceptance of myself that I now feel may not be about leadership *per se*, and yet it so could be. It could be about *my* style of leadership because it involves the way that I work, which is inextricable from the way that I live. Each of us has our way of working, our own standard operating procedures, our own value systems that we cannot prize ourselves away from. It is this aspect of ourselves that will make the journey and methodology of every leader different and unique. We are perhaps at our best if we simply stay true to ourselves and find our niche and a place where we fit and there is harmony.

The irony that I had my epiphany and came to the realisation that I was 'enough' at the age of 46, whilst on a junior officer leadership development weekend with some wonderful people from my military unit, and during the rainiest day in recent history (maybe not, but it felt like it) whilst walking to the peak of Ingleborough, as the third peak of the English Yorkshire Three Peaks, is not lost on me.

In finding that I no longer want to push myself in a formally academic way, I now know that I will have more time to pursue other interests. Re-doing my Summer Mountain Leader qualification in the near future with the Army won't just benefit me in a personal sense – reacquainting me with the hills and mountains – but it will enable me to take people with me safely in a professional sense to enjoy the very thing that I found so enriching almost three decades ago, that opened my mind and my eyes. Sharing joy, awe and wonder, whilst talking to and coaching others in the elements – will there be a more purposeful way to spend my spare time in future years? Choosing to believe finally that I am enough does not mean stopping, ending and finality – in fact, it means a whole new untrodden path as I look forward and head towards 50. Our age should not necessarily be a limiting factor or a reason to be overlooked or become complacent.

What's it all about?

When my children, who are now adults, were small, I would ask them, 'What's it all about?' (Bless, even at an early age they were being challenged by me to consider the existential concept of 'life' – is it any wonder my children would ask me questions in the car like 'Mummy, do cows only know one word?' Or 'Mummy, what comes *AFTER* space?'). They learned early on, whilst we rubbed our noses together in 'Eskimo Kisses', to respond: 'Love, Mummy, it's all about love'.

And here is the thing: in my limited view, most things are indeed about love, or its absence.

Our pursuits, when fuelled by love, are what put us into what positive psychologist Mihály Csíkszentmihályi describes as a state of complete immersion in an activity, a state of 'flow', and what Maslow calls 'peak experiences'. While in this state, we are completely involved in and focused on what we are doing. You may already know that for me, this is being in the outdoors, near or on water of any sort, or in the hills, regardless of the weather; or exercising; or cooking; or reading. You will all have something that you do that transports you into an almost entranced frame of mind where you are untroubled and at peace – if I could make a suggestion, do more of whatever this activity is, and see how it impacts on your mindset and outlook, your happiness and productivity!

Purpose

Our work, the activity that gives our life purpose, is similarly linked to what creates a state of engagement and focus – and excelling in our work can simultaneously create not just 'flow' but also increased self-esteem and momentum in social capital as our professional credibility escalates with our experience and reputation. In increasing our own self-esteem and professional credibility, we can enhance that of others around us. It is one of the many joys of my role to be able to facilitate and then actually see this happen. Again, if I could offer any kind of advice here, find a job that aligns with your morals and values – find something to do where you can earn money and also find increased levels of self-respect and self-esteem. Let professional reputation take care of itself, simply focus on giving maximal effort to your job in an ethical and pragmatic way.

With whom we actively choose to make time for and spend time with is fuelled by love (duh!); our families, friends, life companions, lovers – all permit us to be our true selves and encourage us to grow with them as we navigate both the obstacles thrown in our way and also the enjoyment of shared experiences when we spend precious moments together. As I am chucking advice around like confetti, don't just seek people out when you are fed up, or bored – seek them out to share fun and happiness; don't just tolerate companions or partners because they have been in your life for some time, seek people who light you up. If they are not growing with you, find courage to gently let go of and move on from them. Find people who ignite the curious in you, who want to see you succeed and shine, who support you and challenge your thinking. Seek people out to *live* and grow with, not to exist and then die with.

Gifting

We are as able to choose who not to invest time in as we are the opposite, and as earlier suggested, time is our most precious gift – it really is not worth spending it on anyone or anything that does not enrich our short existence on the planet. Compassion and kindness should underpin how we behave, although this is not always the case. If we are no longer satisfied in our job, friendships, relationships, if we have mentally moved on, then we can physically move on in a kind way, without compromising our values and morals – hurting others on purpose is no way to live and no legacy to leave.

If, like me, you like rounded and even numbers, the fact that we are finishing this book on Chapter 17 may well be irritating to you, for which I apologise, and for which there is no rhyme or reason! I have talked about the last 47 years, and how each experience I have had, mistake I have made, and opportunity I have seized or lost, has shaped me to be the human being and leader I am. In sharing a few of those experiences, and what they have taught me as a reflective person, I hope to have brought to life some of the reality of what so many of us will have embraced – I may be unique, but numerous elements of my history will resonate with many of you, and thus we are collectively human, fallible and not unique at all.

Au Revoir!

To summarise, if you have skipped chapters or dozed off reading them, to live an authentic life and lead with love, I believe that that we must firstly have love and compassion, forgiveness and understanding for ourselves, embracing our early personality-forming experiences, forgiving ourselves for the people we have hurt in our ignorance and lack of self-awareness, forgiving our mistakes and antisocial behaviours as we were growing (yes, we all have those skeletons in our closets!!), and finally learning to love even the prickly parts of ourselves that we may struggle even to like. If we can do this for ourselves, the chances of us doing it for others increases.

We need to ensure that we are careful and proactive with our language, keeping in the centre of all that we do the knowledge that we have the ability to alter the course of someone's life and affect life chances and outcomes for other people through our words and deeds. We can exercise and train our ability to do this, in the same way that we can train our muscles, and for far more rewarding results!

We need to take care to dream big and then influence bigger, always reaching a step out of our comfort zone to keep pushing our capacity and development, to feel the fear and do things anyway. Our bodies and brains can do this – but they will try to fool you into not doing so with false messages of 'can't' – ignore them and tell yourself you can. In doing this we are modelling how to break down the seemingly unattainable into manageable chunks, paving the way for others to follow suit. In doing so, our influence is exponential, and we will never even see it.

We must literally seize opportunity and continue to learn, in all domains, never allowing ourselves to submit to imposter syndrome and other negative self-sabotaging behaviours but remaining humble and not allowing ourselves to pendulum the other way into self-aggrandisation and narcissism. We are all successful because of luck, influence of others, being in the right time and the right place – we do not exist in isolation, and much of what we achieve is made possible and realised through a combination of events, not simply how innately wonderful we are (or tell ourselves we are!). Acknowledge the part others have played in your success, and then explicitly and overtly be a part of the success of someone else.

When we make people feel valued, we pay forward so much love for humanity that it is a force for good, a force multiplier, a quiet tsunami of free investment that sees a huge return because each of those people will naturally go out of their way to be kind to and value others – a self-licking lollipop as they say (what is not to love?). Valuing others means practicing gratitude and being thankful for the gifts others give us, those priceless gifts that cannot be bought.

We have a duty of care to invest in our own mental and physical health; if we don't, we cannot possibly expect others to. If we do, then no matter what life throws at us, we are giving ourselves the best opportunity to fight back and overcome adversity. Exercise and reduction in stress hormones in our body naturally support our immune system and therefore our ability to remain physically healthy, as does eating well and not putting too much into our bodies that we cannot filter out. All things in moderation mean that we are able to support ourselves and others as effectively as possible – this is self-explanatory yet often overlooked. We can focus all we like on mental health, but if physical health is not cared for also, then it is futile. Equally, we can be physically fit, but without mental health it makes no difference to our ability to conduct ourselves effectively in our lives.

If we make choices based on calculated risk, hope and positive self-talk, rather than fear and negativity, we will facilitate not just our growth and success, but that of all who rely upon us – friends, family, colleagues, communities and so on. Always living in a 'small' way so as not to offend others, or because we are afraid to fail, will mean always doing what we have always done, and this inertia gets us nowhere. Lack of growth may lead to despondency, depression, dissatisfaction and melancholy – sorrow at the opportunities missed and lost futures.

We need to build teams both within and across organisations, all based on knowing that people are the change, not policy and politics. One of the most daunting and yet rewarding parts of the job of any leader is curating a team and empowering others to make decisions, forge ahead and succeed. The success of individual members of any team, if cohesively nurtured, can maximise the collective success of the entire organisation – like a car engine with all components finely tuned, well lubricated and regularly maintained. The lubrication in any team is made from trust and respect, routine and methodical maintenance delivered by the leader with knowledge and respect of how each component performs an essential role.

Anyone can do it

My life has been filled with enriching experiences, but it has at times been tricky to navigate. What I hope I have done here is create a narrative where you can all see that if I could do it, then it really is possible for you to do it, for anyone to do it. I hope that I have illustrated the conceptual with anecdotes from my own life, leadership experiences, and challenges and from reading about them that you can see that not only is leadership attainable, it is also (perhaps more importantly) sustainable and something that each of us is able to do in our own unique way.

There is no mysterious magic, no recipe for success to leadership; there is no 'one-size-fits-all' manual, so in answer to all those who have asked me how I do it, how they should do it – this book should tell you. All that I have done is applied the wisdom gained from a million mistakes in a life well lived, whilst carrying several battle scars, to the mundane and everyday and hopefully brought the pseudo-mystique and elusiveness of leadership to the fingertips of each of you who has stuck with me and read this far.

In developing emotional literacy, a values-based concept epitomising both the individual knowledge and skills of a leader, and how this influences the processes and practices of a leader in their organisation, a leader can ensure that their organisation embodies values such as equality, respect, inclusion and compassion – essential as we look to the future development of our world. Each of us is capable of developing and enhancing their emotional literacy and working on improving equality, respect and inclusion. Each of us is capable of contributing to and ultimately changing the culture of our workplace and wider society.

Schools are eco-systems; the complexities of interactive factors that create the cultures within them are significant, but positive discourses, initiated by leaders, around love, understanding, development and healing allow staff to feel respected and valued. This is made more powerful still where leaders model high expectations and articulate them because we all know that leadership only exists if there are followers prepared to follow.

Followership these days can become confused with social media 'followers', and whilst these are inevitably important in terms of networking and sharing practice and ideas, they should not be confused with the people who follow you in your real-life endeavours. Followers only follow those they fear, love and/or respect. Followers tend to emulate those they love and respect, and therefore, we have a duty and a responsibility to be the best versions of ourselves that we can be, both in the virtual and real worlds.

Thus, leading with love and a sense of moral imperative absorbs the ability to build teams within an organisation and the networks created with the outside world that can transform an organisation, in my case a school, from a 'failing' or an ordinary establishment to a thriving and committed community, with the leader able to withstand the relentless pressures of the macro-level governmental policy.

There is a range of research exemplifying the dangers of when this does not happen, including burnt out teachers, reduced financial resources, increased accountability demands and staff who become disenfranchised from their 'authentic' selves and from each other, ultimately quitting the profession. But it is not just schools; my academic lecturing and latterly my military journey has shown me that what endures about leadership does so across generations and across professional fields because it is usually based on values.

The Army values that I now embody are no different to those from my life and my teaching career, and this makes my knowledge and skill set eminently transferable. What I do now only amplifies the message of leading with love, and I feel eminently humbled, proud and privileged to be able to work in several fields where I can have tangible influence over the future of members of society.

I am able to care now for the career pathways not just of those in the educational profession, coaching the staff who work with me, the student teachers who aspire to careers in education and social care, and those keen to do post-graduate study; I also contribute to the career cultivation of each of the soldiers that I am responsible for.

Equally, this influence is as far ranging as junior soldiers at the Army Foundation College, Harrogate; to directing staff who train soldiers at Pirbright; to those at my Battalion – I say the same things to everyone and live by what I say. A hierarchical system exists in the Army for battle, and clear lines of communication and responsibility, in the same way that the hierarchical system exists in schools for accountability, with clear lines of communication and responsibility – this does not detract from how we work with one another or the respect and values that underpin that work on a daily basis when not on operations.

Extolling these values is key in a world where how people feel about their education setting, or workplace, and how they position themselves within it, influences both wider society and individual academic attainment or social outcomes. Thus, an emotionally intelligent leader who creates a dialogue of emotional literacy within their organisation and wider community is active in creating an emotionally literate society.

So leading with love matters. It matters that the interpersonal capacities of school leaders, and their intrapersonal abilities make positive impact on the members of, and ethos within, their schools. Love, after all, is what it is all about.

What has all of this to do with leading with love, with you?

The main point of this chapter is:

- I came from humble beginnings, theoretically not destined for success, and I have succeeded through following the doctrine exemplified within this simple book and shared without hesitation (which means that you can . . .)

- Follow your own leadership journey and never let anyone tell you that you are unworthy or incapable, not young enough, not the correct gender or colour (because . . .)

- Simply put, YOU ARE ENOUGH (because . . .)

- Life is filled with opportunity that you only need to take in order to change your direction; the possibilities are endless (also . . .)

- You are the master of your own destiny, and whilst travelling on your own path, you have the privilege of influencing people you come across every single day (to make the best team you can).

Further reading/listening

If you like a podcast and 'leading with love' is something you want to know more about in terms of leadership:

1. The High Performance Podcast. https://tinyurl.com/MoralCourageRichardD
2. TED Radio Hour. https://tinyurl.com/TED-Radio-Hour

3. The Challengers with Amy Brenneman. https://tinyurl.com/The-Challengers
4. Mihaly Csikszentmihalyi: "What Makes a Life Worth Living?" Noting that money cannot make us happy, he looks to those who find pleasure and lasting satisfaction in activities that bring about a state of "flow." https://tinyurl.com/What-Makes-Life-Worth-Living

If you like a book and want to get the best potential out of your team in a number of levels:

1. Brown, Brene (2015). *Rising Strong*. Vermillion. ISBN: 978-0091955038.
2. Manson, Mark (2021). *Everything Is F*cked*. Harper. ISBN: 978-0062888433.
3. Godin, Seth (2007). *The Dip*. Piatkus. ISBN: 978-0749928308.
4. 4 Minter, Dial (2021). You Lead: How Being Yourself Makes You a Better Leader. Kogan Page. ISBN: 978-1789666250.
5. Strickland, Samuel (2020). *Education Exposed: Leading a School in a Time of Uncertainty*. John Catt Educational Ltd. ISBN: 978-1912906291.

Index

Printed in Great Britain
by Amazon